Global Children, Global Media

# Global Children, Global Media

## Migration, Media and Childhood

Liesbeth de Block

and

David Buckingham
*Institute of Education, University of London*

macmillan

First published in hardback 2007
This paperback edition published 2010 by
PALGRAVE MACMILLAN

Palgrave Macmillan in the UK is an imprint of Macmillan Publishers Limited, registered in England, company number 785998, of Houndmills, Basingstoke, Hampshire RG21 6XS.

Palgrave Macmillan in the US is a division of St Martin's Press LLC, 175 Fifth Avenue, New York, NY 10010.

Palgrave Macmillan is the global academic imprint of the above companies and has companies and representatives throughout the world.

Palgrave® and Macmillan® are registered trademarks in the United States, the United Kingdom, Europe and other countries.

ISBN-13: 978-0-230-50699-2 hardback
ISBN-13: 978-0-230-27344-3 paperback

This book is printed on paper suitable for recycling and made from fully managed and sustained forest sources. Logging, pulping and manufacturing processes are expected to conform to the environmental regulations of the country of origin.

A catalogue record for this book is available from the British Library.

A catalog record for this book is available from the Library of Congress.

Printed and bound in Great Britain by
CPI Antony Rowe, Chippenham and Eastbourne

*For Daniella*

# Contents

# Preface and Acknowledgments

Children today are growing up in a world of global media, in which the voices of many cultures compete for attention. Media produced specifically for children are increasingly marketed on a global scale; while media aimed at a more general audience give children access to an unprecedented range of international events and experiences, as well as offering visions of other countries and cultures. Increasing numbers of children are themselves citizens of the globe: they inhabit multicultural societies, and many have migrated themselves and now live within active diasporas and transnational networks. Children are also using media, particularly new media, to reaffirm their 'local' domestic identities as members of particular communities, nations, transnational or ethnic groups. These developments are likely to have a significant impact on their understanding of the world beyond their immediate circumstances, and on their relationship with it.

This book seeks to address the complex and multi-faceted relationships between childhood, media, migration and globalisation. Our primary focus is on a specific group that has often been invisible or misrepresented in the debate: that is, migrant children. We are particularly concerned with children who have migrated in their own lifetimes – that is, first generation migrants – rather than the more established 'ethnic minority' communities that now exist in many parts of the world. In this respect, we are addressing an issue that is of considerable concern in contemporary public and political debate: it is an emotionally charged topic that raises challenging questions about social cohesion, nationhood, belonging and citizenship. Yet despite the intensity of these debates, the experiences and perspectives of children themselves are rarely brought to bear – except where they are portrayed as passive victims or (increasingly) as a threat.

By contrast, we argue that children are often central actors in the process of migration. They are in the 'front line' as migrant families come to terms with their lives in their new location; and they are often the focus for parents' fears and aspirations for the future and for the tension between cultural continuity and change. The media are frequently a crucial element in this process. Children in migrant families are likely to experience a wide range of media, from local, national, transnational and global sources. These media provide them with some quite mixed messages and some very diverse 'symbolic resources' with which to build their own identities. For migrant families, the media can serve as a powerful means of sustaining connections with their countries of origin; but particularly for children, they can also offer a means of learning about, and participating in, the new cultures to which they have come. The media offer them multiple representations of 'otherness' and 'sameness', which cannot be reduced simply to a binary opposition between 'us' and 'them'. And yet children also use and appropriate media in diverse ways, in light of their needs and circumstances and in relation to the dynamics of the family and the peer group.

Our primary focus here is on the 'old' medium of television which remains the most significant medium for younger children in particular. However, we also draw attention to the possibilities of new media, especially in terms of creative participation. Digital technologies provide significant new opportunities for young people to become producers of media, rather than just 'consumers'. Potentially, they can enable young people to 'find a voice' and to represent their experiences in their own terms – and this may be particularly important for groups such as migrant children, who are often rendered invisible in the public sphere. Yet as we shall indicate, access to media technology is only the starting point in a much longer process of learning. What children do – and indeed what they *want* to do – with these media depends very much on their social circumstances and on the social contexts in which they gain that access.

In this book, we set out to provide a comprehensive critical review of previous research and debate in this field; but we also present new data from our own empirical research, in which children's voices and experiences are featured prominently and directly. In doing so, we hope to cast a new light on well-established academic debates about globalisation, cultural identity, diaspora and transnationalism presenting a perspective on globalisation 'from below'. We also hope to provide insights for scholars, educators and media practitioners who work directly with children and young people in this field. The immediate impetus for the book emerges from several projects based at our university research centre in London. We draw particularly on a major European-funded research project, 'Children in Communication about Migration' (CHICAM), which we co-ordinated between 2001 and 2004. CHICAM had partners in six European countries (Sweden, the Netherlands, Germany, Italy, Greece and the United Kingdom). We set up media-making 'clubs' in each country, in which children met on a regular basis to create and share short videotapes representing their interests, experiences and concerns.

Each club had a media educator, who taught the children basic filming and editing techniques; but all the videos were produced by the children themselves. The children we worked with were aged between 10 and 14, and were recent migrants or refugees from all over the world – Latin America, Africa, the Middle East, Asia and Eastern Europe. We also set up a project intranet through which the children could share their productions with the club members in the partner countries. Many of the children's productions from CHICAM are on the project websites at www.chicam.net and www.chicam.org.

Our use of media in the CHICAM project was twofold. On the one hand, we were using media as a method of research – a means of gaining insights into aspects of these children's lives more broadly. By giving children the means to represent themselves, we hoped to gain a more direct access to dimensions of their experience that might have been harder to reach through more traditional research methods such as interviews (although we used those methods as well). We can therefore analyse the videos, and the process of making them, in terms of what they tell us about the children's experiences of home and family life, of schooling, and of the peer group – and, of course, more directly about their experience of migration itself. On the other hand, we were also interested in the process of media production in its own right. As educators, we wanted to know more about how children learn to use media technology and how they use the 'languages', generic forms and conventions of media to create meaningful statements or representations. We also expected that this process would tell us a great deal about how these children interpreted and made use of the complex media environments in which many of them lived. We will be saying more about the basic philosophy and the methodology of this research, as well as its findings, as the book proceeds.

We also draw here on data from other projects we have been involved with over the past several years. Prominent among these is Liesbeth de Block's research (funded by the Economic and Social Research Council) about the role of television in the social lives of migrant and refugee children in the United Kingdom, which features in Chapter 6.

David Buckingham's work on projects about the production and consumption of global media such as Disney and Pokémon features in Chapter 4; while his work on an earlier international 'video exchange' project, VideoCulture, appears briefly in Chapter 7. This research has involved contact with children and young people, and engagement with media, from many parts of the world. Nevertheless, our perspective on these issues is unavoidably a European – or at least a 'Western' – one.

There are many global experiences and perspectives that are not represented here; and the ways in which the debates and issues are framed inevitably reflect the cultural position from which we write. In common with many authors who engage with this topic, we have yet to find a completely 'globalised' way of speaking about globalisation; and we will discuss some of the consequences of this as the book proceeds.

Broadly speaking, the book moves from the general to the particular. The first two chapters address broad questions to do with how we understand migration, globalisation, childhood and the media. Chapter 3 reviews previous research about how migrant and ethnic groups use media; while Chapter 4 looks at the global production and consumption of media specifically targeted at children. The remaining chapters focus more specifically on our own empirical research. Chapter 5 presents findings from the CHICAM research about migrant children's uses and interpretations of media; while Chapter 6 presents some more in-depth case studies of individual children drawn from Liesbeth's doctoral research. In Chapter 7, the focus shifts to production, as we consider research about children's creative uses of media; and this is followed in Chapters 8 and 9 by some further detailed case studies from the CHICAM project. Our conclusion pulls together the threads of the argument, and suggests some directions for future research, and for policy and practice.

We would like to thank the many people with whom we have worked on these projects. We are particularly grateful to our many colleagues on CHICAM, whose work we have drawn upon and quoted directly in several chapters: Jonathan Chaloff, Antonella Passani and Giuseppe Ganino (CENSIS, Italy); Nadina Christopoulou, Maria Leonida and Litsa Kourti (Greek Council for Refugees); Peter Holzwarth, Bjoern Maurer and Horst Niesyto (University of Ludwigsburg, Germany); Sonja de Leeuw, Frouke Rijsdijk, Ad van Dam and Frans van Lokven (University of Utrecht and MiraMedia, Netherlands); Ingegerd Rydin, Rigmor Nilsson, Fredrik Olssen and Charles Westin (University of Stockholm, Sweden); and Julian Sefton-Green, Steve O'Hear, Tobi Fosdyke and Simon Aeppli (WAC Performing Arts and Media College, UK). We are particularly appreciative of the participation and enthusiasm of the children who formed the media clubs. The reports from which we quote are accessible via the project website. CHICAM was funded by the European Commission under Framework 5; and we would particularly like to thank our long-suffering Scientific Officer in Brussels, Angelos Agalianos, for his support. Our colleague Shakuntala Banaji also played a key role in the project, not least in helping us write up the final report, from which we have drawn various points.

Other thanks are due to Joe Tobin, Julian Sefton-Green, Rebekah Willett and Helen Bromley (on the Pokémon project); Janet Wasko, Hannah Davies and Peter Kelley (on Disney); Horst Niesyto, JoEllen Fisherkeller, Issy Harvey, Julian Sefton-Green and Alison Murray (on VideoCulture). We would also like to thank the Japan Foundation for funding the UK part of the Pokémon project; and the Regional Government of Baden-Wurttenburg in Germany for partly funding the Video-Culture project. Particular thanks go to the schools, youth and cultural centres where much of the research was based. Finally, particular thanks are due to the friends and colleagues who provided helpful feedback on the manuscript: Shakuntala Banaji, David Block, Marie Gillespie and Celia Willem.

A different version of Chapter 4 was published as 'Childhood and global media' by David Buckingham, in the journal *Children's Geographies* 2007; and parts of Chapter 9 appeared in 'Digital rapping in media productions: intercultural communication through youth culture' by Liesbeth de Block and Ingegerd Rydin, in David Buckingham and Rebekah Willett (eds) *Digital Generations: Children, Young People and New Media* (Mahwah, NJ: Erlbaum, 2006).

# 1
# Changing Spaces: Globalisation, Media, Identity and Childhood

An Armenian girl in the Netherlands watches a Brazilian *telenovela* on a Russian satellite TV channel. A Kurdish boy living in Athens records a video of himself singing a lyric by a Turkish poet, translated into Greek. In London, two girls, one Sri Lankan and one Kenyan, debate the merits of popular Hindi films. A Romanian family in Italy watches a Spanish soap opera – although none of them can follow the language. In a small town in Sweden, two Kosovan/Albanian girls act out a scenario for the video camera based on the Swedish version of *Big Brother*, originally a Dutch television format. An Angolan boy now living in London reminisces about watching Disney cartoons in his former home in Portugal. Turkish children in Germany, in Sweden and in Greece celebrate the Turkish winner of the Eurovision song contest, praising her ability to mix traditional Turkish music with contemporary Western pop. A Kenyan girl in the United Kingdom keeps in contact with her friends and grandparents in Nairobi through chat rooms and e-mail.

These are merely some of the scenarios we have encountered in our research on migrant children and their uses of media. Like all children today, migrant children are exposed to a wide range of global media. They enthuse about Eminem, and debate whether Tupac Shakur is still alive; they laugh about *Friends* and *South Park*; they share the complexities of Pokémon and Yu-Gi-Oh games; and, often with their parents, they tune in to Al-Jazeera and CNN. At the same time, they proudly display their enthusiasm for the media of their countries of origin, which are themselves increasingly globalised – for Arabic music, Turkish television and Colombian dance moves. And they use media – mobile phones, e-mail and the Internet, as well as videos and photographs – to communicate and share experiences with friends and relatives who may be scattered around the world.

1

Are the modern media creating a homogenised global childhood, in which national cultures and traditions will eventually disappear? Or are they fostering the development of new local or 'hybrid' or transnational identities, expanding the range of cultural options and forms of expression available to us all? Are they enabling migrant children to integrate within their new locations, or are they merely creating a new generation gap, as their parents fall prey to a nostalgic longing for their homeland? Are they creating greater tolerance and mutual understanding, or are they merely reaffirming incommensurable differences and inequalities?

The debate about media and globalisation, and specifically about the implications for migrant communities, has often been drawn in such starkly polarised terms. Yet, as we hope to show through our discussion of a range of research in this book, the realities are both more complicated and more ambivalent. In this first chapter, we intend to give a broad – and necessarily brief – overview of the issues at stake. We look in turn at debates about globalisation and culture, and the role of media within it; at questions of migration, diaspora and transnationalism; and at issues to do with ethnicity and identity. And in our final section, we come to focus specifically on the position of children – a group that is arguably affected by many of these phenomena in very profound ways, yet which has often been neglected.

## Going global

Discussions about globalisation have taken two broad directions; one primarily concerned with economics and trade and the other focusing on culture and tradition. In studies of the processes and effects of globalisation, there is an emphasis on one or the other although of course their interdependence is also recognised. However, in both the economic and cultural discussions, there are disagreements about the historical roots and development of globalisation that broadly adopt three contrasting perspectives.

Several authors maintain that the nation state and the structures of modernity remain influential, pointing out that global trade, migration and the mutual influences between national cultures can be dated back to ancient times (Cowen, 2002; Robertson, 1992). From this perspective, globalisation is seen as merely a development of the imperialist strategies of the western economic superpowers.

By contrast, Nederveen Pieterse (2000) argues that contemporary globalisation is different from nation state imperialism: while the latter was 'territorial, state-driven, centrally orchestrated and marked by a clear division between coloniser and colonised', globalisation is 'multidimensional, non-territorial, polycentric' and 'involves multiple intentionalities and criss-crossing projects on the part of many agents'. Nederveen Pieterse argues that globalisation is a long-term historical process that is too often seen from a Eurocentric and western point of view, ignoring the fact that early international connections were part of a very different economic and cultural power axis: 'Europe, until the fourteenth century was invariably the recipient of cultural influences from the "Orient". The hegemony of the West dates only from very recent time, from 1800 and arguably from industrialization' (Nederveen Pieterse, 2000: 70). His approach prioritises the cultural mixing that has always been part of trade and cultural contact, and that is often the result not of peaceful merging but of contest and conflict, an argument we return to later in this chapter. The difference now is that through modern communications technologies, these contacts are increased and deepened as well as accelerated. Even so, as Doreen Massey (1991) points out, its effects on the majority of people in poorer countries – or indeed on the poor in wealthier nations – may well remain the same.

However, others argue that globalisation is a distinctive new phase, in which fundamental social, cultural, economic and political transformations are occurring (for example, Giddens, 1990). From this perspective, globalisation is seen to represent a growing interconnectedness between different parts of the world, from which new forms of global community are arising. Harvey (1989) describes how, as constraints of physical distance are reduced, space and time come to seem compressed; while Giddens (1990) describes the same process as 'time-space distanciation', arguing that with new global relationships society can no longer be seen as 'bounded'. At least some social relations, Giddens argues, can be characterised by 'disembeddedness', 'the lifting out of social relations from local contexts of interaction and their restructuring across time and space' (Giddens, 1990: 21). Local involvements, in which people are physically co-present, certainly continue; but interactions across distance are giving rise to new forms of interdependency.

Within the children's lives that form the basis of this book, we recognise aspects of all these arguments. National policies relating to social welfare and education, as well as immigration law, form the local experience while at the same time these are influenced by international treaties, economic and political pressures and international military alliances. These in turn are the products of historical forces, conflicts and interconnections (for example, commodity trades in such goods as spices, sugar and salt, the slave trade, religious wars dating back to before the crusades, colonialism and post-colonialism). They also create their own contemporary patterns of migration, trade and remittance.

Thus following Held and McGrew (2000), we regard globalisation as 'a product of multiple forces, including economic, political and technological imperatives as well as specific conjunctural factors such as the creation of the ancient silk route or the collapse of state socialism.' Furthermore, 'since it pulls and pushes societies in different directions it simultaneously engenders co-operation as well as conflict, integration as well as fragmentation, exclusion and inclusion, convergence and divergence, order and disorder' (2000: 7).

The media that our children experience are also a mixture of the national, regional and global. These media can serve to maintain national allegiances as well as offering a view of the world that reconnects children with another history or opens a window to a new world. We are concerned with recent media developments (both economic, ideological and cultural) and changes in children's immediate experiences of migration and everyday living. The tension between the cooperation and conflict that globalisation engenders in everyday lives is the central focus of our work.

## Globalising media

Among other things, globalisation clearly entails new means and patterns of communication, and new forms of movement, whether physical or imaginative. As such, the media are bound to play an important role here. Indeed, it is generally accepted that globalisation and increased communication possibilities are inseparable. This is not to suggest that the media simply produce new forms of global consciousness; but it is to imply that changes in media are likely to have consequences in terms of our awareness of the world beyond our immediate national boundaries. Terhi Rantanen (2005) draws on James Lull's (2000) 'timeline' of developments in media, to argue that the inherent characteristics of electronic and now digital media – particularly in terms of distribution and circulation – have resulted in a significant acceleration in the process of globalisation.

However, this is not simply a matter of technological change; it is also important to take account of the political, cultural and economic dimensions of the changing media landscape. In its early days, broadcasting was often regarded as a distinctly national project. For example, Lord Reith, the founder of the British Broadcasting Corporation (BBC), explicitly conceived of broadcasting as a medium for national bonding and national identity formation (Morley and Robins, 1995; Schlesinger, 1987); while the BBC's World Service was an important means of spreading British values to the wider world. With the advent of commercial television, and subsequently with new distribution technologies (cable, satellite and digital), broadcast channels have proliferated. National governments, themselves often explicitly committed to 'free market' policies, were obliged to deregulate – or, as some have argued, to 're-regulate' – in the interests of global corporations (Barker, 1997a,b; Murdock, 1990). While national and local public broadcasting continues to exist, the media can no longer be considered only as a national or local resource. The same programmes can be seen worldwide and the same products advertised, albeit in different time frames and configurations, alongside local productions (Morley and Robins, 1995). At the same time, the potential for 'niche marketing' – both locally and on a global scale – has also increased: media produced for mass global markets, giving access to faraway places, now sit alongside new forms of specialised or locally relevant programming. All these have set the scene for the expanding array of new media, which are offering both more choice and a greater range of types of communication and production.

Accounts of the role of media in globalisation reflect the polarities of the debate as set out in the previous section. Those aligned to theories of *cultural imperialism*, point the finger of blame directly at the United States, as the world's leading superpower. As the title of one influential early book expressed it, *The Media Are American* (Tunstall, 1977). From this perspective, the United States media are powerful agents of cultural homogenisation: they eradicate local or indigenous cultures by imposing a singular ideology and worldview. This development is seen as an inevitable consequence of capitalist expansion, as corporations restlessly seek out new markets, and as economies of scale result in a steady growth of monopolisation. Rather than relying simply on physical occupation, the United States is now seen to sustain its hegemony through a process of ideological and cultural domination, or 'Coca-colonisation' (Ritzer, 2004; Wagnleitner, 1994).

This kind of argument has been widely criticised. Nederveen Pieterse (2004), for example, argues that the flow of cultural goods is not so straightforwardly unidirectional; that the relations between global trade, nation states and local markets are more complex and diverse; and that *economic* power does not necessarily result in a form of *ideological* domination. The media imperialism thesis also tends to ignore the agency and diversity of audiences: as Tomlinson (1991) points out, such arguments effectively infantilise consumers, implying that they are somehow powerless to resist colonial ideologies. Evidence from audience research illustrates the diverse ways in which global audiences use and respond to (and, in many situations, resist) US-made cultural products (for example, Liebes and Katz, 1990; Miller, 1997), interpreting 'American' cultural values in the light of their own cultural and subcultural affiliations. This mirrors discussions about the ways in which cultures have historically incorporated, subverted and resisted colonising and conquering powers.

In more recent years, the cultural imperialism thesis has been challenged by a much more optimistic account of the global spread of media. Advocates of this approach point to the dominance of home-grown media products in domestic markets (Chadna and Kavoori, 2001; Shim, 2006; Silj, 1988); the historical and continuing popularity of non-US cultural products around the world (French paintings, African and Latin American music and Hindi films) (Cowen, 2002); and the emergence of new 'cosmopolitan' global cultures (Hannerz, 1996). They also proclaim the new forms of 'hybridity' that emerge as global media forms (such as hip-hop: Bennett, 2000) are merged with local idioms and traditions. From this perspective, globalisation actively produces cultural diversity, rather than homogeneity; and cultural identities are accordingly fluid and open to change. As we shall see in Chapter 3, the advent of the internet – and, most recently, of 'social software' – has again brought these claims to the surface in a celebration of the possibilities of virtual communities (Block, 2004).

Nevertheless, as the obverse of the cultural imperialism thesis, this 'pluralist' position tends to overestimate the power of audiences, and to underestimate the continuing inequalities that characterise the global trade in media (Karim, 2003). In regions with their own effective media industries such as India (Hassanpour, 2003), Turkey and Mexico with its international Spanish-speaking audiences (De Santis, 2003) this is more possible than for those with little home-grown media production, minority languages and poor economies, as in parts of Africa, Latin America and Eastern Europe. To give just one example, in the Caribbean island of St Lucia, 95 per cent of the TV programming is from the United States, while the most read newspaper is the Miami Herald (Kaufman et al., 2002).

In addition, some critics have pointed to the commodification that continues to apply here, for instance in the marketing of so-called 'world music' (Feld and Keil, 1992); and they challenge the superficial 'exoticism' (or 'ethnic chic') of some such developments (Hutnyk, 2000). It is certainly possible to argue that this more optimistic account neglects the economic dimension of the media – that is, their function as a means of generating profit for already-wealthy nations, which was a key concern of the cultural imperialism thesis – and slides into an easy form of celebration that is characteristic of some postmodern cultural theory.

Others have sought to find a way beyond these opposing positions, however. Rather than the global replacing the local, or the local vanquishing the global, the two have been seen to converge and complement one another in a process of 'glocalisation' – a term that has its roots in 1980s Japanese business, where it was first used to describe the ways in which marketing global goods becomes successful on the basis of adapting them to local tastes. (Featherstone, 1995; Robertson, 1995). It is argued that this can lead to 'hybridised' cultures and identities (Huq, 2005; Nederveen Pieterse, 2004) – although, here again, it could be argued that this process has a very long history, rather than being a development unique to contemporary capitalism. From this perspective, we need to consider the multiple relationships that now exist between the local and the global, rather than simply conceiving of this as a linear one-directional flow. For example, in the experience of many of the children in our research, globalisation has redrawn the relationships between 'being away' and 'being here'; and new localities are forming, both in geographical spaces and in the space of the imagination.

From this perspective, global developments are seen as multi-centred or 'nodal'. Rather than remaining with established polarities of north/south or centre/periphery, we can conceive of different places being centres of different types of 'globalities'. This also allows us to think in a more flexible way about how societies and people adjust to the demands of globalisation. Several observers cite India (Chadna and Kavoori, 2001) and Japan (Tobin, 1992) as examples of the possibility of retaining the traditional, whilst still addressing and being central to global transactions. Indeed, Japan is itself the centre of its own economic and cultural globalisation, and thus challenges the West's sense of privilege and security (Featherstone and Lash, 1995; Morley and Robins, 1995; Robertson, 1995). As we shall see in Chapter 4, children's media phenomena like Pokémon or Yu-Gi-Oh provide telling instances of the 'glocalisation' of Japanese media products as they are exported around the world.

## Adapting the global to the local?

As Kevin Robins (1991) points out, global media have increasingly taken account of local differences and, in fact, thrive on the commodification of difference. For instance, global TV channels have had to adapt to keep a market edge and retain local audiences: both CNN and MTV had to recognise that their future progress as market leaders would demand the production of different editions, in different languages, in different parts of the world (Morley and Robins, 1995). The same is true of children's programmes like *Sesame Street* and *Teletubbies*, as we shall see in more detail in Chapter 4. Many programmes (such as *The Simpsons*) also thrive on the intertextuality and transnational images that are only possible through the increased global awareness of their audiences. Robins (1991) thus argues that globalisation is a matter of the re-relating of local, regional, national and global alliances, and the redefining of previously fixed national borders:

> globalization entails a corporate presence in, and understanding of, the 'local' arena. But the 'local' in this sense does not correspond to any specific territorial configuration. The global-local nexus is about the relation between globalizing and particularizing dynamics in the strategy of the global corporation, and the 'local' should be seen as a fluid and relational space, constituted only in and through its relation to the global.
>
> (ibid.: 319)

This raises two issues. First, it could be argued that the 'local' in the glocal is only recognised or encouraged when it works in the interests of the global, when global forces recognise it. Where the local does not have any power or influence, or is too different, it becomes invisible and ignored. Secondly, Massey (1999) also raises the question of who in fact is telling, experiencing and owning this story of the meeting of differences in the first place. It could be argued that most people's sense of home and place has always been characterised by negotiation and formation in relation to the 'other'. The difference now, according to Massey, is that this has only recently been recognised by the white, the rich and the powerful (Massey, 1992).

These struggles in turn can lead to a protective reaction to try to limit cultural contacts. The meeting of 'difference' can produce adaptations and hybridities but it is also the source of conflict across borders, regions, beliefs and cultures. In fact Nederveen Pieterse (2004) maintains that this process of conflict and potential cultural regeneration is a necessary and unavoidable aspect of globalisation. The rise in nationalism and fundamentalist movements within religions, are the most obvious contemporary examples of such defensive reactions. Faced with global media and cultural practices that do not necessarily reflect local beliefs and values, either bringing foreign people in or making you yourself the foreigner, people may tend to withdraw into tradition. These traditions are not necessarily national, but may well reflect regional differences. They might also be more to do with nostalgia and imagination than reality (Bauman, 1995). Ironically many of these movements are also dependent on transnational connections, as we discuss in Chapter 2. Many nationalist campaigns often live by the support of those no longer living in the home country but who continue long distance political activities as in the case of Somalia and Sri Lanka (van Hear 2004;) or Kurdistan (Hassanpour, 2003). Space and locality are therefore again re-formed in the interaction between the local and the global (Appadurai, 1996); and new media technologies are potentially facilitating even closer, ongoing alliances and connections across distance.

In such examples, the one directional and purposeful flow that char-acterised much of the early discussion of globalisation simply does not match the reality particularly in the area of media and culture. In response, Appadurai (1990) proposes looking at global development and relations in terms of five zones or 'scapes': ethnoscapes, medias-capes, technoscapes, financescapes and ideoscapes. This allows greater flexibility in the conceptualisation of global processes. There is scope for movement, overlap and conflict here, rather like Venn diagrams with no fixed edges that shift composition with each new phenomenon. Crucially for our discussion, he sees the imagination as acting as a social force in globalised interactions allowing people to draw on different media and other cultural resources to construct new identities and to challenge boundaries (Appadurai, 1996). Appadurai's approach also allows some scope for individual agency – and for focusing on the exper-iences of people such as migrants, who may be living on the sharp end of globalisation.

Rantanen (2005) goes further, arguing that the understanding of glob-alisation needs to incorporate a nuanced notion of *time*, which includes age, generation, time zone, memory and 'media time'. By tracking the 'mediagraphies' of three families over four generations, including her own, she illustrates how different places, times, personal circumstances, political contexts and ages affect the experience of globalisation and the role that the media play. In the case of her own family, her great-grandmother grew up in a rural peasant village in Finland governed by the seasons and an agricultural calendar, and by Russian imperialism. Rantanen herself grew up influenced by stories of this earlier life, but separated from it: her main media influences were foreign pop music on Radio Luxembourg, the Eurovision song contest and television news (which included stories of the Soviet Union). She now lives a cosmo-politan life in London, but is still aware of different time zones and influences when she calls her son in Finland and teaches her inter-national research students. Comparing her own experiences with the other families in her study (originating from China and Latvia), she is able to illustrate the different times and paces of change, the inter-linking of media developments with migration, and their consequences for different families.

## Travelling lives

While the media are becoming significantly more globalised, migration is also a growing phenomenon. We will be looking in detail at patterns of global migration, and particularly the role of children in migration, in Chapter 2; but the broad picture is clear. The International Organ-isation for Migration (2005) estimates that the number of international migrants – that is, people living in countries different from their coun-tries of origin – is likely to be over 190 million, around 3 per cent of the world's population. This figure has risen by more than 250 per cent since 1960. Global tourism is also significantly increasing: the World Tourism Organisation (2006) estimates the figure of international arrivals in 2005 at 808 million, an increase of 5.5 per cent on the previous year.

Of course, migration and tourism are not new. Trade and economic transactions involving capital and labour have always been an integral part of international human relations and politics. However, new tech-nologies of transport and communication have brought about increased intellectual, commercial and diplomatic travel. Hannerz (1996) celeb-rates the rise of what he terms the 'cosmopolitan', new types of travellers that he claims are building new 'habitats of meaning'. He claims that the resultant transnational cultures are creating new opportunities for inter-cultural understanding. He argues that this is not limited to one group of people at the 'centre' (that is, wealthy Western nations) but, increas-ingly, to people from both the centre and the 'periphery'. Hannerz's view is clearly applicable to some categories of travellers. These people are able to move relatively freely across borders because they possess documentation from one or more states. Ironically, however, their legal 'belonging' to a nation state or states may have less and less personal resonance in their everyday lives.

However, others have argued that this conception of the cosmopol-itan (as well as such terms as 'centre' and 'periphery') is both implicitly male and implicitly Western, and entails an elitist rejection of the value of local experience (Tomlinson, 1999) and discrepancies of class and economics. Indeed, the very terminology both distances those at the 'periphery' and homogenises them. Pilkington and Bliudina (2002a,b) argue that this distancing of the 'local' is illustrated by the way the study of these unnamed 'peripheral' places is often situated within the discipline of anthropology. Bauman (1998) criticises theories of globalisation on similar grounds. He maintains that there is not enough consideration here of the real lives of people at the local level, particularly those at the 'centre'. According to Bauman, the process of globalisation has often been framed in passive terms. It is seen as simply something that is done to us, rather than specifying who is doing what and what role we ourselves are playing. The result, he claims, is that those disadvantaged people remaining in the local, the 'vagabonds', are caught with no means to either improve their condition or move out. Their only access to 'far away' is on screen, divorced from agency and responsibility.

To be sure, cosmopolitanism is only one aspect of the increased mobility that globalisation has encouraged; and in the case of children, it only applies to a very small group. Adelman (1999) argues that the implementation of the nation state was itself a major primary cause of forced migrations (many of which – as in parts of Africa and the Balkans – are still continuing). Individuals or groups who were persecuted within one nation state were forced to move to another, often with the protection of international conventions. The resultant tensions between the nation, the state, and a growing world population proved to be more or less manageable via the globalisation of concepts of individual human rights. However, expanding economic globalisation has brought further increases in migration that, alongside increasing numbers of refugees, are creating what is now widely seen as a migration crisis – an issue we shall explore more fully in Chapter 2.

The tourist, the cosmopolitan, the migrant, the vagabond and the refugee all represent very different experiences of travel, but the contrast between them usefully raises the question of how individuals now relate to the nation state. To what extent can inclusion in the life of the community – however defined – still be dependent upon allegiance to one place and one nation? Through increased possibilities of travel and communications, migrants often have the potential to keep in touch with 'back home' in more immediate ways than before. They can build continuities between the different places in which they live, and which they imagine. They can also build lives that involve a continued economic and emotional connection to two or more locations. But what do these continuities consist of? What particular localised uses of global and local media have people developed through migration? If media are able to 'transport' them imaginatively to different locations, who is choosing to visit where, and why (Morley, 2000: 149)? What, in short, are the relationships between our local lives and our global connections? Such questions are particularly pertinent in relation to children, many of whom have access to an expanding range of media and communications possibilities and who might therefore develop new and different forms of allegiance from those of their parents.

## Defining diaspora

Discussions about diasporas, what they are and how they might be changing are an intrinsic part of debates about globalisation, migration and culture. The notion of diaspora is a way of conceptualising the unresolved tensions between maintaining connections between where you live (home), where you come from (birthplace) and the wider dispersed communities of which you are a part (which might be defined through ethnicity, culture, nation or religion). As we shall see, the dynamic relationships between these factors shift and change but are held together through the lived experience. The word 'diaspora' itself comes from the Greek verb *speira* (to sow) and the preposition *dia* (over). As Robin Cohen explains, the term has taken on diverse meanings over the years:

> the ancient Greeks thought of diaspora as migration and colonization. By contrast, for Jews, Africans, Palestinians and Armenians the expression acquired a more sinister and brutal meaning. Diaspora signified a collective trauma, a banishment, where one dreamed of home but lived in exile. Other peoples abroad who have also maintained strong collective identities have, in recent years, defined themselves as diasporas, though they were neither active agents of colonization nor passive victims of persecution.
>
> (Cohen, 1997: ix)

Cohen outlines five different types of diasporas that encapsulate these very different experiences: victim/refugee (Africans, Armenians); imperial/colonial (Ancient Greek, British); labour/service (indentured Indians, Turks); trade/business/professional (Venetians, Lebanese, contemporary Indians); and cultural/hybrid/postmodern (Caribbean peoples, contemporary Chinese).

There are two reasons why discussions about diaspora are significant in our research. First, media have always played an important role in sustaining diasporic contacts and this is even more the case with developing new media technologies allowing cheaper and more direct contacts. Secondly, more frequent and sustained contacts are facilitating more flexible modes of belonging and of national consciousness. Families are able to maintain frequent family contacts across several countries discussing family relationships, business relations and educational arrangements for their children. Children who previously only met at occasional family celebrations are able to develop more sustained and ongoing relationships that enable them to feel located both in their current place of residence but also to build connections with the family place of origin as well as other locations (Gardner and Grillo, 2002; Mahler, 1999).

Yet despite this challenge to national boundaries, there is some contradiction in the fact that we still tend to refer to diasporas by their countries of origin (the Somali diaspora, for example). This implies a fixed national identity, even when the contemporary country itself may no longer be directly familiar or have significance in everyday life (especially for children). The term also continues to be used in relation to second or even third generations of immigrants. Diasporas are associated with nostalgia and a desire for past times and places.

There is also a sense that internationalised communities are defined as diaporas when they are not privileged in global relations and media. Karim (2003:2) argues that a 'transnational group's non-dominant position in global cultural contexts generally remains a key indicator of its status as a diaspora; the global English or French are usually not treated as diasporas since their languages and cultures have privileged places in the transnational media and other mechanisms of globalisation from above'.

So what is defined as diaspora and what is defined as the diasporic experience varies widely. Avtar Brah (1996) usefully stresses the diversity of personal experiences contained within specific diasporas. In her account, diaspora refers to 'dispersion from' a point of origin: it necessarily implies a home or a centre from which the journeys begin. It is not only the when, why and how of the leaving that we need to consider, but the different experiences within each diaspora:

> All diasporic journeys are...embarked upon, lived and re-lived through multiple modalities: modalities, for example, of gender 'race', class, religion, language and generation. As such, all diasporas are differentiated, heterogeneous, contested spaces, even as they are implicated in the construction of a common 'we'.
>
> (ibid.: 183)

Importantly, Brah also argues that the diasporic experience implies a location in which the journey will end, even if temporarily. The question implied, then, is how this location is experienced and settled. Often this process of settlement is depicted in terms of binary opposites. The new arrivals are seen in essentialist terms as Black, Jew and Muslim – in some way Other – while the dominant culture which they meet is seen as a binary opposite (White, Gentile, Hindu and so on). By stressing the differentiated experience of migration, Brah highlights the fact that there is never only one Other but 'multiple others embedded within and across binaries'. As diasporic communities increasingly meet and intersect, we need to consider not only their differentiated pasts but also how 'location' becomes 'home', and how it incorporates the influences of these crossing paths. As we will see in later chapters, this negotiation of place and varied differences was clearly evident in children's media uses and their video productions.

Like Cohen, Brah stresses the fact that diasporic experience is not all about trauma, but also about new beginnings. The question then remains as to how the receiving community is changed by contact with immigrants and if the new beginnings sought by the new arrivals are allowed to take shape (de Block, 2006). Diasporic communities may be particularly capable of adapting to the new demands of globalisation, but with increasing migration they too are under pressure both from within and through the increased cross-currents of diasporic connections. As Castles and Miller (2003) emphasise, migration inevitably brings with it a greater diversity within the receiving country and a greater number of connections beyond the national borders.

In this context, many scholars have drawn on Benedict Anderson's (1983) idea of the nation as an 'imagined community', arguing that it is particularly applicable to the role of the media in the creation and sustaining of diasporic consciousness. For example, Appadurai (1996) focuses on the role of the media as a channel for the imagination that facilitates and cements connections within diasporas. The role of myth and idealisation are regarded as important aspects of the diasporic experience. They become not merely presenters of past and current ideas and images but creators of them:

> the story of mass migrations (voluntary and forced) is hardly a new feature of human history. But when it is juxtaposed with the rapid flow of mass mediated images, scripts, and sensations, we have a new order of instability in the production of modern subjectivities. As Turkish guest workers in Germany watch Turkish films in their

German flats, as Koreans in Philadelphia watch the 1988 Olympics in Seoul through satellite feeds from Korea, and as Pakistani cab drivers in Chicago listen to cassettes of sermons recorded in mosques in Pakistan or Iran, we see moving images meet deterritorialised viewers. These create diasporic public spheres, phenomena that confound theories that depend on the continued salience of the nation-state as the key arbiter of important social changes.

(Appadurai, 1996: 4)

Appadurai (1996) expands Anderson's notion of 'imagined communities' to 'imagined worlds','the multiple worlds which are constituted by the historically situated imaginations of persons and groups spread around the globe'. By thinking beyond the local/global nexus and beyond the national, he maintains, we are more able to conceive of diaspora and the consequences of deterritorialisation. For Appadurai (1996), mediascapes facilitate the work of the imagination in 'diasporic public spaces' and in the re-alliances of the global, national and regional. They are thus increasingly central to ethnoscapes – that is, the international movement of people. These spheres are described by Appadurai as 'postnational orders', that emerge as media producers and audiences create transnational linkages, and as media audiences engage in conversations involving both those who move and those who stay behind.

Prioritising the imagination and media is useful in revealing the complexity of contemporary diasporas – although Appadurai has been criticised for being too 'top down' in his approach, and privileging the imaginations of the cultural elite (Fog Olwig, 2000). Other critics have challenged the idea that the diasporic experience is necessarily infused with a kind of backward-looking, nostalgic imagination of the homeland. Contrary to Cohen's argument, it has been argued that the links between migrants and their countries of origin, and the fantasy of eventual return, are less powerful than is often assumed (Hall, 1993) – not least because the homeland is itself likely to be caught up in the process of global modernisation. Thus, Annabelle Sreberny (2000) argues that the experience of migration and diaspora is not simply a matter of 'looking back' to the homeland, but also of 'looking around' at other possibilities – 'a scoping all-round gaze, [that is] multi-directional' (ibid.: 182).

This has significant implications in terms of how we understand the idea of diaspora. Rather than conceiving of diaspora simply as a matter of dispersal from a national 'home', we should perhaps be focusing on the emergence of new forms of transnational consciousness. Thus, Roza Tsagarousianou (2004) argues that contemporary diasporas are characterised not so much by dislocation or mobility but by connectivity: via media technologies, diasporas are undergoing a constant process of reconstruction and reinvention. Rather than enabling people to be 'in two places at once', media enable them to create 'new spaces where remote localities and their experiences come together and become "synchronised"' (62). Insisting on the primacy of people's connection to the homeland, and on the experience of loss and displacement, effectively denies this process of ongoing change, and the potential for creativity and self-invention. As Tsagarousianou argues, diasporas are not simply given: members of diasporas have to construct or mobilise themselves as such, and this is a social, political and cultural process in which the media are playing an increasingly important role.

Kevin Robins and Asu Aksoy (2005) go further, asserting that the notion of diaspora is itself 'a category of the national imaginary', and that notions of collective ethnic identity are simply abstract, administrative categories. They call for 'a thinking of self beyond identity', arguing that the relationship between the individual and the group is always problematic, rather than something that is simply fixed and given. Drawing on their research with Turkish migrants in London, they posit an 'emerging transnational sensibility' that can no longer be contained within the national frame.

## From diaspora to transnationalism

This 'transnational' emphasis has come to the fore in recent work in migration studies (for example, Guarnizo and Smith, 1998; Levitt et al., 2003; Vertovec, 2001). It entails a recognition that migration does not always involve a finite 'leaving' and 'arriving' at some set moment in the past. Nor does it necessarily entail a nostalgia for a 'homeland' that is forever lost. On the contrary, with increased possibilities of travel, communication and economic interdependence, growing numbers of people keep active commitments to several places at the same time. This has enormous implications for economic relations, development and citizenship, as national borders and affiliations are challenged and reconceptualised in everyday experience. As Fog Olwig (2002: 216) states: 'Whereas diaspora denotes a largely mental state of belonging, which may be grounded in physical movements that took place many generations back, transnationalism is shaped by present-day movements between two nation states and the resulting cross-border relations.'

Transnationalism clearly depends on advanced means of communication. As Mahler (1999) points out, transnational connections became possible for families living between El Salvador and New York when a transmitter facilitating mobile phone connections was installed. Similarly, in the case of Aksoy and Robins' (2003) research, the availability of Turkish media systems beyond national borders makes it possible for Turkish migrants across Europe to sustain connections with changing contemporary realities in Turkey. Much research in this area is now focusing on the diverse ways in which people 'do' migration and connection in everyday life (Fog Olwig, 2002; Gardner and Grillo 2002), rather than on more rarified experiences of imagination and emotional longing. As we discuss in Chapter 2, family life, and the formation and the sustaining of households, can be re-shaped within this framework. Yet what is so far missing is any detailed examination of how *children* experience this kind of transnational living.

However, not all migrants are engaged in transnational connections and not all transnationalism is experienced in the same ways and with the same intensity (Levitt et al., 2003). As Portes (2001: 183) notes, 'not all immigrants are "transmigrants" and claims to the contrary needlessly weaken the validity of empirical findings on the topic. It is more useful to conceptualize transnationalism as one form of economic, political and cultural adaptation that co-exists with other, more traditional forms.' As we shall see, these differences are also played out in the ways in which migrants who come from different national settings, and have different motivations for leaving, use the media in their everyday lives.

## Rethinking ethnicity and identity

The idea of diaspora has often been connected with the aftermath of colonialism – with peoples who already had a political and cultural connection with their immigration countries. It is also within this frame that much of the research and debate on ethnicity has been conducted. In recent years, however, there has been a growing challenge to essentialised notions of ethnic and cultural identity. This has arisen partly as a result of broader theoretical challenges – most notably in the form of poststructuralism – but also from the experiences of migrants themselves. Rather than focusing on the past and on heritage, the thinking here concentrates on the ways in which migrants relate to their new setting, and how this changes both the immigrant and the receiving community.

This is particularly important in relation to children and young people. Many of the children in our research were developing identities that drew on very different cultural experiences in order to negotiate their current relationships both within and beyond the family. One of the resources they used were the media available to them as consumers but also, as we discuss in later chapters, media that allowed them to create and play with their own self representations through production. Stuart Hall has been a particularly influential figure in this reconceptualisation of identity. Hall (1992) challenges the exclusivity of traditional notions of national identity – ideas that he argues have become significantly weakened as a consequence of globalisation and the undermining of the traditional nation state. For example, he argues that received notions of 'Englishness' are currently being forced to change as a result of the decline of colonial powers, the rise in immigration and new regional alignments such as the European Union (Hall, 1991). Alongside this, Hall (1992) also employs poststructuralist arguments about the 'decentring of the subject' to challenge essentialised notions of national identity. Rather than a unitary notion of identity, the emphasis here is on the multiple strands and contradictory influences that make up the modern subject. Hall (1996) talks of the separation of the subject from the nation and the growing importance of 'difference' in identity formations:

> We need to situate the debates about identity within all those historically specific developments and practices which have disturbed the relatively settled character of many populations and cultures, above all in relation to the processes of globalization … and the processes of forced and 'free' migration which have become a global phenomenon of the so-called 'post colonial' world. Though they seem to invoke an origin in a historical past with which they continue to correspond, actually identities are about questions of using the resources of history, language and culture in the process of becoming rather than being: not 'who we are' or 'where we came from', so much as what we might become, how we have been represented and how that bears on how we might represent ourselves. Identities are therefore constituted within, not outside representation.
>
> (ibid.: 4)

Hall argues that identity, like culture, 'is always in the process of formation' (Hall, 1991: 47), and as such it becomes possible for individuals to claim agency in these formations. We actively perform identity – albeit only within the terms of the available resources and representations. Yet as new representations and narratives become available, new forms of imagination and fantasy become possible, and new kinds of identity can be developed. Difference is no longer seen in terms of clear oppositions but in more complex nuances: it is a matter 'of the trace of something which still retains its roots in one meaning while it is, as it were, moving to another...' (1991: 50). Yet Hall also highlights the need to engage with the 'hard game' of the politics of identity. This returns us to Nederveen Pieterse's description of the meeting of difference as a point of conflict and struggle, whilst also being a catalyst for new beginnings and transformations.

The idea of the trace and the translation from one meaning to another is the basis of the thinking behind the concept of 'new ethnicities' – an approach that became particularly significant in the wake of Hall's work during the late 1980s and 1990s. Building from an identity that is centred in one ethnic experience to incorporate another and thereby forge yet another, this new, changed ethnicity challenges any essentialist notion of ethnicity itself. While the idea of new ethnicities is most often associated with British Black or Asian youth, it also questions the assumed invisibility of white ethnicities. Ethnic 'hybridity' becomes a matter for positive celebration, rather than a form of corruption, or the dilution of some essential, authentic identity.

The idea of new ethnicities has its roots in a particular historical and political moment in the United Kingdom. Hall situates these discussions firmly in the arena of race and cultural politics, motivated by the political realities of Britain in the 1980s. Responding to Thatcherism and the resurgence of an aggressive political nationalism, the idea of new ethnicities challenged the prevailing ethos that to be Black meant you were not British. However, it also challenged the related assumption that if you were Black you belonged to a specific 'elsewhere'. The emphasis moved from where you came from to where you were. For example, Paul Gilroy's concept of the 'Black Atlantic' – as opposed to the 'Black diaspora' – emphasised the in-between-ness and the intercultural nature of Black people living in Britain (Gilroy, 1993a): it was a matter of 'routes' (journeys, transitions and becomings) rather than 'roots' (fixed origins). Seen in this way, the notion of new ethnicities was a directly political challenge, with the aim of changing perceptions of race and belonging in late twentieth century Britain and undermining essentialist notions of national cultural identity. As Gilroy (1993b) put it:

For a brief moment to claim the right to be black and English at the same time was a gesture of insubordination crucial to the task of changing what England is.

(ibid.: 147)

It is in this sense that Phil Cohen (1999) has termed it the new ethnicities *project*, because it was conceived with a clearly defined political aim. However, there was some criticism that such theorising did not have a strong enough empirical base and did not relate to the complexity and changing influences in the lives of young people themselves. As Back (1996: 2) states, 'contemporary theory needs to be brought closer to the experience of its youthful censors and in doing so offer an account of a cultural politics that avoids banal optimism while holding on to the possibility of transcendence'. Back's research examined the relationships between youth in two south London youth clubs and the ways in which race, anti-racism, nation and locality operated as conflicting influences in their everyday lives and loyalties. He describes the 'liminal and mixed cultures' that marked the youths' local social relationships but also how unstable and fragile these were, remaining vulnerable to essentialised notions of ethnicity and nation at particular points of political and personal crisis.

The new ethnicities project was also, crucially, about the more individual changes needed to challenge internalised perceptions of belonging. The ideas of difference and the ways in which we form a real-isation of the self in relation to the 'Other' are central to this rethinking. Fanon (1968) raised the issue of how colonial subjects internalise the ways that the 'rulers' see them; and he argued that it is only by freeing themselves from the power of that gaze that they can free themselves politically. This idea was taken up and used by others, not only in rela-tion to 'race', but in recognition of the psychological and subjective aspects of identity formation. For example, Brah (1996), who grew up in Uganda, relates how she encountered this in the questions she was asked in an interview for a scholarship. For the first time, she had to justify being both Indian and African. What she had lived as a unified experi-ence became separated under the gaze of the 'Other'. Forming cultural representations of this personal experience and placing them within the political domain – and in the process, challenging dominant media representations – were therefore crucial to the new ethnicities project in the United Kingdom: films such as *Handsworth Songs* and *My Beautiful Launderette*, and the work of visual artists such as Isaac Julien and David A. Bailey, were a key part of this challenge. More contemporary British media products such as the films *East is East* and *Bend it Like Beckham* and the music of Nitin Sawnhey and Talvin Singh continue to challenge essentialist notions of ethnicity and belonging; and, as we shall see in Chapter 9, this is also manifested in the global appropriation and reworking of hip-hop and rap music.

## The relevance of new ethnicities

The notion of new ethnicities and associated terms such as 'hybridity' have increasingly been taken up in accounts of migrants' experiences of media, an issue that we explore in detail in Chapter 3. However, there are significant questions about how far these debates are still relevant to today's situation and to the new reasons and routes for migration. In many ways, the thinking behind the new ethnicities project may relate more to those who have already settled, to the second and third generation migrants, usually from former colonies; and it may also relate more directly to the specific situation of the United Kingdom and other former colonial countries. To a large extent, this may well limit its wider application.

Hall clearly conceives of new ethnicities as a form of cultural politics, whereby local formations and struggles can be brought to bear on the global. However, in the celebration of the new 'routes' of second generation Black and Asian young people in the United Kingdom, the importance of politics and 'the links between structural and cultural racisms' that were the basis of Hall's analysis were arguably lost. Phil Cohen (1999) describes how the social mobility of a 'youthful multicultural intelligentsia' has left behind a black and white underclass who, by not achieving mobility, are disconnected from the global society even if they are part of a diasporic community (and who come close in some respects to Bauman's 'vagabonds' (1998)). For the most part, the forms of cultural expression associated with the new ethnicities project have remained – or perhaps been ghettoised – into the safety of the artistic avant-garde. Cohen argues that this 'multicultural intelligentsia' is divorced from the institutional discrimination that still operates for many young people, and that (among other things) actively prevents them from participating in the new ethnicities project. He argues that it is not until both cultural *and* structural or institutional anti-racist work rebuilds these links that the new ethnicities project can make any impact.

Meanwhile, Gayatri Spivak (1987) draws attention to the global inequalities that are at stake here. Where there is an imbalance in the meeting of cultures, she argues, or where one culture is too damaged or too different from the other that it cannot be 'read' by the other culture, there can be little genuine exchange. In the context of the media, for example, many poorer nations and cultures are excluded from being represented at all, often even within their own borders. Where they are, they are predominantly represented through the eyes of the more powerful. Broadly speaking, mainstream global television programmes portray ethnic differences within strict limitations. Culturally different ways of living, definitions of family, goals and aspirations are marginalised (Shohat and Stam, 1994). While popular global television products are open to multiple readings, they are created primarily for the Western market; and there is a stark absence of other depictions of difference from other places. In this context, 'hybridisation' comes closer to assimilation by the more powerful of the less powerful.

Finally, it can be argued that the celebration of hybridity and new ethnicities simply does not take enough account of the pain and dislocations that can be experienced by migrants and their families. Children can find themselves negotiating on both sides. They can be accused of not fulfilling the expected family roles and taking on too much of the new culture while at the same time being reminded in school, with peers and on the street that they do not quite belong there either. Again, the negotiations are unequal. The feelings of never really belonging, while being a resource for much cultural expression, are not always resources for joy. Even for those who do settle, and who do become part of a reforming receiving community, there is a residual awareness of the processes they have been through that do not apply to those originating from the immigration country. This pain of 'unbelonging' is explored in many novels by authors such as Salman Rushdie and Caryl Phillips, and in some international art films; but it is rarely reflected in mainstream popular culture. Unfortunately, such issues also seem to have been sidelined in academic celebrations of the cultural hybridity of a small cosmopolitan elite.

The challenge to fixed, essentialist conceptions of identity that is central to the 'new ethnicities project' remains topical and relevant today. In the context of discussions about transnationalism, these ideas need to be extended to incorporate the experience of ongoing connections. Yet in the current situation, where debates about multiculturalism, assimilation and integration are at the top of political agendas in all immigration countries, it is vital to avoid collapsing the diversity of migrant experiences into a single 'migrant identity'. Massey's (1991) emphasis on the power relationships that are at stake in globalisation continues to be of central relevance. Migration has always meant the meeting of difference and the creation of new identities. The difference is in the power relations of who is meeting whom, in what locations and under what political circumstances.

## The place of children

The issues we have discussed thus far may well have particular implications for children. Yet discussions of globalisation, migration and ethnic identity rarely address the specific experiences of children. Clearly, we need to take account of the wider context: the global flows of populations, the international trade in media and the social and political dimensions of the national setting are obviously key aspects of the contexts into which immigrant children arrive. However, these factors may impact on children in specific ways. Children are often in the 'front line' in migrant families' attempts to deal with their changing circumstances. They carry with them past and continuing experiences that are powerful influences on how they build their new lives. The ways in which they play with the new identities they meet may lead them to challenge stereotyped notions of where and how they belong, both within the home and in other institutional settings such as the school.

The migrant children whose experiences we discuss in this book have mostly moved from the economically poorer countries to richer ones, both for safety and to find a better life and access to a better material future. Their experiences are individual and particular, but they all have aspects of their present geographical locality in common. They also have to make the necessary adaptations to new cultural demands, in terms of both language and customs. At the same time, through a globalised media and continuing family connections they are all linked to different, other 'locals'. These are actual places but also new connections of affiliation and imagination, which provide both continuity and conflict.

For a Turkish child living in London, for example, the local mosque is linked to a wider Islamic community, not least through media of various kinds. Cartoon Network, which she watches on cable television, is both linked to a previous 'local' but also to an imagined and distant dominating cultural centre. The choice between watching English television at home or Turkish television at a friend's house constitutes an experience of living with different places within the same geographical space. As this implies, the media facilitate a diversity of global experience; although this focus on experience at a distance could be at the expense of living effectively within the locality. Learning to live with difference next door may take second place to the global experience, and this in turn has particular implications for the development of a sense of 'home' and of cultural identity.

Our approach to analysing children's mediated experiences draws on two main sources. First, we would locate our work within the 'new sociology of childhood' (for example, James et al., 1998). In broad terms, this means that we regard childhood itself as a social and historical construction, and not as a timeless or universal state. Historical and cross-cultural research clearly shows that the ways in which childhood is defined – and hence the ways in which children experience it – are both diverse and variable. Cultures vary significantly in terms of the extent to which children are separated off from the adult world, how they are disciplined, trained and regulated, and the expectations that are made of them. At different points in history, children have been variously defined and represented as innocent, incompetent, vulnerable and dangerous, in ways that tend to serve the interests of adult power (Higonnet, 1998; Holland, 2004). Yet the age at which childhood is deemed to end – and fears about its premature demise – have also been subject to much broader social and historical variations.

Despite significant evidence of diversity – or perhaps as a bulwark against it – the discipline of psychology has historically sought to establish universal norms of physical, social and cognitive development. The child is treated here as an isolated individual, and measured in terms of clinical tests and observations that are assumed to be culturally neutral. Children who fail to conform are deemed to be deficient, and thereby pathologised. Yet while mainstream developmental psychology is effectively institutionalised within education and the caring professions, it has been increasingly challenged within the academy, both by those who have paid closer attention to the social and cultural nature of development and (from a different direction) by psychoanalytic approaches, that have questioned normative ideas of childhood as a stage on the way towards adult rationality (Burman, 1994; Morss, 1996; Rogoff, 2003). This kind of work disputes essentialist notions of children's 'needs' – notions that are increasingly being globalised and exported through the work of aid and development agencies (Boyden, 1997; Stephens, 1995; Woodhead, 1997).

To challenge such universalising positions, and to claim that childhood is a social construction, is not in itself to deny the importance of biology. Children share certain biological experiences which affect the social discourses that are used in relation to them, particularly in respect of adult power. Likewise, it is not to sanction a wholesale celebration of children's competence or agency. Sociologists of childhood are keen to challenge notions of childhood innocence and vulnerability; but they also draw attention to the fact that children's lives are framed by broader structural forces. There is a significant danger here of romanticising and overplaying the power that children might have. As Alan Prout and Allison James suggest:

> It is important to recover children as social actors (and their activity as a source of social change); as interpretivists have insisted, this in itself is not adequate. We need also, however, to grasp childhood as a social institution that exists beyond the activity of any particular child or adult. There must be theoretical space for both the construction of childhood as an institution and the activity of children within and upon the constraints and possibilities that the institutional level creates.
>
> (Prout and James, 1997: 27)

The sociology of childhood has also encouraged an approach to research with children based on participation and children's rights. There is a strong emphasis here on 'listening to children's voices', and attempting to understand the world from their perspective. As we shall see in Chapter 7, this has been particularly important in our own work, where we have often sought to give children access to the means of representation, in the form of still and video cameras and other new media.

Even so, there are important questions to be raised here about who defines children's interests. The discourse of children's rights – for example as defined in the UN Charter for Children's Rights – tends to separate the rights of the individual child from a more holistic consideration of the child in relation to role, function, place and community. This view of rights and needs has been criticised as highly culturally specific. One concept of childhood thus appears to be more powerful internationally and institutionally than another, and so the importance of the relativity and specificity of childhood itself is in danger of being lost (Stephens, 1995).

Furthermore, sociologists of childhood have largely neglected the increasingly mediated nature of children's lives (Buckingham, 2000a; Livingstone, 1998). The fact that children spend increasing amounts of time engaged in play and talk about toys, games and media is hardly mentioned. There is an implication that such activities are external, adult impositions that somehow corrupt the 'natural' experience of childhood itself. In this respect, we need to look towards our second major source, which is that of Cultural Studies.

Our interest here is not in analysing the putative 'effects' of media on audiences. This does not mean that we believe the media have no effects at all. It simply means that we are more interested in the ways in which people use, interpret – and, in this instance, actively create – media (see Buckingham, 2000a: Chapter 6). We are concerned with how children use media to construct their identities and to make sense of the social and cultural contexts within which they live. While we would broadly agree that children are 'active' users of media – in the sense that they select, interpret and make judgments about what they watch and read – we do not believe that they are all-powerful. The texts they encounter, the institutions that make them available, and the 'interpretative resources' children use to make sense of media are not socially neutral. To paraphrase a well-known saying, children make meanings (and pleasures), but they do so in conditions that are not of their own choosing.

We also see the use of media as inextricably embedded within everyday life and social practice. Indeed, we would regard the use of media as itself a symbolic social practice, which cannot be separated from broader relationships of social power. The media form the basis of much social interaction; and while they may confirm individual, group and national identities, they can also provide resources for challenging and reshaping them. The struggle over meaning is one whose outcome cannot be predicted in advance, simply by analysing texts or the institutions that produce them: we also need to look at the myriad ways in which young people incorporate media within their everyday lives, and in the context of their relationships with family and with peers.

In these respects, this book builds on a series of earlier studies of children and media (Buckingham, 1993a,b, 1996, 2000b; Buckingham and Bragg, 2004). These studies have sought to wrest the debate about children and media away from simplistic questions about 'effects' and to address the role of media within children's everyday social worlds. While questions of identity formation have been a central focus in these investigations, cultural and ethnic differences have only been explored in passing. This book seeks to make good this absence, and to build on other relevant work in Cultural Studies (for example, Gillespie, 1995). In the process, it also addresses questions about the emotional and even psychic functions of media for children – questions that are often ruled out of court within broadly sociological analyses.

Another significant development here is methodological. For many years, the most common approach to audience research in Cultural Studies has been the in-depth interview, either one-to-one or using focus groups. While these approaches have important benefits, they tend to limit the kind of access the researcher has to the everyday practices of their subjects. In recent years, there has been a turn to more 'ethnographically styled' methods, including observation; although it has been rare for media researchers to engage in the kind of long-term, in-depth research that characterises ethnography in the discipline of anthropology. By contrast, much of the work we describe in this book does make a significant move in this direction; and some of it does so by adopting a participatory approach, in which we worked with children over an extended period of time, helping them to develop their own media productions. This kind of work is not unprecedented, either in education (for example, Buckingham and Sefton-Green, 1994; Buckingham et al., 1995) or in media research (for example,Gauntlett, 1997); but it is nevertheless relatively novel. We discuss the value and some of the limitations of this approach in some detail in Chapter 7.

## Conclusion

A Somali girl arrives in London as a refugee. Her family makes connections with a new Somali community that reflects the section of Somali society of which they were members back home. This new community has connections in other countries, although it is also distinct from other Somali groups in this country. Her parents often talk about the news broadcasts they have all watched on Al Jazeera or CNN, although there are few portrayals of Somalia itself, except in periodic images of war and starvation. Even so, her parents listen to Somali music, read Somali newspapers when they can obtain them, watch videos sent from the home country and keep in e-mail contact with families in Italy and Canada.

Outside the home, the girl wears her hijab, although she is aware of the hostility it can evoke from some segments of the host community. She is also aware that her father is not allowed to work in this country and of the personal and financial tensions that this causes in the home. She reads hostile newspaper headlines about 'bogus asylum seekers', and her parents are often frightened for her to leave the house.

At school she meets children from many different parts of the world who reflect different aspects of her life and personality. She speaks the same language as some of them, and attends the same mosque. One of her friends is Muslim but attends a different mosque. They both speak some Arabic. She enjoys the same television programmes as many of the children at school and enjoys some of the same popular music – and both serve as an important means of learning English. She watches Cartoon Network, occasionally sees 'tween' girl magazines, and listens to chart hits on the radio; although she rarely sees representations of 'herself'. She meets different expectations of herself as a child, as a girl, and as a Muslim.

After a year, she considers herself to be both Somali and a Londoner, but not British. This might happen later, and it may wait for the next generation – although this too will depend on her experiences as a resident in the United Kingdom. Her sense of place is simultaneously global and extremely local, embedded within the streets and public spaces and people of her immediate neighbourhood.

This case study is one that we explore in much greater detail in Chapter 6, but it illustrates several of the key themes and issues that are at stake here. At home, in school and in the wider community, the media promote existing connections and new formations, while also offering windows on the world of the past, present and future. Both the media and direct social contacts allow the 'looking around' (Sreberny, 2000) that is a central part of the migrant experience. It is through the use and interpretation of media images and these connections within family, community and friendships that children begin to make sense of their experiences of migration, place, home and belonging and to forge their identities.

The work we describe in this book explores the ways in which children's uses of media reflect and are formed by their experience of migration. In this chapter, we have put this discussion into the wider framework of debates arising from the globalisation of culture. As we stated above, we are primarily concerned with the social, personal and cultural experiences of children in migration – a group that has in the past been somewhat marginalised within sociological research. At the same time we see these forces within the wider frame of national and global historical, political and economic influences and conflicts. The book focuses on children. It explores children and media, addressing new questions about cultural difference and using more participatory methods. In each of these respects, we hope this book can make a modest, but nevertheless innovative and useful contribution to the continuing debate.

# 2

# We Are the World?: Children and Migration

In this chapter, we review some of the research on migration as it relates specifically to young people, and briefly present some evidence from our own and others' work. Like Castles and Miller (2003: 25), we see migrations as 'collective phenomena, which should be examined as subsystems of an increasingly global economic and political system'. Even so, we believe there is a need to focus on the particularities of young peoples' experiences and concerns, and to recognise their agency in this process. We start by situating our discussion within the changing causes, patterns and power structures of migration more broadly, and consider the importance of taking into account child migrants in particular. We then move on to discuss the different categories of child migrants; and finally we consider the more personal ways in which migration changes family relationships, and how migrant children are positioned by the institution of the school.

## Migrants in the media

At the time of writing, in mid-2006, our news screens were dominated by images of the young poor of Africa arriving by boatload in Tenerife and on the islands off Sicily, attempting to reach Europe and its promise of work and a better life. Most of them were single men, but occasionally the camera focused on women and children who were also swept up in the need to migrate, reminding us that migration is not an individual act but one that connects large groups of people.

Such images of migrants and refugees are now rarely absent from our television screens and newspapers; although it is still unusual to hear the voices of migrants themselves. On the contrary, these stories are typically framed in ways that define migrants as being essentially to blame for their predicament and the problems they encounter. Research on newspaper coverage in the United Kingdom, for example, has pointed to the systematic disparaging of migrants, and particularly of refugees, whose motives for coming to the country in the first place are routinely seen as suspect or illegitimate. The figures of the 'bogus asylum seeker', of the migrants who have come simply to deprive natives of work, or to sponge off our supposedly generous welfare state provision, and of the 'lost generation' of migrant youth who represent a violent threat to law-abiding, civilised citizens, are part of the stock-in-trade of mainstream media coverage (Kaye, 2001). In much of this coverage, race and migration continue to be conflated, and racism is seen as the result of migration.

Yet in recent years, with the diversification of migration this simplistic creation of the 'other' has become more complex. In Europe, the expansion of the EU and the commitment to internal labour mobility has, to some extent, changed the debate. These new migrants from Europe are often portrayed as hard working, wealth producing and as filling a skills gap. These migrants are also often portrayed as temporary and therefore less of a threat (King and Wood, 2001). However, it is Muslims in particular who have increasingly been singled out by Western media as an undifferentiated group who are culturally alien and unwilling to assimilate – a perception that politicians of many persuasions have readily disseminated and exploited. Since the September 11th attacks on New York in 2001, the Afghan and Iraq wars and terrorist attacks in European cities and centres of Western tourism, this situation has become even more acute: immigration has increasingly come to be seen as an issue of security rather than merely one of economics or culture (Castles and Miller, 2003). Of course, the perception of migrants and refugees as 'illegals' and scroungers (Harding, 2000) – and now as potential terrorists – has in turn made them more vulnerable to racism and exclusion, thereby appearing merely to exacerbate the 'problem'.

In this climate, debates about multiculturalism, citizenship, nationality and national values have taken on a new urgency; and much of the focus of concern is directed at young people. As we shall see, children are often central to the reasons why people migrate, and a crucial factor in the whole experience. Yet in the official statistics, they are often conspicuously absent. Understanding the experience of child migrants in its own terms is therefore a far from straightforward task.

## Changing patterns of migration

There is no doubt that the globalising effects of increased travel and communication technologies (discussed in Chapter 1), as well as continuing natural and human disasters, have precipitated an enormous increase in migration worldwide. Escape from poverty and conflict remains the primary motive for migration. The majority of migrants move either within their national boundaries (generally, from rural to urban settings) in search of employment, or to neighbouring countries within their region in search of safety and work. Only a minority begin the journey further afield to the richer industrialised countries of immigration. Traditionally, their main destinations were Europe's former colonial or trading countries (United Kingdom, Netherlands and France) or those encouraging temporary labour migrants (Germany, Switzerland and Austria), along with the United States. However, this picture is changing. While the United States remains the largest industrialised country of immigration, new immigration countries have emerged. With the formation of the EU, countries in southern Europe (Spain, Italy and Greece) now have substantial numbers of migrants staying within their borders, rather than passing through to the richer nations of the north such as Germany or the Nordic countries. Rather than being countries of emigration, they are now having to adapt to a newly arrived and much more diverse population. In addition, former emigrants from these countries are now returning 'home', often with children who were born and grew up abroad and who may not speak the language fluently, if at all.

Other industrialising countries are also experiencing greater numbers of migrants from new and old areas of conflict or poverty. This no longer means a South-to-North movement of people: increasingly, the picture is more complex. South Africa, for example, is receiving large numbers of immigrants from across Africa; and while Nigeria is a net emigration country, it is also a centre for immigration, receiving people from its poorer neighbours.

For official purposes, migrants are categorised as economic migrants, refugees and asylum seekers (the notion of transnationalism does not feature here). Since 1951, refugees have been protected by the 'UN Convention Relating to the Status of Refugees', and by the related 1967 Protocol, to which 145 countries have currently signed up. The Convention defines a refugee as a person who is unable or unwilling to return to their country because of a 'well-founded fear of persecution on account of race, religion, nationality, membership in a particular social group, or political opinion'. Asylum seekers are those who are seeking protection under the Convention but whose claims have not yet been decided.

The Convention came into being primarily because of the numbers of refugees needing resettlement at the end of the Second World War, but it was also used for effective anti-Soviet propaganda by the West during the Cold War. Since then, the numbers of refugees have increased dramatically, as have the countries from which they originate – although the picture is constantly changing. The UNHCR (2006b) has recently reported an increase in what they term 'populations of concern' (currently at 20.8 million), which include internally displaced people. Almost the entire population in Colombia is classified in this way, while Iraq currently has 1.6 million displaced people. Relative to these, refugee numbers have actually declined in recent years. In 2006, they constituted 40 per cent of this total population of concern, while during the period 1997–2001 the figure was between 55 and 61 per cent. By the end of 2005, the global number of refugees totalled an estimated 8.4 million, the lowest level since 1980: this constitutes a net decrease of more than one million refugees (−12 per cent) since the beginning of 2005, when 9.5 million refugees were recorded. Part of the reason for this relative decline, however, is due to more restrictive policies on the part of immigration countries.

In Europe and the United States, the 1970s saw an economic recession due to the oil crisis and a resultant closing of the doors for migrant workers who had previously been encouraged to come. The 1980s saw increased numbers of asylum seekers coming independently from the world's trouble spots rather than as organised groups through international agreements. In the 1990s, European countries began to implement several restrictive measures (UNHCR, 2000a,b). First, 'carrier sanctions' were imposed to prevent people without documents from reaching Europe. Secondly, western Europe began to shift responsibility by drawing up lists of 'safe third countries', which meant that refugees could be returned to countries through which they had passed in their attempts to reach western Europe. Thirdly, governments began to reinterpret the UN Convention and practise a more restrictive definition in their assessment of asylum applications. Fourthly, several measures were introduced that saw the detention of asylum seekers, denial of social assistance and a restriction in employment opportunities. One consequence has been a growing number of illegal immigrants and a significant increase in human trafficking. The costs of migration have increased, and it is only those with resources who can travel the further distances out of their immediate regions (Van Hear, 2004).

In this situation, there is a contradiction between the increasingly globalised flows of finance (and therefore of migrants seeking work) and national or regional measures that are seeking to restrict immigration. Indeed, such restrictions are keeping out a workforce that is often positively required: there is growing concern in the traditional immigration countries about an ageing demographic, and a recognition that a younger workforce is needed. As a result, in some sections of the economy there is an increasing dependency on a poorly paid and illegal immigrant workforce. In Europe, there have been calls for a more realistic assessment of employment needs, on the basis that this would automatically reduce the illegal workforce and the possibility of obtaining work illegally, and thus illegal immigration. At the other end, international recruitment of professionals to fill the gaps in health and education services in the ageing, richer industrial nations is also leaving sections of the health and education services short-staffed in African and east Asian countries. So while travel and transnational employment are offering increased choice for those with the economic and social resources, there are growing numbers for whom migration means difficult, illegal and expensive journeys to poorly paid, illegal work.

## Belonging: the naturalisation debate

While there has been a growing acceptance of dual and multiple nationalities, regulations surrounding the granting of legal citizenship vary greatly from country to country, as do the ways in which states view the rights of second generation migrants. But, crucial as they are, legal papers saying you are part of a society do not ensure what Castles and Davidson (2000: 84) term 'substantial citizenship', by which the immigrant is assured of equal chances to participate in the politics, employment, welfare and cultural life of the nation. As they argue, a certain level of social and economic welfare is needed before meaningful participation in civil and political society and the take-up of political rights are possible:

> the nation state has an in-built tendency to create difference and to racialise minorities. This is achieved not only through discourses that ascribe difference to the Other, but also through various forms of political and social action that separate and differentiate members of minorities from the mainstream population. These discursive and material practices create the Other, and then take the prescribed Otherness as a justification for the differential treatment. In turn

the excluded minorities tend to constitute themselves as collect-
ives – sometimes using the very symbols of exclusion as a focus of
resistance.

(Castles and Davidson, 2000: 82)

These debates about migration and citizenship reflect some fundamental
contradictions that are part of the wider cultural climate in many
nations experiencing substantial immigration. On the one hand, there
is a growing nostalgia for (or perhaps merely a fantasy about) a simpler,
less diverse form of national belonging. There are calls for stronger
restrictions and controls on immigration, and a resurgent emphasis on
the need to assimilate immigrants into the 'national culture' – itself a
construct that is based on an imagined national history, destiny and
values that are presumed to be shared. Far right parties are gaining
ground and influencing centrist governments to 'toughen up' (van
Donselaar and Rodrigues, 2001). Yet at the same time, the economic
and social interrelationship of countries through globalisation means
that national boundaries and cultures are no longer so powerful in the
imaginations and actualities of many people's lives. Remaining in one
place can no longer mean insulation from the rest of the world (if indeed
it ever did). This contradiction has been exacerbated by recent world
events, but it has always been reflected in the educational and social
welfare policies of immigration countries, as we shall see below.

However, for the most part, children and young people are absent
from these debates. Migrant children occasionally figure here as victims –
vulnerable, innocent and at risk of corruption and exploitation. By
contrast, once they approach the age of majority, migrant youth tend
to be perceived more as a threat to the established social order. Yet, as
for migrants generally, there is little recognition here of the diversity of
their experience, and little attempt to understand the issues from their
perspective. In terms of social and educational policy, the overriding
tendency is not to recognise the skills that these children bring from
their own diverse backgrounds and cultures, but rather to insist on their
conformity to perceived national norms. As in so many other areas, children are predominantly seen here as mere recipients of adults' attempts
at socialisation, rather than as social actors in their own right.

## Children at the centre

Nevertheless, as Orellana et al. (2001) suggests, children play a very significant role in migration and transnational living; and in turn, children

themselves (and childhood more broadly) are shaped by these experiences. As she argues, 'scholars who ignore children's presence and participation in processes of migration…neglect a central axis of family migration, and an important reason why families move across national borders and sustain transnational ties' (ibid.: 588). As we shall see in more detail later, statistics on the issue are limited and unreliable, but it is clear that growing numbers of children are migrating, either alone or as members of families. Across the world, the large majority of migrants and refugees are young people aged under 25 years. Information on the age breakdown of UNHCR's 'populations of concern' is available for some 5.6 million persons: of these, some 44 per cent are children under the age of 18 years, while 12 per cent are under the age of 5 years (UNHCR, 2006a).

Children are frequently central to the experience of migration. In the decision to move, families are often motivated by the desire to build a better educational and material life for their children (Yeoh et al., 2005). Planning family migration takes time and money, and children are often actively involved in working with the family to raise the cash. Indeed, children are increasingly financed (often with great hardship) by the extended family to lead the way on their own, taking responsibility for improving the lives of their families. Alternatively, when it is parents who relocate, remittances are often used to maintain the younger members of the family and sometimes extended family members back home. Transnational parenting facilitated via phone, e-mail and letters is also increasing (ibid.: Mahler and Pessar, 2001; Vertovec, 2004). Children represent the cohesion that motivates much family reunion. When whole families move, children form the front line in the place of arrival, often learning the language and social mores before their parents, acting as interpreters and negotiators for family members.

Likewise, when and if the opportunity comes to return to the home country, it is often the children who might prevent this from happening. Having formed a new life in the immigration country, and feeling more detached from their parents' country of origin, they may be reluctant to return and the family often decides to settle permanently (Castles and Miller 2003). In discussing the possibility of return with the children in our research, many could foresee that as they grew older they would be reluctant to move back to what they increasingly saw as their parents' country of origin. They wanted to visit (where possible) and to keep contact with the extended family and the culture, but most were more concerned with their present lives and futures in their new location than with the idea of return.

In all these ways, children are central actors and participants in the processes of migration, while at the same time their own lives and relationships are fundamentally altered through the experience (Orellana et al., 2001). Their presence and needs influence social policy in the receiving countries; and they are often the focus of conflict between cultural maintenance and cultural change. It is therefore increasingly anomalous that in accounts and statistics about migration, children and youth are largely invisible. Where they do appear in such statistics, and in academic and policy debates, it is as refugees and asylum seekers – as unaccompanied minors or victims of trafficking – and in discussions about education, welfare provision and social unrest in the immigration countries. As in much of the media coverage, they are seen either as victims in the leaving or vandals in the settling.

Several researchers have addressed the unequal power relations that are inherent in contemporary forms of migration. Doreen Massey (1994: 149) refers to this as a 'power-geometry', in which there are some 'who are really in a sense in charge of time-space compression, who really see it and turn it to advantage, whose power and influence it very definitely increases ... but there are also groups who are also doing a lot of moving, but who are not "in charge" of the process in the same way at all.' However, the recent emphasis on transnationalism (discussed in Chapter 1), and the recognition of the active ongoing connections that migrants maintain between locations, suggest that migrants are nevertheless able to exert some forms of power and control. This suggests that we need to attend to the complex relationships between broader global structures and individual agency at the local and personal level. As Levitt et al. (2003: 567) remind us, 'transnational migrants are embedded in multi-layered social fields and ... to truly understand migrants' activities and experiences, their lives must be studied within the context of these multiple strata ... it is not simply that global forces influence local actors but that local economic, political and religious practices of individuals act back'. In studying the role of children in migration, researchers similarly have to deal with what Rizzini and Bush (2002: 372) call 'the tension between the particular and the general, between that part of the world of children the researcher is exploring and the larger forces that affect the microcosm'.

## Defining child migrants

So who are the child migrants? In one sense, it is not possible to consider them as a group since they vary with origin, age, social class, gender, religion, ethnicity and so on. Their heterogeneity reflects that of all migrants and reconfirms the fact that behind the main trends and statistics, migration is also a deeply personal experience (Brah, 1996; Kaufman et al., 2002). This diversity is complicated further as a result of the methodological difficulties entailed in gathering and comparing data. For example, migration is frequently seen in terms of ethnicity, and yet categorisations of ethnicity (for example, in ethnic monitoring) are often confusing, appearing to mix nationality, language, region, skin colour and religion. This means that certain groups are highlighted while others become invisible. For example, in some countries (like the United Kingdom) 'Turkish' people are often classified under 'white', so they do not appear as a separate group, although their circumstances and needs might be different from those of the mainstream 'white' population. In addition, the category Kurdish/Turkish might not appear at all. To give another example, 'white' immigrants from the so-called old Commonwealth countries of Australia, Canada and South Africa become invisible, although they are one of the largest immigrant groups in the United Kingdom (as indeed are 'white' Europeans). As a result, they do not become part of public debate and concern about immigration: in the public eye, migration is seen as 'black' or increasingly as 'Muslim' (as the new 'Other'). Strict categorisations also disallow self-determination, and tend to ignore 'mixed' racial backgrounds and serial migrations.

In such discussions, terms like 'minority' and 'majority' also tend to become fixed, immoveable categories (Castles and Davidson, 2000). This implies that the 'majority' is somehow homogeneous, while minorities will have more in common with other minorities than with the majority. Such categorisations take no account of differences of class, region, gender, age and so on within each category. Likewise, many documents do not differentiate between newly arrived ethnic migrants and those who have been here for several generations. This implies that all ethnic minorities are somehow 'foreign', and makes it difficult to take account of the different experiences of first and second or third generation immigrants.

Several of these difficulties are compounded when it comes to children. As we stated above, children generally do not appear separately from adults in the statistics, and it is often necessary to read between the lines in order to get a picture of where children sit or the main issues that affect them. These difficulties further contribute to the marginalisation – or indeed invisibility – of migrant children. For example, the International Federation Terre des Hommes (2005) notes that in an

EU Green paper (COM, 2004: 811 final) seeking to identify 'the main issues at stake and possible options for an EU legislative framework on economic migration', the specific position of children was totally ignored. In response, Terre des Hommes pointed out that children could also actively choose to migrate for economic reasons, or indeed be encouraged to do so by their families, and that they should necessarily be considered as part of the flow of migrant workers.

A good practice guide published for immigration lawyers in the United Kingdom points out that this invisibility continues into immigration statistics:

> The task of compiling statistical and other information about children and young people who are subject to immigration control is difficult. Existing information is patchy and different agencies who are in contact with children and young people collect different information depending on their organisational needs. In addition it may be difficult to collate information because comparable definitions are not used.
>
> (Crawley, 2004: 98)

Nevertheless, there have been some recent moves to ensure that children are seen and treated as a distinct category with particular needs. The aim here is to use the UN Convention of the Rights of the Child and its key principle of the 'best interests of the child' in order to integrate a children's rights perspective into the processes affecting migrant children (not just asylum seekers) (Swedish Migration Board, 2001). This 'child first – migrant second' approach has also been taken up in discussions in the United Kingdom in relation to the detention and legal treatment of unaccompanied minors and the children of asylum seeking families. For example, a recent report by the United Kingdom charity Save the Children (Crawley and Lester, 2005) draws on interviews with children, parents, policy makers and practitioners to describe the criminalisation of refugee children and its detrimental effects on their education, physical and mental health that run counter to the terms of the Convention.

However, the United Kingdom Refugee Council has highlighted continuing problems with establishing this principle. As a result of moves by the EU designed to harmonise asylum policy and processes across Europe and ensure that asylum seekers can only claim asylum in one EU state (the Dublin II regulation), children are being treated primarily as migrants. The following example is a good illustration:

Michael, an unaccompanied child from the Middle East, had sought asylum in Greece and was held in detention for three months, where he was beaten and exploited. He was released from detention after signing a document saying he would leave Greece immediately, despite no decision having been made on his claim for asylum. Still unable to return to his home country because of a fear of persecution there, Michael fled to the UK. The Home Office asked Greece to 'take back' Michael despite being aware of his experiences. Michael was removed to Greece earlier this year.

(Refugee Council, 2006)

Even so, this emphasis on children's rights is not straightforward. As we argued in Chapter 1, definitions of childhood are culturally specific; and it is not always easy to see how the interests of the child are to be defined, or indeed by whom (Boyden, 1997). The UN defines a child as a person between the ages of 0 and 18 years, yet in many parts of the world adolescents aged well under 18 years take on major responsibilities and are no longer considered minors. The discourse of children's rights as defined in the UN Convention also tends to separate the rights of the individual child from a more holistic consideration of the child in relation to role, function, place and community. The idea that children have certain 'needs' that must be met runs together with the discourse of children's rights and underlies many international policies and aids initiatives formulated in the West. Yet this view of rights and needs has been criticised as highly culturally specific (Stephens, 1995).

In practice, then, child migrants take on two, often conflicting, legal statuses, that of a child and that of a migrant. Yet in both respects, they can be stigmatised:

In the first place there is an initial focus whereby the minor is conceived as a victim that must be subject to protection through models that infantilise and are excessively protectionist. Contrary to this, there is a second view, the legal focus, whereby the UMM (unaccompanied migrant minor) is conceived as a public order problem due to their legal situation, their provisional legal status and also their condition as a young person and its implications.

(CON RED Project, 2005: 16)

## Categories of child migrants

If there are problems in defining the categories of 'child' and 'migrant', we also need to take account of the diverse forms that migration can take. In this section, we look at some broad categories of child migrants – although we need to bear in mind that these may overlap, and that other factors of locality, class, gender, culture and religion also play a part in defining the migrant experience.

### Third culture kids

By no means are all child migrants disadvantaged or socially excluded. So-called third culture kids (TCKs) can be seen as a category of exclusive cosmopolitans of the kind mentioned in Chapter 1. According to Pollock and van Reken (2001: 19), a third culture kid is the one who has 'spent a significant part of his or her developmental years outside the parents' culture. The TCK builds relationships to all of the cultures, while not having full ownership in any. Although elements from each culture are assimilated into the TCK's life experience, the sense of belonging is in relationship to others of similar background.' TCKs are the children of (for example) diplomats, international business executives, military personnel, religious missionaries, students studying abroad or aid agency workers. They might be born in Hong Kong and raised in Nigeria and England, an Indian living in Japan, an American reared in France or a German growing up in Ghana. These children of expatriates often attend international schools, and have varying degrees of integration into the places in which they live. The idea implied in their name is that through their migration experiences they develop a 'third culture' that allows them to integrate different aspects of their experiences and contacts with others into a culture that is not fully connected either to that of their parents or to the place in which they are currently living.

Studying the experiences of repatriating Germans from these elite backgrounds, Knorr (2005) notes the cultural adjustments they are required to make. Many feel they are having to adjust to different racial and social hierarchies. Having been part of an elite white minority, they are now part of a large middle class that in some areas might be racially mixed. One 16-year-old boy recalls that having lived in Africa for most of his life, it was only on returning to Germany that he made friends with a black classmate from Guinea. Another describes the experience of repatriation in terms of loss of identity:

> I felt different but I looked the same. I wanted to show I am different. So I got dreadlocks to make me look African...well in a way, I suppose I wanted to show my African part. I had a friend who was half Ghanaian, half German. He had never been to Ghana, but he was always considered an exotic person somehow, whereas I, having

spent 15 years in Africa, was considered the same as everyone else. I felt I was more different than him. So I got myself dreadlocks and a Rasta cap. I also became an expert in Reggae and Highlife music. In fact, that's when I started to feel at home somehow. After turning my African part inside out... Yes, I turned my African part inside out.

(Knorr, 2005: 74)

It is significant that in the case of these children the creativity of developing a 'third', new culture is so easily recognised. This is related to the notion of new ethnicities we discussed in Chapter 1: here, the experience of living with two or more different cultures is not seen as potentially schizophrenic or a matter of 'culture clash' but as a creative process. By contrast, when it comes to other immigrant groups this potential is generally either ignored or becomes a source of controversy. As Knorr (ibid.: 54) states, 'There is an implicit – and qualifying – distinction made between TCKs on the one hand and other young (im)migrants on the other. With regard to the former, (appropriate) cultural creativity is emphasised; with regard to the latter (inappropriate) cultural conservatism.'

### Refugees and asylum seekers

At the other extreme are those children who have been forced to move because of conflict or natural disasters, either as part of large population movements, with their families or alone as unaccompanied minors. As we outlined above, most of these refugee children will move within their geographical region, usually to neighbouring countries, many living for long periods in refugee camps, relying on international aid efforts for food, shelter and education. However, many others form a significant presence in all industrialised immigration countries. As we have seen, UNHCR figures state that refugee numbers dropped by one-third between 2001 and 2006. This is partly due to refugees returning to their countries of origin, especially to Afghanistan, Liberia and Burundi. Interestingly, Afghanistan is also the country producing the largest numbers of refugees with 1.9 million in 72 countries. However, the number of people 'of concern' has risen globally to 20.8 million mainly due to the increasing numbers of internally displaced people, with Colombia, Iraq and Sudan being top of the list. In 2005 the United States and most western European nations were each receiving over 10 000 asylum applications. These figures do not separate out children as a special group although the UNHCR states that 'usually more than half of any refugee population are children' (UNHCR, 1994).

With increasing demographic movement, it has become difficult to differentiate between refugees, as narrowly defined by the UN Convention on Refugees, and other migrants (UNHCR, 2000a). Over the years, immigration authorities have developed operational categories that refer to different reasons for immigration – labour, refugees, family reunifications and so on. Policies of immigration and integration have differed with regard to these categories. Whereas the intake of labour migrants is regulated by domestic needs and economic considerations, the acceptance of refugees and family reunifications is justified by international conventions and humanitarian considerations. In this climate, Europe, for example, has increasingly sought to exclude 'economic migrants' (except those within an expanding EU) who are not covered by the Convention, and to keep successful asylum applications to a steady small percentage. However, such administrative distinctions can be hard to sustain. People, including children, can migrate for a variety of reasons closely related to their own and their families' survival, but not always related directly to the actions of oppressive governments (for example, due to torture and human rights abuses). The dilemma here is that, while recognising the complexity of these issues, it is also vital to maintain the legal status of 'refugee' (as defined by the UN) in the interests of protecting international human rights.

A small number of refugee children with financial resources and social networks in the destination countries travel beyond their immediate regions. For example, in Greece, traditionally a country of emigration, the figures for 2003 (ECRE, 2003) show that between 2002 and 2003 asylum applications went up by 44 per cent to 8178. The Greek Council for refugees reported that in 2000 (CHICAM, 2002) nearly one-third of the then 3000 applicants were below the age of 20 years, the majority being young men. The ECRE figures state that in 2003, there were 314 unaccompanied minors arriving primarily from Afghanistan, Iraq and Nigeria. Meanwhile Home Office figures (2005) in the United Kingdom for 2004 show that the majority of principal asylum applicants were under 35 years. Out of a total of nearly 41 000 asylum applications (a drop of 32 per cent on the previous year) the majority of dependents (6665) were under the age of 15 years. The largest groups came from Iran, Iraq, Somalia, China and Zimbabwe. There were 2990 asylum applications by unaccompanied minors (below the age of 17 years), mainly from Afghanistan, Iran and Somalia. Within this picture it is difficult to gauge the number of child refugees and asylum seekers. Children generally migrate with their families, often through the legal entitlement to family reunification, and clear figures of exactly how many do so are not readily available.

The discourse of child rights (discussed earlier) has been used to highlight cases where child asylum seekers are being mistreated as a result of their migration status. For example, in Australia a group of parents and citizens formed an organisation called ChilOut in 2001 to oppose the mandatory detention of children in Australian immigration detention centres. They state that 'between 1992 and 2005, thousands of children and their parents were locked in remote desert facilities surrounded by razor wire fences in Australia and islands to Australia's north. Most of the children were from Iraq, Afghanistan and Iran and nearly all were found to be refugees' (*www.chilout.org*). Again, they base their protest on the fact that Australia is a signatory to the UN Convention on the Rights of the Child (1989). As a result of this pressure, there are now no longer children behind razor wire, although the policy of mandatory detention remains and families and children are held in community-based centres.

The ChilOut campaign successfully personalised children's experiences of detention by making them visible through drawings and personal accounts that appeared on their website. These highlight the physical and mental suffering they were experiencing:

> Shayan's picture (right), which he drew as a 6 year old, shows Shayan and his sister crying, with their parents. The van at bottom right is the ambulance that would take Shayan to and from Westmead Children's Hospital, when he needed to be rehydrated because he would not eat or drink properly. Top left is a guard with a baton. Bottom left is a detainee bleeding where he has cut his wrist. All along the top is the razor wire that sits across the fences at Villawood.

> (ibid.)

In the United Kingdom, the experience of children in detention has also been a matter of concern. The Save the Children report *No Place for a Child* (Crawley and Lester, 2005), discussed above, highlighted similar individual cases. One of these was Jacques who arrived in the United Kingdom at the age of 16 years after spending time in prison due to his family's religious affiliations. He was placed in detention where his mental health deteriorated: 'I spent eight months and 24 days [in detention]. It was the hardest time of my life. It's hell. Prison is better than detention ... In prison you have rights not veiled rights. In detention you have no rights.' As these accounts suggest, the treatment of such children may be little more humane than the cruelty from which they have fled. It also negates the positive role that children play in migration and in settling into the new country.

## Unaccompanied minors

A matter of concern in immigration countries is the increasing number of unaccompanied minors (or separated children) arriving both as refugees and as economic migrants (discussed below). The UNHCR classifies separated children as 'children under 18 years of age who are outside their country of origin and separated from both parents or their previous legal/customary primary caregiver' (2000b). The 2003 OECD report on international migration trends highlights this issue. Again, the authors stress the difficulties in gathering accurate data, since different countries use different definitions and methods of assessment. They also note that the increase in trafficking and disappearances from reception centres, both of which directly affect children, complicates the issue. However, they note that at any one time there 'may be up to 100 000 non-accompanied minors in Western Europe alone' (OECD, 2003: 87) and that although this number is increasing, only a very small percentage claim asylum.

Interestingly, the pattern of migration for children in this category appears to be different from the main trends. In the Netherlands, for example, the number of unaccompanied minors increased by 34 per cent in 1999 and almost doubled in Hungary. Most of the inflow in the Netherlands comes from China (67 per cent), whereas there are relatively few unaccompanied minors among Chinese asylum applications in the United Kingdom (3 per cent). However, the Chinese account for only 3 per cent of all asylum applications in the Netherlands but for 5 per cent in the United Kingdom (OECD, 2003: 87).

In other immigration countries, the pattern of growing numbers of unaccompanied minors is similar. Both Australia and Canada have seen a substantial increase in recent years, mainly young men from Afghanistan, and the United States has seen at least a doubling of arrivals (5400 in 2001) most coming from China, Mexico, Guatemala, Honduras and El Salvador. Approximately one third of these are detained in secure units. As the report points out, this presents a challenge to receiving countries (especially since these official figures probably hide a reality of greater numbers).

In our own research, we have worked with several children from Angola who were sent unaccompanied to join extended family members in the United Kingdom. Two of these had witnessed their parents' death and were fortunately receiving counselling through a refugee support agency. In another case, it was unclear under what circumstances the boy had left Angola, as he was unwilling to talk about his past. His school was concerned about his progress but had no contact with the family with whom he was living. This is not unusual: as Rutter (2006) points out, services for unaccompanied minors in the United Kingdom are very variable and often poor, which has a detrimental effect on their mental health and educational attainment.

## Economic migrants

The majority of migrants are what is termed 'economic'. This is the category that causes the most controversy but it is also the one that most clearly demonstrates the growing interdependence between sending and receiving regions. As mentioned above, children are often central to the motivation to migrate in order to try to improve employment and educational prospects and achieve a better standard of living. Yet as Castles and Miller (2003: 32) argue, it is increasingly difficult to distinguish between refugees and economic migrants, as there are links between the various reasons for migration: 'underdevelopment, impoverishment, poor governance, endemic conflict and human rights abuse are closely linked. These conditions lead both to economically-motivated migration and to politically-motivated flight'.

Economic migration affects whole communities of children. For example, in a study conducted in one region of El Salvador, Mahler (1998) found that 97 per cent of school children in the area had one or more relatives living in the United States, with an average of more than six relatives for each child. This pattern is not new or specific to Central or Latin America. Many children of workers coming to the United Kingdom from the Caribbean in the 1960s and 1970s were initially left behind with extended family members. The children would be sent for after a few years, joining parents they hardly knew. Meanwhile, in South Africa this pattern of long separations was a harsh reality for many workers under apartheid, and is still continuing. In Europe, the Middle East, Africa and the United States, there have long been domestic workers unable to keep their children with them. In our CHICAM research, for example, our Italian partner worked with several children from Latin American countries who were living in an orphanage while their mothers worked as domestic servants, unable to have them living with them.

On the other hand, as for many non-migrants, children are actively involved in the economic survival or well-being of their families, working in shops, as street vendors or assisting in the home while parents are out at work. Dropping out of school or absenteeism is often related to urgent financial needs at home. For example, several of the children in the CHICAM research helped in the family business (for example, a kiosk or a restaurant). A boy in the German club talked about helping his father with his delivery job during the school holidays, while in the Swedish club some children sought temporary work in the summer in order to make extra money for their families. The issue of child workers and children's relationship to the economy, like that of childhood itself, is often perceived differently in different cultural settings and circumstances (Boyden, 1997). In many cases, the horror stories of 'child slave labour' are not distinguished from children who work, and the role of children in the family and community economy becomes invisible or alternatively demonised. In many cases, the economic contribution of children is part of the overall survival and improvement plan for the wider family, of which migration can of course be an integral part.

Migration itself demands economic resources to begin with, and this can determine how far and where it is possible to migrate to. Van Hear (2004: 2) cites the example of 'a Ghanaian would be asylum seeker who wound up in Lebanon, not because he particularly wanted to go there, but because this was the destination he could reach with the financial resources and connections he had at his disposal. He had hoped to use Lebanon as a stepping stone to a more prosperous destination, but ran out of money and had to go back to Ghana'. Van Hear draws on Massey's notion of 'power geometry' and on Pierre Bourdieu's (1986) thinking on capital, arguing that in migration one form of capital can be converted into another. Thus, the ability to reach more wealthy countries can be made possible either through greater access to funds – economic capital – or through access to contacts and know-how – social capital; and the ability to work there, and send remittances to family members back home, can in turn fund the education of other family members (educational capital) or community and political enterprises. In these ways, migration can increase the social power and capital of certain families and particular family members, affecting the emigration country and changing or reinforcing the power balance of whole communities and nations. This kind of continuing but distanced involvement in the politics of the country of origin, termed 'long-distance nationalism' (Anderson, 1998) can reach extreme forms whereby armed conflicts are prolonged by emigrants' financial and political support, thus in turn perpetuating the reasons for migration.

The overall point here is that social class is a central but often forgotten factor in migration patterns. It has a profound affect on children in terms of who moves and who stays, their access to education, health and housing – and this applies both to the migrant family that moves and to the wider community that stays and to those who return. It also applies to refugees in the same way as it does to economic migrants. Van Hear (2004) highlights how these differentials played an important role in the situation in Somaliland. The majority of refugees returning from neighbouring Ethiopia to Somaliland when it declared its separation from Somalia were returning to difficult economic and physical circumstances, having lost property and land because they had had to flee. Meanwhile, a group that had managed to travel further and were returning from Scandinavia successfully obtained EU financial assistance to buy land, build houses, improve infrastructure and provide schooling that would continue instruction in their children's Scandinavian languages. While the whole community might have benefited from the physical improvements, it is clear that an elite was created that would have long-term effects on the society.

As we have argued, in certain circumstances it may prove very difficult to distinguish between children who are economic migrants and those who are refugees and seeking asylum. Perhaps more to the point, these groups' experiences of settling into their new countries of residence, of negotiating new institutions, educational and social expectations, and dealing with racist responses from the host population, are likely to be similar. In the following sections, we consider the implications of this in terms of family life, and then in relation to schooling.

## Migration and family life

The fact of migration changes family relationships. The economic and social factors that bring about migration in the first place also determine to a large extent the ways in which families are affected by it. The ability to get well-paid, legal employment, live in decent housing and find good schools depends on economic and social capital. The majority of migrants move to where they can receive support. If there are already family members in the immigration country, this eases the entry; but even where there are not, there is a tendency for people from a particular region to follow each other to particular locations. For example, large numbers of migrants from Carriacou, a small island off Grenada in the Caribbean settled in the port town of Hull in the north-east of England;

while the families who migrated from an area of Northern El Salvador all tended to live in the same neighbourhood of New York City.

In these cases, community members begin to take on the role of extended family, children growing to see them as 'aunts', 'uncles' and 'cousins'. These were terms frequently used by the children in the CHICAM research, but they were by no means confined to blood relatives. In this situation, 'family' and 'household' become more fluid and take on a different form from that widely held in Western social welfare and educational institutions, where family is still seen as a collection of closely related individuals remaining within one national context (Gardner and Grillo, 2002). In the case of CHICAM, the children used quite diverse definitions of 'family'. These included: the international extended family that has developed through migration, who are in contact from time to time; the immediate group who live under one roof on a daily basis (which could be nuclear); and people from the same country who are not blood relatives, but who had formed part of a new community in their everyday lives – a form of 'constructed family'. As Fog Olwig (2002) suggests, understanding transnational and diasporic identities among migrants requires a greater awareness of this 'multi-sited and multi-dimensional character of home making'.

Migration can have complex and ambivalent consequences for power relationships within the family. Rather than liberating women from gender-based dependencies and unequal power structures, migration has arguably reinforced them, changing family patterns in ways that are not always to the advantage of women and children. For example, in her study of the wives of El Salvadoran, migrants Mahler (1999) points out that before their husbands migrated to the United States, family and community survival depended on the success of the agricultural crops. After the husband's migration, families were dependent on the uncertain arrival of the letter containing money, and because of the men's absence crops were no longer being grown, thus making the women even more vulnerable. In other situations where the feminisation of migration has become an established pattern, for example, with women from India moving to take up domestic labour in the Gulf States and leaving their partners and children behind, the pressure to maintain family connections remains with the women, placing an enormous emotional and financial burden on them and on the children they leave behind (Yeoh et al., 2005). In our own research in the United Kingdom, we found mothers describing their loss of power both in and outside the home, and particularly in relation to their children. One group of Turkish/Kurdish women talked of their fear when their children threatened to phone a child advice agency (Childline) when there was a family disagreement (de Block, 2002).

However, the implications of migration for children's position in family power-relationships may be more ambiguous. Migration can place more responsibility onto children. Children frequently act as interpreters for parents or other community members; and they can become the interface between the family and the social institutions of the immigration country. In migrant families, certain roles may be reversed, as the educative function of the parents is often taken up by the children. The children are frequently charged with the responsibility of educating their parents in the ways of the new society (Hamilton and Moore, 2004). As the father of one of the CHICAM children told us: 'being a refugee is to learn from your children instead of teaching them yourself'.

In the case of our research, many of the children played a crucial role in helping the family to learn the language of the new country (cf. Murad, 2002). They were the ones who learnt the language first (mainly at school but also through everyday use in the neighbourhood, playground or their other activities), and who in turn acted as translators and mediators for older family members. The parents often had to rely on their children to make contact with the locals. This was an important factor affecting the distribution and negotiation of roles within the family. Although learning the new language was one of the primary prerequisites in terms of adapting to life in the new country (for example in Sweden, immigrants are expected to pass tests in Swedish), it was often the case that adults did not learn it, nor did they ever speak it at home. This inevitably led to a heavy reliance on the children for dealing with public services and legal procedures (Vera, 2002). For the adults, learning a widely spoken language (such as English) was often more valued than learning the language of the country in which they lived (such as Italian), as it would be more useful for their further plans as opposed to what they considered a temporary residence.

For both parents and children, this renegotiation of roles can bring great frustration and unease. On the one hand, parents want their children to conform to their own way of life and standards; yet on the other, they want them to be successful in the new country, to build new social contacts and understand the new systems. This brings the risk that they will cease to conform (de Block, 2002; Gillespie, 1995). Likewise, children want to maintain the family connections, but also to fit in with their new friends and the demands of the new environment. These are sometimes incompatible desires, and they can create significant tensions in the home. Meanwhile, from outside, families are often faced with hostility and racism that breed fear and resentment. Although there are some exceptions, refugee and migrant families are also disproportionately likely to live in conditions of relative deprivation. In our CHICAM research, several families were living in very difficult physical circumstances. In Greece, a family of nine lived in a one-bedroom flat, with most of the children squeezing into the living room and the corridor. Another family of five lived for a while in an elevator service room without any windows. Even when the situation was not so bad, the children often lacked a private space. Very few children had a room of their own. Yet the need to create small spaces where they could install their own microcosm, as for any other children, remained: many maintained cupboards of memorabilia, in which pictures, posters and gadgets were placed side-by-side with toys and small symbols of identity.

In several countries, refugees (once their status is established) are better off than economic immigrants, as they are offered accommodation in public housing or receive support with rent payments. In countries like Greece where these are not offered, there is a greater pressure to move elsewhere. Unemployment is also a major source of stress within refugee and migrant families. Even when employment is found, it is not offered on the basis of qualifications and skills. In most cases, the level or the status of employment in the new country is much lower than it was in the place of origin (there were several instances in our research of university graduates being employed in manual work). Issues such as these, which affect the parents of refugee and migrant children, have a consequent effect on the social and psychological well-being of the children, sometimes leading to further social exclusion.

All the families in our research had limited means, while some lived in conditions of poverty. For many families, further migration to another country, especially one that appears to be wealthier or more supportive in terms of rights and opportunities towards immigrants and refugees or where there are existing family and community connections, is often a desired option. In turn, this imagined future mobility makes integration into one place difficult. Attempts to become established somewhere and to form social relations are threatened by the lack of resources and the uncertain outcome of asylum or residence applications, as in the case of one girl in our UK CHICAM club, who was deported during the course of our research.

In such circumstances, long distance family connections can often take on powerful emotional and symbolic significance. Increasingly, it is women who are the migrants and remittance senders; and this has consequences for maintaining familial bonds and connections with children. There is a growing number of studies of the ways in which women migrant workers work to maintain a sense of connection with their children through phone calls, letters and e-mail. As Yeoh et al. (2005: p310) point out, 'the changing technologies, economic acts and emotional pains and gains of "staying connected" in order to "do family" and perform care work across national borders are central concerns to understanding the inner workings of the transnational family' (see also Asis, 2002; Orellana, 2001). Similarly, Mahler (1998) describes children writing letters for their illiterate mothers in El Salvador to send to their fathers in New York.

Family rituals and religious festivals are used by migrants in conventional ways to display social success and power, but they take on additional importance in confirming continuing connections across the globe (Gardner and Grillo, 2002). For example, Fog Olwig (2002) followed the events surrounding a Caribbean wedding that brought family members together from several continents to participate in the celebrations acted out in the home village in Nevis. She notes the various ways in which power was displayed through the process, both to other family members and to the community who were still based in the home village where the ceremony took place. Of course, it remains to be seen whether the children of such transnational families will feel the need to continue this type of display or whether they will be more focused on the country in which they grew up, although this kind of continuing connection is certainly a central part of their experience of migration.

For the children in the CHICAM research, religious observances served as an important way of sustaining cultural identity and as a reminder and a fortifier of habits and traditions that had been forcibly left behind. When religion or religious persecutions and exclusion have been the reason to leave the country of origin, the practice of that religion offers a legitimate basis of existence in the new country and plays an affirmative role (Murad, 2002). Yet children also experience pressure to give up traditional habits, particularly at school, as they may be perceived as backward and conservative, or even threatening to the host culture. Thus, some children talked about celebrating the major festivals of their own religion but also those of the majority Christian society of which they were now part. Two Syrian Kurdish brothers in the Greek club, who kept all the Kurdish celebrations but also went from door to door to sing traditional Christmas carols, stated: 'We are Muslim but also a bit Christian as well!' Similarly, Western teenage fashion and media symbols were often taken up by the migrant children in our clubs, particularly in their attempts to establish themselves within their peer groups.

As we shall see in Chapters 3 and 4, media and new communications technologies are a powerful factor in the changing family lives of migrants. In most instances, families can now maintain much more regular contact than would have been possible in the past. Gone are the days when you saved up for the one-minute international phone call that you booked and then waited in line for in the telecommunications office in town, only to come away frustrated by the rushed verbal transactions over crackling lines. Vertovec (2004: 222) argues that this has transformed family life for migrants: 'Whereas throughout the world non-migrant families commonly have discussions across a kitchen table (for example, can we buy a refrigerator? What do we do about the teenagers' behaviour? Who should take care of grandmother?), now many families whose members are relocated through migration conduct the same everyday discussions in real time across oceans. Cheap telephone calls have largely facilitated this. It is now common for a single family to be stretched across vast distances and between nation-states, yet still retain its sense of collectivity.'

Thus, several children in the CHICAM project maintained regular contact with grandparents through the use of e-mail, and one father spoke graphically about the difference his mobile phone had made to him being able to maintain contact with his sons before they eventually joined him in London. Such resources are unevenly accessible, particularly in poorer or more remote parts of the world; but mobile telephones, which do not depend on cabling, may be helping to overcome these differences still further.

Family rituals and ceremonies are also often supported by the circulation of family videos. The significance of these is greater for migrant families, who are separated across continents and meet only occasionally. As we shall see, they often play an important role in including and educating children into the family culture and sustaining cross-generational continuity (Gardner and Grillo, 2002; de Block, 2002). Encouraging family memories and creating a sense of belonging through building family narratives across time and place is an important aspect of migrant family life (Chamberlain and Leydesdorff, 2004; Yeoh et al., 2005). Yet as Morley (2000) argues, the bringing of artefacts and objects from the country of origin reflects not so much a nostalgic desire to recreate the old home, as much as the need to create a safe place to go out from and meet the challenges and opportunities of the new location.

# The role of school

Before we move on to address the role of media in much greater detail, it is important to make some brief observations about the role of schools, since they provide the key link between the child, the family and the wider society. Of course, schools are an integral part of national societies: through their curricula, as well as through teaching methods, space and time management and the student–teacher relationship, they transmit the values that the national society considers central. As Anderson (1991) makes clear, it is partly in school that 'imagined communities' are created and reproduced. However, there is no simple linear transmission from an adult teacher representing a single national culture to a passive student receiver: school is a place where many narratives intersect in potentially conflicting ways (Besozzi, 1993).

Increasing globalisation and migration have significant implications for education. As schools in many areas are becoming increasingly culturally diverse, national narratives from the past are losing their relevance, and schools are being forced to adapt. This is making practical demands. For example, in the United Kingdom, some schools are beginning to include the languages of large immigrant communities such as Bengali as possible exam options. At the same time global economic shifts mean that schools are also offering Chinese (Mandarin) rather than French or German; and many are promoting international school links through the Internet and teacher exchanges. However, at the same time, the skills and experiences that immigrant children bring with them are often undervalued. Particularly in the wake of current global conflicts, discussions about multiculturalism are increasingly giving way to an emerging rhetoric about the role of schools in promoting assimilation and cultural integration. In some of the schools in the CHICAM project, multiculturalism was largely conceived in terms of historical representations of cultural difference rather than contemporary motivations and realities.

Education systems are finding it difficult to adapt to the increasing diversity that migration brings, and to the economic divides that are often the result of poor or overloaded social and educational services. A recent OECD report states that one of the main barriers to educational progress for immigrant children (from both first and second generations) is the fact that the majority attend poor schools in impoverished neighbourhoods:

> Clearly immigrant students in most countries attend schools with less socio-economically advantaged student populations. The differences

between the two student groups are significant in all countries except Australia, New Zealand, Norway, Sweden and the Russian Federation. In several European countries, such as Belgium, Denmark, France, Germany and the Netherlands, the segregation of immigrants across socio-economic lines in schools are large. In some of these countries (Belgium, Germany and the Netherlands), the pattern likely reflects tracking effects within the education system, with the highly tracked education systems having a tendency to sort students by their socio-economic status.

(OECD, 2006: 9)

Here again, social class is a significant dimension of the migrant experience; but as this report states, even after accounting for socio-economic factors, migrant children overall remain significantly disadvantaged in terms of educational attainment. This resonates with Castles and Davidson's (2000) argument, discussed earlier, that legal citizenship is inadequate if substantive citizenship through social, material and educational equalities is denied.

There are also great variations in how receiving countries deal with the integration of migrant children. These differences can be related to histories of immigration, the size of the multicultural population or the size of the community itself (such as in large cities versus small towns). For example, new immigrants may be placed in a mainstream class with their own age group and offered initial language support within the class (generally the policy in the United Kingdom); they may be placed in a preparatory class, and required to reach a particular grade before they move into the mainstream (the practice in Germany); or they may be placed in a special multicultural school and treated similarly to children with special needs (as in Greece). Across the countries in the CHICAM project, very few children received language support beyond the first levels; and in most cases there was no or very little support to encourage children to maintain and develop their first language/s. The OECD report confirms these findings and stresses the importance of sustained language provision: 'it appears that in some countries with relatively small achievement gaps between immigrant and native students, or smaller gaps for second-generation students compared to first-generation students, long-standing language support programmes exist with relatively clearly defined goals and standards. These countries include Australia, Canada and Sweden' (OECD, 2006: 5).

One common practice in several of the countries involved in CHICAM was in the form of 'multicultural days' or festivals in schools. These days shine the spotlight on the culture of origin, providing a space in which it can (re-)present itself. However, in such contexts students can become merely a representative of a culture, its symbol or, at worst, a mascot. In general, this form of shallow multiculturalism in education may be counterproductive to integration, since minority cultures are presented as different and 'special'. It often reflects an implicitly anthropological approach that privileges traditional, historical images above local contemporary realities and further 'exoticises' the representatives. For example, some of the Kosovan children feared that showing ethnic dances could be considered old-fashioned and as evidence that Albanians are backward and 'different'. As we shall see, the children involved in the project stressed repeatedly that they wished to speak as children, rather than representatives of a community or country. This was also confirmed in their refusal to speak of cases of discrimination related to their origins, and their tendency as far as possible to avoid representing themselves as 'different'.

Furthermore, in this context, some cultures (or rather their symbols) may well be viewed more positively than others. In the German school, for example, one girl from the Dominican Republic was in great demand as a salsa dance expert and was viewed in a positive manner by the teachers, while Turkish girls wearing the hijab did not enjoy this flattering attention, and were often the victims of hostile behaviour and questioning. As Rutter (2006) points out, rarely are local 'white' children asked to represent their cultures in this way. In this scenario, there is little recognition that the culture of the immigration country can no longer be isolated (if indeed it ever could) and is itself inevitably adapting to global demands and changes.

Despite these difficulties, it remains the case that migrant children's educational aspirations are often very high (OECD, 2006). While they find themselves immersed in the youth culture of the host country, they also tend to have a feeling of respect for the school and greater expectations than many of their non-migrant peers. This often leads to a sense of tension. On the one hand, they wish to identify with the youth culture of their peers (aspects of which are likely to be anti-school); while on the other, they have high expectations of formal schooling. In fact, the majority of children involved in our CHICAM research (and indeed their parents) saw the school as being an extremely important investment for their future – albeit at the same time, a dull, boring place that did not fully meet their expectations. As one girl from the club in the Netherlands said, the school is 'a gateway to the future'; but in practice it often translated into a daily experience that was not adequately supportive. We will explore some of the tensions here in some of our detailed case studies in Chapters 8 and 9.

The physical space of the school also plays a part here. Children typically make clear distinctions between central (public) spaces and marginal (private) spaces in schools; and this has particular implications in terms of whether children feel safe and able to participate in school life, both socially and academically. For many children, it is the marginal spaces that are central because this is where social relationships are negotiated: the small corridors hidden from the teachers' eyes, the unsupervised spaces and the toilets are places where the children's own culture comes to the fore. As some of their video productions clearly showed, these marginal spaces can be re-appropriated by migrant pupils in the same way as their local peers; although the fact that they are unsupervised can also make them arenas for bullying and intimidation, especially for refugee and migrant children.

Finally, it is worth noting that there are occasions on which the pressure is less on education and more on turning towards the labour market in order to contribute to the family's needs. Particularly for girls, there is often a high level of expectation in terms of fulfilling duties within the family (for example, looking after younger children), when parents have to be away for work. Family economics often necessitate a choice about which of the children will focus more on education and which will have to offer assistance to the parents (Black, 1994). For example, Balkys, an Iraqi girl in Greece who was part of our CHICAM research, did not attend school and stayed at home in order to assist her mother with her medical problems, to act as a translator in sorting out their documents, to do household chores and to help her younger brother, who did go to school.

## Conclusion

The specific experiences and perspectives of children are often absent from the broader debate about migration – whether this takes place in the popular media, among policy-makers or in the academy. Of course, migrant children will share a great deal with their parents, and with other, non-migrant children. In this chapter, however, we have sought to draw attention to some issues that are specific to such children's lives – particularly in relation to their place within the family and the school. This has provided a broader context for our discussion of what we regard as the third significant socialising influence in children's lives: the media. It is to this issue that we turn directly in the following chapter.

# 3
# Between the Global and the Local: Young People, Media and Migration

As we have seen, academic discussions of globalisation and its consequences have been quite strongly contested. For some authors, globalisation is merely a further logical stage in the development of modern capitalism; while for others, it represents a distinctive break with the past, as embodied in the form of the traditional nation state. For some, it is primarily a cultural phenomenon, while for others it is essentially driven by economic and political forces. And while some are keen to celebrate the emergence of new global dialogues that will create tolerance and mutual understanding, others see only an extension of already well-established relationships of oppression and inequality.

Interpretations of the role of the media in these developments have been equally double-edged. On the one hand, there are those who view media globalisation as the belated arrival of McLuhan's 'global village': it is seen to encourage the free flow of images and ideas, to offer new possibilities for self-expression, and to foster the development of inter-cultural understanding. On the other hand are those who see it merely as a further extension of 'Coca-colonisation' – that is, as a form of cultural imperialism that only consolidates the economic and ideological power of (primarily US-based) multinational corporations.

Generational or age differences may be particularly significant in this respect (Drotner, 2001a). For British audiences, the most popular TV programmes among adults generally remain those which are domestically produced; but this is less the case with children and young people, whose preference for imported programming may represent a more general rejection of the more paternalistic approach of domestic children's television. Furthermore, children and young people are likely to be the most enthusiastic users of new media technologies, particularly those (like the Internet and mobile phones) that offer possibilities for interpersonal communication. In these respects, we might expect younger people to be more oriented towards a globalised media culture: globalisation can be seen to have encouraged the emergence of forms of youth culture (and children's culture) that transcend national and cultural differences. Here again, some popular commentators have welcomed these developments as evidence of a growing 'global consciousness' among the young (Tapscott, 1998); while others fear that the continuities between generations may have been lost – and that children today may have more in common with children in other countries than they do with their own parents (Ohmae, 1995).

These developments have specific – yet also diverse – consequences for migrant communities. As many media companies are now conceiving of their markets in international rather than national terms, it becomes possible for viable global audiences to be constituted from groups that in national contexts are perceived merely as 'minorities'. In principle, it is possible to watch Turkish or Chinese or Indian television in most parts of the world; although television from less wealthy countries (particularly African countries) is less widely distributed. Meanwhile, the Internet provides new possibilities for cultural expression and dissemination; and migrant communities have been among the first to realise its potential for transnational or diasporic communication – although again we should not forget that domestic access to the Internet is less likely to be available to more disadvantaged migrant groups.

In this chapter, we review previous research in this field: we look at national differences in the use of media, the provision of media for ethnic minorities, and what little is currently known about how ethnic minority and migrant young people actually use media. (Our focus here is primarily on screen media – television, film and the Internet. Music – certainly a significant medium for older children – will be discussed more specifically in Chapters 5 and 9.) Broadly speaking, this research clearly shows that children are not passive recipients of transnational media output: like adults, they select, interpret and filter global media through their own local cultural experiences (Tomlinson, 1991). Furthermore, different cultures continue to perceive and define 'childhood' in diverse ways, not least in terms of the kinds of access children gain to the media. Different media systems, as well as different definitions of childhood, mean that children live in distinctive 'media cultures' that combine the global and the local in quite particular ways. This is obviously the case when we compare the lives of Western children with those of children in the global South (Stephens, 1995); but it is also the case across Europe, which is our primary focus here.

# Europe: the big picture

The major Europe-wide comparative study *Children and their Changing Media Environment* (Livingstone and Bovill, 2001) quantifies and explores many of these similarities and differences in great detail. These researchers see children's media use as a phenomenon that is situated in the context of other social activities; and as such, it can only be understood in the light of broader social and cultural differences. Thus, the media that are available to children depend upon factors such as the size of the country or the language community (and hence the ability to sustain national production) and the average level of income among the population, as well as on policies concerned with media regulation and technological innovation. Family structures and education systems vary between countries, creating different opportunities and constraints in terms of children's leisure experiences. The ethnic and linguistic diversity of the population is also significant here – as is the extent to which that diversity is acknowledged in cultural policy in the first place. All these factors affect the kinds of media that are available, and the extent to which children can gain access to them.

Among the 12 countries they studied, the authors identify four broad 'clusters', as follows:

1. Countries with a strong focus on national television and relatively low dissemination of new technologies: Spain, Italy and France.
2. Countries with a multi-channel environment and moderate uses of new technologies, but with different preferences regarding television and newspapers: Germany, Switzerland, Belgium and Israel.
3. Countries that are pioneers of new technologies, but are integrating them within a media environment focused primarily on newspapers and radio, rather than television: the Netherlands and the Nordic countries.
4. The United Kingdom, which combines a strong orientation towards television with relatively high figures for new technologies.

These differences clearly reflect several of the broader cultural differences identified above. Thus, countries with smaller language communities tend not to define screen media as inherently inferior to print media, and hence are more enthusiastic about ICTs; whereas larger countries tend to have more invested in older, nationally based media such as broadcasting and the press. Language is also a crucial variable in the response to globalisation: children in countries with smaller language communities tend to favour imported TV programmes, whereas those in larger communities (where more funding can be invested in production) are more inclined to favour domestically produced material. Meanwhile, children in more family-oriented cultures tend to have less privatised access to media, as compared with those in more peer-oriented cultures, where a media-rich 'bedroom culture' tends to dominate. Countries with strong national policies on ICT provision tend to be ahead of others in this respect; although in some instances, there are higher levels of access in schools than in homes.

Despite these differences, the study identifies a number of general patterns that seem to apply across Europe. These include the increasingly restricted, domestic character of children's leisure time; the 'privatisation' of children's media use, via the growing provision of television and other media in the bedroom; inequalities of access to new media (ICTs) in the home, in terms of socio-economic status; gender differences in uses and preferences for particular media or genres; and the ongoing struggle for control over access to media between parents and children. While acknowledging the exponential take-up of digital media, the study also confirms the continuing dominance of television, particularly among younger children, who are far less likely to have independent access to the Internet.

In general, the study suggests that European children are increasingly participating in a global or transnational culture of childhood and youth. Indeed, it is likely that several of the national differences these researchers identify have already become less significant since this study was undertaken almost 10 years ago. However, the study entirely fails to address the issue of cultural diversity, and the ways in which all the European nations involved in the research are steadily becoming less homogeneous: 'race', ethnicity or migration status do not feature as variables in any of the national studies. This absence is not unrepresentative of research in this field in general – or indeed of the official statistics gathered by governments or broadcasting companies. 'Children' are often seen as a singular category, defined only by their age. Yet when it comes to addressing ethnic groups specifically, research often seems to ignore the specific experiences of children. Studies of ethnic minorities' uses of media have rarely addressed children as a distinct group: here, as in so many other areas of social research, children are largely subsumed within the family or the community. From both points of view, it would seem, migrant and ethnic minority children are effectively invisible.

## The provision of 'ethnic' media

Of course, children from migrant backgrounds are bound to be experiencing a similar media 'diet' to children in general. Much of their media consumption is likely to be focused on the mainstream *national* media produced in the host country; and they will also be exposed to *global* media imported from other countries (particularly the United States) as part of the wider international trade in media. However, they are also likely to experience media that are specifically targeted at their own ethnic group. These media are of two main kinds. First, there are what can be termed *ethnic minority* media, produced in the new country of residence. This would include programming produced in community languages by public radio and television channels (generally as part of an explicit 'multicultural' policy), as well as local ethnic newspapers and other media produced by migrant groups themselves. Secondly, there are diasporic or *transnational* media, generally produced in the country or region of origin – a phenomenon that has significantly expanded since the advent of multi-channel cable/satellite television and the Internet, and the more general deregulation of broadcasting (cf. Naficy (2003) for a similar categorisation).

Riggins (1992) suggests that media may have a dual role for ethnic minority audiences. National media can function as a means of integration or assimilation, insofar as they enable minorities to inform themselves about the dominant values and practices of the host society. This may be an explicitly intended effect, as in the case of programming provided by public channels specifically targeting minority ethnic groups; although of course it may also be a consequence of exposure to mainstream media more generally. On the other hand, both transnational and 'ethnic minority' media can function as a means of cultural maintenance or survival – a way of maintaining connections with 'home', and with the language and the cultural and religious traditions of the country of origin. This can be particularly important for parents who may be keen to prevent their children from losing their home language or more generally becoming 'Westernised'. For example, research on South Asians' use of video in Britain and the United States suggests that parents may use media quite self-consciously in this manner (Bhattacharya, 2004; Gillespie, 1995). These two functions of integration and cultural maintenance apply – albeit in different ways – both to immigrant groups and to indigenous or 'aboriginal' minorities, whose claims to cultural and linguistic protection may be perceived as more valid by the majority population (Riggins, 1992). The balance between these two roles and the ways in which they may be combined are likely to change over time; and this is clearly dependent upon issues such as levels of access to media, the training of media workers, and the existence of support from the state or from social movements.

When it comes to *national* media, research from many countries suggests that ethnic minority audiences are often critical of the ways in which they are represented (see, for example, Jakubowicz, 2001; Ogan, 2001; Tufte, 2001). In the United Kingdom, several studies have criticised mainstream media for failing to reflect the multicultural nature of modern Britain (for example, van Dijk, 2000; Ross, 1996) – and this view is echoed in the arguments of ethnic minority audiences themselves (Halloran et al., 1995; Mullan, 1996; Poole, 2001; Ross, 2000; Sreberny, 1999). There are frequent complaints about stereotyping, 'negative images', marginalisation and tokenism, and the way in which individual characters are made to carry the 'burden of representation' for entire groups. However, others have suggested that, when compared with some other European countries, representations of ethnic minority groups in the United Kingdom are found in a wider range of programming, rather than simply being confined to news and current affairs (Hargreaves, 2001b). Following vigorous debates on these issues during the 1970s and 1980s (Daniels and Gerson, 1989; Mullan, 1996), there are now industry codes of practice governing the representation of ethnic minority groups, and equal opportunities policies are slowly leading to increases in the proportions of such groups both on screen and in production roles – although progress in this respect has been fraught with obstacles and resistances (Campion, 2005; Cottle, 2000). Across Europe, there are several networks and projects seeking to improve the representation of ethnic minorities in the media (for example, the work of Mira Media in the Netherlands: *www.miramedia.nl*).

There is also a long history of mainstream broadcasters in Europe – particularly public service channels – attempting to provide *ethnic minority* programming for particular communities (Husband, 1994). In Britain, for example, specialist 'ethnic' programming on mainstream channels dates back to the 1960s (Cottle, 2000); and Channel 4, which has a specific remit to address ethnic minorities, offered significant support for ethnic minority film and video production workshops during the 1980s, although this has since been dissipated (Hussein, 1994). Nevertheless, this provision has also frequently been criticised as tokenistic and inadequate; and ethnic minority producers and audiences are both keen to see greater representation in mainstream programmes, not least because they believe this serves an educational function for the population as a whole (Halloran et al., 1995; Mullan, 1996; Ross, 2000; Sreberny, 1999). Research suggests that ethnic minority audiences do not wish to be 'ghettoised' – although as audiences for television and other media have become increasingly fragmented, the notion that the media might serve as a form of social integration may itself be somewhat outdated (Mullan, 1996).

In the more established countries of immigration, it appears that this kind of state-funded ethnic minority programming has declined in recent years. This was certainly apparent across the European countries involved in our CHICAM research. In Germany, for example, the minimal state broadcasting aimed at the Turkish community, broadly with a social education aim, has largely disappeared as satellite take-up has increased; although there are also so-called 'open channels' that offer people from migrant backgrounds the opportunity to create and screen their own productions (cf. Kamp, 1989). In the Netherlands there is no specialist public service minority programming, although general programming has a multicultural 'gloss', and presenters from minority backgrounds are now widely found. In Sweden there is official recognition of the need for multicultural media output, but its provision is minimal. However, in both Greece and Sweden large and socially significant minorities (Albanians and Russians, and Finnish and Lappish respectively) have put political pressure on government to achieve some limited specialist provision from the public service channels – as is the case in the United Kingdom with Welsh and Gaelic television. On the other hand, minorities that do not form either a lucrative global niche market or a significant group in the host countries, such as the Moroccan Berber speakers in the Netherlands or Sri Lankans in the United Kingdom, have much less choice.

Nevertheless, more established ethnic minority communities often have their own thriving economic infrastructures, which support the production of local ethnic minority media. In the United Kingdom, for example, there is a strong 'ethnic' local press (for instance, among the Pakistani population in Bradford: see Husband, 1998); and the concentration of Britain's ethnic minority populations in urban centres results in a 'critical mass' of potential consumers for local radio services (Hussein, 1994) – such as, in areas of London, Greek Cypriots and South Asians (Tsagarousianou, 1999). Increasing numbers of locally based organisations hold licences for provision specifically targeting particular ethnic groups, although many of these organisations are relatively short-lived. Licenses for such channels must be granted by the relevant authorities (now in the form of Ofcom, the Office for Communications), and in some instances there have been political disputes surrounding this (as in the case of Turkish opposition to the United Kingdom's Kurdish channel: see Hassanpour, 2003). In an increasingly crowded, competitive market, the funding of local programming is bound to remain limited; and as Tsagarousianou (1999) indicates, the economic pressure to maximise audiences seems to result in a homogenising of diverse communities. This may be particularly acute where the audience is relatively small in the first place (Cunningham and Sinclair, 2001). Even so, the rate of expansion of such services does suggest that some at least are highly economically viable.

At the same time, the provision of specialist *transnational* media continues apace in many European countries. As Frachon and Vergaftig (1995) point out, the existence of more than 13 million people 'of foreign origin' across Europe represents a lucrative market for niche channels. In the United Kingdom, for example, cable/satellite providers now offer a wide range of Indian, Bangladeshi, Greek, Arabic, Chinese, Turkish, Kurdish, African, Iranian and other subscription channels, some of which target several nationalities; and there is a large video, DVD and CD market among many of these communities as well. To a large extent, this form of 'global narrowcasting' has been commercially driven: it could be seen as a direct consequence of the deregulation of national media and the demise of state monopolies (Chalaby, 2005a; Karim, 2003; Tsagarousianou, 1999). Economic and technological developments suggest that there is likely to be even greater segmentation of the audience in the coming years, not just along the lines of ethnicity, but also in terms of generational differences (Husband, 1998).

Ultimately, these transnational media – like niche media in general – are subject to the commercial logic of global media markets. As Mullan (1996) points out, the high start-up costs mean that transnational TV channels tend to operate by recycling old material (particularly music, soap operas and movies), or constantly repeating newer programmes (although of course this is a feature of cable/satellite channels in general). In some instances, they are able to rely on the enormous stock of films and programmes from countries like India and Hong Kong, which may be particularly attractive for first generation immigrants; although second generation immigrants also wish to see the realities of their current lives represented in locally produced programming (Frachon and Vergaftig, 1995; Mullan, 1996; Tsagarousianou, 2001b). It is also important to be wary of assuming that these 'minority' audiences are homogeneous: for example, as Tsagarousianou (2001a) points out, Greek Cypriots in London have been critical of what they see as the overemphasis on mainland Greek issues on London Greek Radio, while Muslim South Asian viewers have criticised what they perceive as the anti-Muslim bias of some transnational channels. Yet although some of these channels are owned by powerful global players (for example, Rupert Murdoch's Star TV), they can nevertheless provide a powerful alternative to the mainstream channels – not just in the receiving country, but also in the country of origin. In this respect, the controversies surrounding the role of the Arabic channel Al-Jazeera in reporting the Afghan and Iraq wars provide a telling case in point (Sakr, 2005).

What are the consequences of these developments in terms of cultural identities? In many instances, these media are seen to assist in the creation and maintenance of transnational or diasporic communities and cultural attachments – albeit ones that may be partly based on nostalgic or merely 'imagined' ideas about the home nation (Sreberny, 2000). Yet while they may enable migrants to feel 'at home' in their situation of exile, and hence to combat feelings of isolation, it has been argued that they can also undermine the assimilationist aims of the host country (Wood and King, 2001). In Germany, for example, there has been concern that older Turkish migrants are choosing to retreat into their own 'private media world' rather than participating in mainstream (that is, German) social life (see Aksoy and Robins, 2000). Similar concerns have been voiced in relation to Islamic groups in France (see Hargreaves, 2001a) and Turks in the Netherlands (see Milikowski, 2001). However, these complaints typically appear to blame migrants themselves for their failure to assimilate, rather than looking at the limited opportunities available to such groups to participate in public life.

Even so, it may be a mistake to see this debate in either/or terms. Aksoy and Robins (2000) argue that – at least in the case of Turkish television – the picture is more complex. These channels do not in fact offer an homogeneous image of Turkey, catering to traditional (and supposedly nostalgic) ideas of the 'imagined community'. On the contrary, they argue, the commercial channels in particular offer diverse images of modern Turkey: by providing ordinary, even banal representations of everyday life, they effectively 'demythologise' idealised notions of the homeland (see also Aksoy and Robins, 2003; Milikowski, 2001; Robins and Aksoy, 2005). Likewise, Banaji (2006) shows how young British-Asian viewers can use elements in popular Hindi films to help them criticise or challenge various aspects of their traditional culture – and that they may choose these films precisely because the older generation are likely to be less suspicious of them. How far this argument applies to other migrant groups – particularly those whose home countries may have less developed media industries – is open to question, however. Aksoy and Robins also seem to promote a rather benign view of Turkish diversity (they do not discuss the blocking of Kurdish satellite signals by the Turkish in the United Kingdom, for example: see Hassanpour, 2003); and they do not address the need for television that addresses the specific experiences of migrants.

Ultimately, as Hargreaves (2001c) suggests, this is not a 'zero sum game': a heightened interest in one society may not necessarily mean a loss of involvement in another. Aksoy and Robins (2003) go further, challenging the notion that migration necessarily implies a radical dislocation or 'splitting' from the culture of the homeland – and that it necessarily results in feelings of loss and nostalgia, or in yearning for an idealised image of the past. They suggest that transnational television makes a significant difference in migrants' ability to manage separation and distance. Thinking of migration in terms of dichotomies between 'here' and 'there' or 'now' and 'then' is, they argue, too simplistic: migrants are increasingly living and thinking transnationally, rather than being 'caught between cultures' – although they acknowledge that some migrants do nevertheless opt for 'monocultural, national identifications and attachments' (Robins and Aksoy, 2005: 25).

The debate on these issues thus implicitly raises broader issues to do with access to the public sphere (Silverstone, 2001). The presence of diverse ethnic voices within the public sphere potentially disrupts the seamless production of the 'imagined community' of the nation. Yet the question of how ethnicity itself is defined and recognised in debates around media policy is very complex. 'Ethnic groups' are clearly heterogeneous in themselves; and ethnicity is only one dimension of identity, that is likely to come into play (and indeed be deliberately invoked) in specific situations for specific purposes (Husband, 1994). As such, it could be argued that there is no such thing as an essential ethnicity – or a singular 'ethnic experience' – that can be unproblematically represented or reflected in the media. Traditional notions of a singular national 'public sphere' may be giving way to a more pluralistic conception of multiple public spheres, some of which are defined in terms of ethnicity (Cunningham, 2001); yet there is clearly a need for ongoing dialogue, not just *within* ethnic groups, but also *between* them – and of course, between minority groups and the majority population as well. There is justified concern among ethnic minority groups that the provision of specialised media may come to serve as a substitute for more satisfactory representation in the mainstream media (Mercer,

1989). As Husband (1998: 31) suggests, 'a viable multi-ethnic public sphere ... requires *both* a media infrastructure that can address and reflect the interests of specific ethnic communities, and media which facilitate dialogue and engagement across ethnic boundaries'.

## Patterns of media use

Here again, however, much of this debate relates to adults rather than specifically to children. As a minority within a minority, migrant children are unlikely to be well served even by public channels – although in Sweden, specialist children's programmes are produced in Finnish and Lappish, and some other countries (including the United Kingdom) have explicitly 'multicultural' shows for children. Of course, many transnational cable/satellite channels also carry programming for children – or at least for 'family viewing'. In general, however, relatively little is known about migrant or ethnic minority children's access to, and use of, media.

Across the countries involved in our CHICAM research, ethnic minority children's access to television appears relatively comparable to that of the host populations, although there are some notable differences. In Germany, for example, television is effectively universal among Turkish households; and, even by the mid-1990s, around three-quarters had access to cable or satellite (Zentrum für Türkeistudien, 1996). Research conducted by the West German Broadcasting Company (WDR), found that television consumption was somewhat higher among ethnic minority groups than among the host population (Holzapfel, 1999). In Italy, research for RAI (public television) found that the use of television among ethnic minority children was quite similar to that of their Italian peers (Mauri et al., 1999). While the penetration of television was again almost universal, more advanced technology (such as VCRs and PCs) was less likely to be available in migrant families. Furthermore, while immigrant children tend to watch TV with family members, Italian children tend to watch TV alone: this may be because immigrant children are less likely to have separate rooms (and hence separate viewing facilities), or because Italian families are smaller in size (the Italian birth-rate is currently the lowest in Europe). Likewise, in Sweden, there is relatively little information relating specifically to children in ethnic minority communities. Research with adults (Weibull and Wadbring, 1999) suggests that migrant communities have higher levels of access to cable television than the majority population, although access to satellite TV is fairly similar. However, they have rather less access to other media, such as computers and the Internet and (particularly) newspapers.

In the Netherlands, a study by the Veldkamp market research company found that first generation Turkish, Moroccan and Surinamese children watched considerably more television than Dutch children. Because of their access to a large number of television stations, these children were able to watch whatever they wanted, and tended to focus primarily on entertainment programmes. Turkish children also watched channels from their country of origin, while Moroccan and Surinamese children mainly watched Dutch (commercial) stations (Veldkamp Marktonderzoek, 1998). Turkish children watched Turkish channels both for Turkish news and for sport; whereas Moroccan, Surinamese and Antilles/Aruban youths did not follow the news in their own-language media. Many young Moroccans have problems with the Arabic language spoken on most Arabic or Moroccan channels, because many of the Moroccans living in the Netherlands speak Berber rather than Arabic (d'Haenens et al., 2000).

A later study by d'Haenens et al. (2001) explored the media uses of Turks, Moroccans (who tend to be more culturally distanced from indigenous Dutch youth) and Surinamese (who are less distanced). While these groups all had similar levels of access to 'old' media (such as television), when compared with Dutch youth, they had significantly less access to new media. Ethnic minority youth (like their Dutch counterparts) were making growing use of the Internet for chatting and e-mailing, as well as searching for information for their studies or hobbies; but they were more likely to do so in school or in the library, rather than at home. Antilles and Aruban teenagers also used the Internet to look up information about their home countries: in a number of cases, these young people had come to the Netherlands to study, so the bond with their home country was still very strong (d'Haenens et al., 2000). Furthermore, practically all ethnic minority and indigenous Dutch participants were using mobile phones. In terms of individual media ownership, the Surinamese participants in this study were the most comparable to their indigenous Dutch peers; but other demographic factors such as social class and gender were also significant in this respect (girls and working-class youth having less access to new media, overall). In general, though, this study suggested that television was still the pre-eminent medium in the everyday lives of Turkish, Moroccan, Surinamese and indigenous Dutch youth.

In general, UK studies have tended to ignore or marginalise the position of ethnic minority children. Research conducted in the early 1990s suggested that Asian and African-Caribbean groups were likely to have fewer television sets than the rest of the population, and that sets were much less likely to be located in children's bedrooms – perhaps, according to the researcher, reflecting a greater emphasis on 'family togetherness' (Mullan, 1996). On the other hand, the same research suggested that Asians were more likely to have access to VCRs, home computers and video cameras than the rest of the population; although African-Caribbeans had less of this technology than average. There is also evidence that ethnic minority parents use mainstream national television – particularly news and soap operas – as a tool for cultural acclimatisation, both for themselves and their children; and that, conversely, children might persuade their parents to watch such programmes in order to familiarise them both with the contemporary popular culture of the host country and with their own dilemmas (Gillespie, 1995; Ross, 2000; Sreberny, 1999).

These studies, patchy and uneven as they are, do suggest that ethnic minority children have roughly comparable levels of access to television – which, we would argue, continues to be the dominant medium, particularly for pre-teenagers. On the other hand, they may have lower levels of access to new media such as the Internet – a finding that was confirmed by our admittedly small-scale work with the children in our CHICAM research (see Chapter 5). However, the continuing exclusion of this dimension from more recent large-scale surveys makes it hard to be definitive; and it would certainly be quite mistaken to generalise about 'ethnic minority' children without paying attention to the significant differences within and between such groups. Clearly, access to media depends not only on the amount of disposable income, but on how that income is spent – and this reflects broader cultural dispositions and priorities. As we have implied, media can serve specific social and cultural functions for migrant groups; and hence their patterns of access and use should not simply be deduced from their socio-economic position. In addition, we would need to take a broader view of 'access' – as not simply a matter of access to equipment, but also of the social and cultural capital that is needed to use it.

Even so, there are likely to be different patterns of media use among different generations of migrants. To some degree, these differences appear to follow the 'logic of assimilation'. Hargreaves and Madjoub (1997), for example, found that while parents in Mahgrebi families in France were tuning in to Arabic-language satellite channels, their children were more interested in French or US-style stations (to the extent, in some cases, of repositioning the satellite dish when their parents were out of the house). In Germany, young people from migrant families come closer in their viewing habits to their German counterparts, and programmes from their countries of origin are watched less often than by their parents: this seems to be the case in families from both Turkish and Italian backgrounds (Fritsche, 2000; Granato, 2001; Hargreaves, 2001c). Likewise, second generation Chinese migrants in Britain complain that their parents' preference for the specialist Chinese channels prevents them from keeping up with the British soaps, and hence being able to discuss them with UK peers – although some elements of Chinese popular culture (such as music videos) remain very popular with them (Siew-Peng, 2001). Ogan's study of Turkish migrants in the Netherlands also found that parents were more oriented towards the transnational channels, while their children were generally more interested in Dutch TV. The children criticised their parents' use of Turkish television, arguing that it prevented them from engaging with Dutch society; yet at the same time, they themselves did watch the Turkish channels, for example, for music programmes and sport. Differences in terms of religious affiliation, gender and linguistic ability were at least as important in this respect as generational differences (Ogan, 2001).

Likewise, the young British-Asians in the studies by Halloran et al. (1995) and Husband (1998) also show little enthusiasm for TV programming or newspapers in minority languages, in some cases because they are less fluent in those languages themselves. Some of the young British-Asians in Gillespie's (1995) study were also dismissive of what they perceived as the lack of 'realism' in popular Hindi films. However, the global proliferation of Indian media, the greater investment in production values, and with many channels now broadcasting the films with English subtitles, the contemporary situation may be rather different in this respect (Banaji, 2006; South Asian Popular Culture, 2005). Halloran et al. (1995) and Mullan (1996) also provide some evidence of struggles between parents and children over the viewing of morally 'inappropriate' content – although whether these are any more intense than generational conflicts within any other ethnic group is perhaps debatable. However, several studies suggest that adults may be just as critical as children of 'ethnic' programming (for example, Journal of Ethnic and Migration Studies, 2006; Ogan, 2001; Tsagarousianou, 2001a). Both Aksoy and Robins (2003) and Banaji and Al-Ghabban (2006) argue that migrant or transnational viewers may be more critical of television in general, for example as a result of their ability to access and compare a range of different news sources.

As this implies, this 'generation gap' is not always quite so straight-forward. Children and young people may turn to the media of the host country for some purposes, and to transnational media for others; and this is likely to depend upon a range of factors, not least those of production quality. The overwhelming impression is that the younger generations are taking a 'pick and mix' approach. Where they have access, they do watch transnational satellite or local specialist programming (often for language retention) but not as intensively as their parents, often preferring to watch national programming. Migrants who have come with the intention of staying are also likely to have different motivations in their media use from those who see themselves as temporary visitors. As we have seen above, studies in the Netherlands indicate that historical connections to the host countries are significant here, with the viewing patterns of younger migrants from former colonies being closer to those of Dutch youth than those from countries with no such connection. On the other hand, there is a feeling among second generation migrants that neither the diasporic channels nor the host country programming really meet their needs, and that there is a lack of material specifically for migrant groups (Frachon and Vergaftig, 1995; Ogan, 2001; Tsagarousianou, 2001a).

## Making identities

What are the implications of these different uses of media in terms of the development of cultural identity? Much of the work in this field tends to subscribe to the 'new ethnicities' approach discussed in Chapter 1 – and not all of it manages to escape the pitfalls and limitations we identified there. There appears to be general agreement that the media are playing a positive role in young people's development of 'hybrid', 'cosmopolitan' or even 'floating' identities (cf. Hannerz, 1996).

Thus, Sreberny (2000) describes how Iranian migrants in the United Kingdom use a range of both majority and 'ethnic' media to construct a more fluid sense of cultural identity. In her terms, they use media to 'look back', to sustain their ties to their country of origin, but also to 'look around' at the new culture to which they have come: identity in the diaspora, she argues, is not fixed or singular, but fluid and constantly in a process of becoming. Likewise, Aksoy and Robins (2000) refute the idea that migrants viewing transnational television are straightforwardly and unproblematically 'keeping in touch with home' – and hence that television functions as a kind of 'cultural holding device'. By contrast, they argue that migrant viewers (in this case, adults) are more self-aware and

ambivalent about this experience, moving between emotional engagement and distanced critique. Meanwhile, in the Australian context,
Cunningham (2001) has analysed the use of 'hybrid' popular media
forms among migrant youth – forms which, they argue, are more
relevant to them than the more traditional aestheticised forms favoured
by their parents. According to these authors, these media generate a
'sophisticated cosmopolitanism'; and, as in Aksoy and Robins' study, it
is the commercially produced rather than the 'official' state-sponsored
media that appear to offer most potential in this respect.

For some researchers, the Internet is seen to offer even greater potential in this respect. For example, Panagakos (2003) describes the role of
the Internet among Greek ethnic communities in Canada: she argues
that it facilitates the creation of new, more diverse, forms of ethnic
identity that go beyond the rehearsal of 'official' stereotypes that can be
found in other forms of community activity such as festivals. Communicating via ethnically defined online communities, or downloading
Greek music that is not available through other means, can help
migrants to reassert their 'Greek' identity; but it may also contribute
to a reshaping of that identity, in a more decentralised manner that
is not controlled by the homeland or by official 'community leaders'
(cf. Tsaliki, 2003). Likewise, Thompson (2002) points to the role of the
Internet in sustaining disaporic communication among South Asian
(primarily Indian) immigrants in the United Kingdom. He argues that,
unlike television or film, the Internet is a decentralised medium: it can
allow migrants to retain 'a sense of community that is rooted in an
original homeland', but it can also be used to create new hybrid cultures.
Thompson argues that 'grand narratives' about India are constantly challenged and disputed on Internet message boards, in a way that may be
much more difficult in mainstream television or newspapers (see also
Mitra, 1997). On the other hand, this can have negative consequences,
in that much of the communication is 'extreme and vituperative', and
may exacerbate differences and divisions within the community. Meanwhile, Mandaville (2003) describes the use of new media (the Internet
and CD-ROMs) as a means of propagating religious texts within Muslim
diasporas. To some extent, he argues, this is simply a matter of packaging
old messages in new forms; although there is an ongoing debate about
its consequences in terms of religious identity. While some argue that
the wider availability of such texts may promote greater understanding
and tolerance within Islam, fostering the 'imagined community' of the
global *ummah*, others suggest that it may divide Western Islam from that
in the Middle East and Asia, and that it may ultimately foster extremism.

When it comes to young people in particular, the 'new ethnicities' argument appears very prevalent. Like most of the other studies relating specifically to young people, Gillespie's (1995) work on British-Asian youth focuses primarily on second generation rather than recent immigrants. Gillespie is primarily concerned with how her respondents use the increasingly transnational array of media available to them, both to facilitate interpersonal relationships and to understand their place in the social world. She notes some perhaps unlikely 'homologies' here – for example, between the representation of extended (and reconstructed) families in Australian and British soap operas and her viewers' perceptions of their own family lives. There are also significant generational differences: while the children participate in parentally governed rituals of 'devotional viewing', they are also quite critical of what they perceive as the lack of professionalism of popular Hindi cinema, as compared with Hollywood. Meanwhile, news viewing is seen to provide a means of access to 'adult citizenship' in the host culture, while also occasionally posing significant dilemmas in terms of young people's political and cultural identifications (as in the case of the media coverage of the first Gulf War).

Gillespie's account offers a relatively optimistic view of the role of media in the construction of 'new ethnicities'. What emerges here is a view of young South Asian viewers not as 'caught between cultures' and hence as deprived of a coherent sense of identity (as they are often described within mainstream 'race relations' literature: for example, Watson, 1977), but on the contrary as positively cosmopolitan, constructing hybrid or multiple identities that enable them to enjoy the best of both worlds (see also Gillespie, 2000). However, since this research was conducted in the late 1980s and early 1990s, the situation has become rather more politically polarised, as Hindi film and televised versions of sacred texts have come to play an important role in mobilising support for quasi-fascist forms of Hindu nationalism (see Banaji, 2006; Thompson, 2002).

Barker (1997b, 1998) develops this approach in his analysis of how British-Asian teenage girls 'reflexively construct hybrid identities' in the process of peer-group talk about soap operas. Their discussions of 'ethnic' representations and moral dilemmas in the programmes enable them to construct a positive identity as *both* British *and* Asian; while these multiple identities are also cross-cut by – and in some cases, in tension with – other identifications based (in this case) on age, social class and gender. In line with the 'new ethnicities' perspective, and with recent debates in social theory (for example, Giddens, 1991),

Barker sees identity not as fixed and given, but as something that is perpetually constituted and re-constituted within forms of representation (cf. Hall, 1992) – and not least by the increasing range of representational resources made available by globalisation. Whether this account can be sustained in the light of other contemporary changes such as the resurgence of ethnic and religious nationalism – and indeed whether it applies to more recent migrants – remains to be seen.

Some recent studies undertaken among different migrant groups in the United States reflect a similar approach, although they tend towards a more celebratory account of the role of the media in creating 'new ethnicities'. For example, Durham (2004) describes how American girls of South Asian origin in the United States use media to move beyond essentialist notions of identity: they use both US and Indian media to 'cut and mix' between different positions, not least in respect of sexuality. She asserts that, by virtue of their position, these girls are more likely to be critical of the sexual mores embodied in mainstream media than their US peers. Shi (2005) provides a similar analysis of the use of media among Chinese-American university students. She argues that 'ethnic' media provide a vehicle for sustaining a sense of community belonging, and feed the desire to return to the homeland; but the media more generally also facilitate a form of 'border-crossing', and potentially new forms of subjectivity. However, both studies seem quite uncritical of the 'new ethnicities' approach, enthusiastically recycling a familiar rhetoric of hybridity, displacement and shifting identities which frequently drifts free of the empirical evidence.

One dimension of this discussion that remains to be developed is the interaction between ethnicity and social class. Many of the participants in the studies mentioned above are middle- or even upper-middle-class; and most come from relatively large ethnic groups. Thompson (2002) suggests that middle-class and professional South Asian immigrants in Britain may be more inclined to resist pressures to assimilation than their working-class counterparts – or at least more able to afford the resources that will allow them to do so. For example, they are likely to be able to purchase specialist educational provision, or to pay for their children to visit the home country, in ways that are not available to less wealthy families; and the same might be said of purchasing access to newer media technology. As Panagakos (2003) points out, access to the Internet (and the 'cyber-capital' that it requires) is not equally available to all – as is also the case with satellite television (Panagakos, 1998). This may give younger, wealthier and more educated migrants who are literate in English a significant advantage over others in their community, creating new relationships of social power.

However, it also likely that these possibilities will be differentially available to different ethnic groups: the options for Indian or Turkish immigrants in the United Kingdom are certainly much broader than for (say) Somalis or Ethiopians. In many cases, access to 'ethnic' media may well depend upon location, with residents in major cities likely to be much better served (cf. Shi, 2005). As many of the studies we have discussed are keen to emphasise, it is vital that we do not essentialise particular ethnic groups or 'communities': such groups are likely to be divided by generation, gender, education, religion and language, as well as by successive 'waves' of migration (cf. Sreberny, 2000).

In this respect, Shakuntala Banaji's work on Indian and British-Indian young people's readings of popular Hindi film provides a valuable example of the kind of grounded investigation that is in need of further development (Banaji, 2006). Refusing simple generalisations about 'Indian' and 'British' (or 'non-resident Indian') readings, her study also pays close attention to the differences afforded by social class, religion and gender. As she indicates, viewers do not occupy singular, uncomplicated spaces of identity, but speak from intersecting subject positions; and as a result, their readings and uses of these films may prove inconsistent and even at times quite contradictory. This might be said to be true of all viewers, irrespective of their cultural location; but it nevertheless provides an important challenge to the common tendency in audience research to regard particular individuals as necessarily 'representative' of broader social categories. Furthermore, she shows that viewing Hindi film, whether in India or in the diaspora, cannot be seen simply as a form of ideological recuperation, through which young people are brought into line with parental or community values; nor does viewers' ideological or cultural critique of the films necessarily preclude their pleasure in the spectacle or the social experience of viewing.

Ultimately, as Hargreaves (2001c) points out – and as several of the studies cited here also suggest – there may be many factors other than ethnicity that influence migrants' use of media: in addition to age, gender and class, these may include factors such as religious belief, linguistic competence and patterns of control in the home, as well as judgments of taste and value. There is a danger here of regarding 'culture' as a fixed, unitary quality that straightforwardly determines people's interpretations and uses of media (Harindranath, 2000). As Aksoy and Robins (2003) argue, migrants cannot and should not be wholly accounted for in terms of their membership of the 'imagined community' of the diaspora. Yet while it is important to avoid such 'ethnic absolutism', we also need to be aware of the problems with generalising the notion of 'new ethnicities', particularly in the more celebratory form we have identified here.

## Conclusion

How are children forming their identities in this global media environment – and, in particular, what possibilities does it offer for migrant or ethnic minority children? For most such children, their media experiences are likely to be a complex mixture of the global and the local. In this chapter, we have focused primarily on their access to transnational media, produced in their country of origin, and ethnic minority media, produced in their new location. Yet they are also likely to share aspects of *global* media (Disney or Pokémon or Harry Potter, for example) with children from the dominant culture – even though these texts may in fact be equally alien to both groups. It is these media that we move on to discuss more specifically in the next chapter.

# 4
# Going Global: Childhood in the Age of Global Media

In Chapter 3, we reviewed research on migrant and ethnic minority children's uses of media – particularly media that are specifically targeted at transnational audiences. In this chapter, the focus shifts to an examination of 'global' media for children – by which we mean media produced for a mass audience of children worldwide. Rather than looking only at the act of use or consumption, we also focus here on the companies that produce these media and the representations they provide: addressing these dimensions is crucial if we are to understand the wider structural contexts in which childhoods are lived out. While outlining some general tendencies in this field, we also look more closely at a few specific instances drawn from our own empirical research on two international projects tracking the global distribution and consumption of Disney and Pokémon products.

As we have noted, globalisation is not merely a cultural phenomenon, but also an economic one: it is about the trade in both material and cultural commodities. Placing children in the debate about globalisation thus inevitably invokes familiar concerns about the 'commercialisation' of childhood. In these debates, children are typically seen as passive victims of the machinations of capitalism: unable to understand or protect themselves against the pressures of advertising and marketing, they are seen as helplessly vulnerable to commercial exploitation. This popular critique of marketing to children has been gathering pace in recent years, not least because of the increasing scale of commercial interests targeting children. Yet, perhaps paradoxically, it is a critique that often seems to deny children's agency or autonomy, and even their competence as consumers (Buckingham, 2007).

Combining this familiar concern with anxieties about globalisation thus invokes fundamental issues to do with cultural continuity.

Commercial forces are seen to have disrupted the process of socialisation, upsetting the smooth transmission of cultural values from one generation to the next. According to the critics, globalisation will inevitably result in the construction of a homogenised global children's culture, dominated by a small number of media superpowers. In this situation, it is argued, cultural differences will be flattened out and erased, and parents' attempts to sustain and pass on their cultural values will be increasingly in vain. For authors such as McChesney (2002) and Kline (1993), this is an inevitable consequence of commercialisation: neo-liberal economics are, in their view, inherently incompatible with the 'real' needs and interests of children.

This view also speaks to the protectionist imperatives of national media producers. Broadcasters typically invoke arguments about children's needs – and even children's rights – in seeking to justify the need for domestically produced programming. Children, it is argued, need to see representations of themselves and of their national cultures on screen; and they need 'quality' programming of a kind that, it is suggested, cannot be provided in a global market that is seen to cater to the lowest common denominator. Gatherings of children's media producers (such as the series of 'World Summits' on children and media that have been held since the mid-1990s) frequently conclude with calls for government intervention to support domestic production for children against the pressure of the global market (von Feilitzen and Carlsson, 2002). Such arguments often seem to rely on judgments about cultural value that are asserted rather than fully justified; and, more to the point, they raise questions about whose *version* of 'national culture' is to be represented.

This issue is particularly acute for national public broadcasters, such as the BBC. On the one hand, they are compelled to satisfy 'public service' imperatives in respect of the national audience – and indeed, they need to maximise that audience if they are to retain their legitimacy. On the other hand, however, they are increasingly called upon to earn revenue from overseas sales, both of programming and of related merchandising – leaving them open to charges of commercial exploitation. This often leads to an urgent need for ideological self-justification, in which traditional notions of childhood and conservative representations of 'national culture' are strongly to the fore (Buckingham, 2002a).

Even so, it could be argued that the globalisation of media is resulting in a *modernisation* of childhood, or at least in the growing dominance of what might be called a modernist representation of childhood. Thus, the global success of the children's channel Nickelodeon provides a symptomatic instance of the ways in which market values have come to be aligned with liberal political arguments about children's rights. The statements of Nickelodeon executives and the rhetoric of its on-screen publicity proclaim its role as an agent of empowerment – a notion of the channel as a 'kid-only' zone, giving voice to kids, taking the kids' point of view, as the friend of kids. In this discourse, the interests of 'kids' are frequently defined as being in opposition to the interests of adults. Yet, this assertion of children's rights is also tied to a consumerist approach, in which the child is defined as a 'sovereign consumer'. In the words of one Nickelodeon executive, 'what's good for kids is good for business' (see Hendershot, 2004).

This 'modernist' discourse has increasingly been adopted by exponents of more traditional children's media, not least in public service television. This is certainly the case in the United Kingdom (see Buckingham et al., 1999); but it is also apparent, for example, in the (possibly unlikely) case of the Minimax channel in post-communist Hungary (Lustyik, 2003). It might even be possible to talk here about the emergence of a globalised 'modernist style' in children's culture that seeks to address children across cultural boundaries – in the same way that critics have talked about 'youth culture' as a global phenomenon (Buckingham, 2004). As we have seen, the Japanese business consultant Kenichi Ohmae (1995) asserts that children's exposure to such a global culture means that they now have more in common with their peers in other cultures than they do with their own parents.

Of course, we should not forget that many children in the majority world – particularly in the more isolated rural areas of poorer countries – still do not have access to many forms of media communication. Such children and their families may lack the economic resources to purchase manufactured toys or printed media and may lack electricity, let alone access to broadcast signals; and as such, their ability to 'buy into' a globalised children's culture is distinctly limited (for example, see Punch (2003) on rural Bolivia). Yet, as modern technologies steadily extend their reach across the globe, the media that these children are likely to encounter first will not be those produced in their own countries, but those produced in the wealthy nations of the West.

## The economic case

There is certainly an economic logic to the globalisation of children's culture. The children's market is potentially large, but it is also by its nature quite fragmented. In terms of age, children are quite clearly divided (and divide themselves) into age segments: what appeals to a five-year-old is unlikely to appeal to a ten-year-old. The market is also starkly divided in terms of gender. Particularly for younger children this is a very 'pink and blue' market, and there are significant risks in attempting to cross the line, in order to appeal to both groups. It used to be the received wisdom among marketers that the way to succeed was to appeal to boys first: girls were quite likely to buy into boy culture, although boys were less likely to buy into girl culture (Schneider, 1992). Analyses of contemporary toy advertising would suggest that – despite decades of second-wave feminism – this continues to be the case (Griffiths, 2002).

While the picture is (perhaps increasingly) complicated, the fact remains that the children's market is strongly segmented; and one way for producers to deal with this – to develop economies of scale – is to build markets globally and to amass 'niche' markets into a larger global market. This tendency is also reinforced by the vertical and horizontal integration of the media and cultural industries. 'Vertical integration' refers to the way in which the market is coming to be dominated by a small number of global players, who integrate hardware, software and means of distribution; and these are largely the same players who dominate the adult market (Westcott, 2002). For example, in the case of specialist children's TV channels, the market is dominated by Disney (who have significant interests in the adult market via subsidiaries like Touchstone and Buena Vista, and own the ABC network in the United States), Nickelodeon (owned by Viacom), Cartoon Network (owned by AOL Time Warner) and Fox Kids (part of Murdoch's News International). These four US-based companies currently run more than 40 branded children's channels across Europe, for example, although none of them invests to any significant degree in local (or domestic) production. This is by no means a risk-free market, and national producers are responding to the challenge; but in homes where children have access to cable/satellite, these US-owned channels are achieving a growing market share.

These companies are also increasingly operating across media platforms ('horizontal integration'). Nearly all the major children's 'crazes' of the last 20 years (Ninja Turtles, Power Rangers, Pokémon, Beyblades, Harry Potter, Yu-Gi-Oh) have worked on the principle of what the industry calls 'integrated marketing' or multimedia 'synergy'. For example, Pokémon was first a computer game, then a TV series, a trading card game, a series of movies and a whole range of merchandise, from clothes and toys to food and bags and all sorts of unlikely paraphernalia. Again, horizontal integration on this scale requires global marketing: outside the United States and Japan, it would be much harder to achieve in one country alone.

Furthermore, it is significantly less expensive for national broadcasters to buy in imported material than to produce their own; and in this respect, home-grown productions are not competing on a level playing field. However, as Westcott (2002) suggests, there are significant constraints on the global strategies of the leading companies. All of them function under strict financial controls and tend to abandon particular markets if they do not receive a fairly rapid return on their investment. In many countries, cable/satellite penetration remains limited, and with a greater number of channels, audience shares are tiny. Competition is steadily increasing, and several European companies have responded by creating their own specialised children's channels and moving aggressively into the global market. In general, Westcott argues, US companies have tended to overestimate the power of their own brand names and underestimate the continuing influence of local producers. Over the longer term, the strategy is likely to evolve in the direction of 'localisation', whereby channels are adapted to local markets and new 'hybrids' emerge (Staubhaar and Duarte, 2005) – although it is debatable how viable this will prove to be in the case of the children's market.

Furthermore, *economic* domination does not necessarily translate directly into *ideological* or *cultural* domination. Punch (2007) shows how, as individuals move across cultures, the purchase of certain commodities (such as clothes) may accompany changes in attitudes; but even here, the direction of any causal relationship between these things is not necessarily easy to establish. In the cultural sphere, globalisation is often a paradoxical phenomenon. As we intend to show, children's culture is characterised not so much by a one-way process of domination, but by an unpredictable and contested relationship between the global and the local – often expressed in the notion of 'glocalisation' (Robertson, 1994). In the following sections of this chapter, we explore this further by focussing on some specific examples. We begin with two instances of commercial culture, Disney and Pokémon, and then move on to look briefly at a couple of 'public service' productions; and we conclude by considering the current global 'craze' of Harry Potter.

## Uncle Walt and his evil empire

For critics of commercialism, Disney is the 'bad brand' of children's culture. It is the McDonalds, the Nike of childhood. Historically, it is hard to ignore the political intentions of the Disney Corporation.

Uncle Walt's involvement in far-right politics is quite well documented (Roth, 1996); and critics have seen some of the early films as little more than ideological propaganda in the service of US foreign policy. Eric Smoodin's (1994) collection, for example, contains some trenchant critiques of the role of Disney movies in promoting cultural imperialism in Latin America: the Donald Duck film *The Three Caballeros* is singled out for particular criticism (Burton-Carvajal, 1994; Piedra, 1994), alongside some of the lesser-known travelogues and educational films (Cartwright and Goldfarb, 1994).

Donald Duck was also the subject of a famous early critique by Ariel Dorfman and Armand Mattelart (1975), whose book *Reading Donald Duck* was written in Chile in the wake of the United States' involvement in the overthrow of the Allende government. They argued that, far from being a harmless fantasy of childhood innocence, Donald was actually a vehicle for the propagation of capitalist ideology and US interests and values. That critique has been questioned, however. Barker (1990) takes Dorfman and Mattelart to task for a kind of conspiracy theory that overemphasises the closeness of the relationship between government and business and, perhaps more importantly, for oversimplifying the ways in which people read these comics – in effect, for assuming that children would simply swallow whole the values that the comics were seen to represent.

Even so, for many adults – particularly middle-class adults – outside the United States, Disney is synonymous with the unacceptable face of American capitalism. Our own research on this was undertaken as part of a global project involving 12 countries, published in the book *Dazzled by Disney?* (Wasko, Phillips and Meehan, 2001). This project found that there was considerable consensus among audiences around the world as to the fundamental values of Disney, and that they generally regarded those values in a positive light. However, respondents often distinguished between Disney as a source of entertainment and Disney as a business – and they were often very critical of the commercial motives involved. There was considerable disagreement about the extent to which Disney was 'universal' or somehow specifically 'American' – and those who were most critical of Disney on ideological grounds also tended to associate those objections with its 'Americanness' (Phillips, 2001).

For many of the older adults (many of them parents) whom we interviewed, Disney was generally seen as safe, sanitised, predictable, inauthentic and somewhat 'corny' (Buckingham, 2001b). It was full of objectionable stereotypes and cheap moralism; and it was leading children away from true (that is, national) cultural traditions towards a homogeneous, mass-produced consumer culture. Disney was all about brainwashing, seducing the innocent – and in this sense, the debate about Disney was tied up with broader arguments about the changing symbolic value of childhood. This is a view that is also apparent in some of the academic criticism, for example in the work of Giroux (2001) – although for our British respondents, it was very much reinforced by a sense of Disney as quintessentially *American*, as somehow inherently alien. Their resentment of Disney – as of McDonalds – was often inextricably connected with their rejection of the United States' political role as a global superpower.

However, this criticism was not without its contradictions and paradoxes. Some of the younger adult participants we interviewed (who were mostly undergraduates) were more inclined to admit to enjoying Disney: they expressed a kind of aesthetic appreciation of the animation and the spectacle, and talked about the emotional appeal of Disney's construction of childhood. Even for the older adults, there was a certain amount of ambivalence, even tinged with a degree of nostalgia. It may be that the symbolic importance of Disney as a bearer of US capitalist values tends to provoke a principled critical discourse, even where that discourse might not actually reflect how individuals respond to the films themselves.

By contrast, this sense of Disney's 'Americanness' was not at all an issue for the children we interviewed. When we asked one group of six-year-olds where they thought Disney films came from, they were quite unsure (despite the US accents). In the end, they opted for France, on the grounds that one of them had been to Disneyland Paris. A similar finding was apparent from Kirsten Drotner's (2001a) research for the same project in Denmark. Her chapter in the book is named after a quote from one of her respondents: 'Donald seems so Danish'. To some extent, she is suggesting that the Americanness – the alienness – of Disney went unnoticed by the young Danes whom she interviewed, partly because the comics are translated and the movies are dubbed (which obviously is not the case in the United Kingdom). However, she also suggests that they read the comics selectively: the good aspects of Donald (his unconventional, politically incorrect style) were read as Danish, as reflecting some kind of national character, while his bad qualities were seen as American, and hence as 'other'.

On one level, of course, this invisibility could be seen precisely as testimony to the power of Disney's cultural imperialism: if, in the words of Tunstall (1977), the media are American, then we are now all American too. It could be that Americanness is the default position, something so universal and so unquestioned that it has become effectively invisible. Yet, it could equally be argued that, as they increasingly engage with world markets, Disney and other cultural producers are having to suppress elements that might be perceived as too culturally specific in favour of those that seem to speak to some universal, transcultural notion of childhood.

There are some elements of truth in both arguments. In fact, what our research and Drotner's shows is that audiences read selectively, taking aspects of the text that seem to confirm a positive self-image or cultural identity to them, and setting that against other aspects that they perceive as problematic or undesirable. And it is these latter aspects that they often seem to define as 'American' – as plastic, fake, kitschy or indeed as ideologically suspect. Obviously, this is also an historical process: it would certainly be interesting now to map young people's changing perceptions of the United States, as they are mediated through popular culture, in the wake of George Bush's so-called 'war on terror'.

However, the actual texts that are being produced for the global market are also more complex. Politically speaking, the key Disney movies of the last couple of decades have moved quite a long way from *The Three Caballeros*. McQuillan and Byrne (1999) read the Disney of the 1980s and 1990s as a set of parables for US foreign policy – so *The Lion King* is about South Africa, *Aladdin* is about the Middle East, *Mulan* is about China, and so on. On one level, it is possible to read all these texts as being about global ideological colonisation – and, if you include *Pocahontas*, about internal colonisation as well. One might argue that they are all about recuperating and sanitising 'other' cultures and the challenges they might represent. However, we would argue that it makes more sense to see them as liberal texts, even as confused liberal texts – as texts which do at least recognise other cultures and which try to construct some kind of dialogue with them. If we see such films merely as a more subtle form of propaganda (as critics like Giroux are wont to do), then we miss much of their ambivalence and complexity.

## Gotta catch 'em all: the case of Pokémon

Pokémon provides an interesting contrast with Disney, on several levels. Walt Disney always maintained that his films were intended for a family audience, and not just for children; and while this was essentially a financial decision on his part, it is possible to argue that the films tell children and adults rather different stories about childhood

(Forgacs, 1992). By contrast, Pokémon was largely inaccessible, impenetrable even, to the majority of adults; and that in itself partly explains some of its appeal to children.

Our research on Pokémon was part of another global project, which involved researchers from Japan and the United States as well as from the United Kingdom, France, Hong Kong, Israel and Australia. This research is collected in Joseph Tobin's book *Pikachu's Global Adventure: The Rise and Fall of Pokémon* (Tobin, 2004a). Among other things, we were interested in how Pokémon was produced and marketed as a global phenomenon, and how it was perceived and used by children. As we have noted, Pokémon began life as a computer game, which was produced by Nintendo, but it rapidly span off into a TV series, movies, books and comics, a trading card game, toys, plus the usual range of clothing, food, lunchboxes, stickers and countless other products. In many ways, it was a classic example of integrated marketing. The Pokémon brand became a means to market a whole range of licensed goods to a very diverse range of audiences: soft toys for younger children, TV cartoons for a slightly older age group, the Game Boy game for the oldest, pre-teens and younger teenagers. There was also appeal to girls as well as boys, with girl-friendly themes and characters as well as the more predictable boy-oriented ones: so Pokémon was about collecting, about nurturing as well as competing, about feeling as well as fighting. For a while at least, it managed very effectively to cut across the divisions and segments in the children's market.

It was also very successful globally. This needs to be understood in terms of the emergence of Japan as a global cultural power – which has become an increasingly important factor in global media markets (see Allison, 2000). This phenomenon is most obviously apparent in the rise of *manga* (the Japanese comic book) and its move from being a 'cult' medium, or a medium just for children, to something more mainstream; and it is also evident in the global marketing of Japanese 'cuteness' (*kawai'sa*), in the form of Hello Kitty, Sailor Moon and even the Tamagotchi (Yano, 2004). Pokémon clearly combines elements of both these forms.

Our research considered how Japanese producers used other countries as a kind of springboard into local markets around the world. In Asia, where there can be resistance to Japanese products, Nintendo marketed Pokémon products via Hong Kong; while it also used the United States, and US franchise holders, to push into other Western markets. So the Pokémon card game was actually produced by an US company, the sinisterly named Wizards of the Coast, who were also responsible for a similar game for older children, *Magic the Gathering*. Likewise, the version of the TV series that is exported globally is a re-versioned one from the United States, not the Japanese original: it is an 'Americanised' version of a Japanese cultural product.

This 'glocalisation' involved two things. First, at the point of distribution, there is a process known as 'localising'. Thus, the distributors employed people in the United States to adapt the TV cartoons for the US market, which involved editing out material that was seen to be too culturally strange or specific. Katsuno and Maret (2004) compared the Japanese and US versions of Pokémon cartoons and found some quite unexpected (and indeed quite bizarre) differences here, in terms of what was seen to be palatable to a US market – particularly to do with the removal of anything remotely sexual or 'violent'.

At the same time, at the point of production, there was a process which Iwabushi (2004) calls 'deodorising': that is, anything that was seen as too Japanese (the 'odour' of Japan) was removed. So, for example, the characters are given Westernised names, the characteristic *anime* visual style (for example, of the faces) is relatively muted, there is no written language, no religious references and some of the settings are rendered less obviously Japanese. There was therefore a distinct effort to create a product that would be exportable, both at the point of local distribution and at the point of production.

Our research showed that children used Pokémon products in diverse and sometimes creative ways in different cultural settings. They actively interpreted the texts, relating them both to broader moral and social concerns (such as good and evil, or friendship and competition) and to specific local issues. In Israel, for example, the children picked up on the theme of 'fighting for peace', reflecting a national context characterised by ongoing military conflict (Lemish and Bloch, 2004); in Australia, Aboriginal children bypassed the competitive elements of the card game and chose to play collaboratively; while in France, the children adapted the game for playing traditional French card games such as La Bataille and La Tapette (Brougere, 2004). Children also used the toys and their knowledge of the Pokémon universe to create play scenarios of their own invention; and in some instances, as in the United Kingdom, they created their own Pokémon-related texts and artefacts (Bromley, 2004; Willett, 2004). While some of these uses were authorised and promoted by the producers, others could well be seen as unauthorised, and even as 'resistant'; and as Tobin (2004b) suggests, this could be seen as a form of 'secondary localisation', in which children share a degree of power with the producers.

To some extent, the diversity and scope of the Pokémon phenomenon seems to have permitted – if not explicitly encouraged – this wide range of possible uses. Here again, the strategy seems to have been one of 'catching 'em all' (in the words of one of the Pokémon slogans). As Ohmae (1995) implies, this may facilitate the creation of a common global culture among children. We observed several instances of children communicating and playing with Pokémon across social and cultural differences: its extensive, specialised mythology provided a kind of common language that transcended cultural barriers. Yet what was interesting was that – unlike our brief experience with Disney – the 'Japaneseness' of Pokémon was something that children definitely recognised and enjoyed. It was strange, but strange–exotic – and, indeed, profoundly cool (see McGray, 2002). Of course, 'cool' has a limited shelf-life; and it is interesting to speculate about how and why some Japanese products come to be defined as cool in this global market, while others do not. In this respect, our project also tracked the complicated reasons why children appeared to drop Pokémon as quickly as they had taken it up – which were more to do with the dynamics of the peer group than with any actions on the part of global marketers. Even so, it would be interesting to consider how this continuing rise of Japan in the cultural sphere (for example, in the form of subsequent 'crazes' such as Digimon and Yu-Gi-Oh) might play out in terms of children's global awareness.

## Glocalisation as public service

This phenomenon of 'glocalisation' is not entirely new, nor are the processes we are describing confined to the more obviously commercialised end of children's media. Our next two examples suggest that public service media companies may also be engaging in similar attempts to reach the global market – in both cases, of pre-school children.

The US series *Sesame Street* is now more than 35-years old. Produced by a not-for-profit company and screened in the United States on public television, its success and survival have crucially depended on global marketing. Just as with Pokémon, there are global Sesame Street franchises and an enormous range of spin-off merchandise – although because of its educational cachet, these tend to be the kind of products middle-class parents are less likely to find objectionable.

Interestingly, *Sesame Street* was also the subject of a forceful ideological critique by Armand Mattelart, the co-author of *Reading Donald Duck* (Mattelart and Waksman, 1978). He saw *Sesame Street*, like Disney, as the bearer of a set of US ideological values and as part of a broader cultural imperialism. Just as Disney's appeal to childhood allowed it to profess an essential innocence, he argued, so the educational intentions of *Sesame Street* served as a kind of alibi. According to Mattelart, the programme was actually putting across a specific set of social values and capitalist ideologies that children were assumed simply to accept. Perhaps surprisingly, this argument was also made in the United Kingdom as well, albeit in slightly different terms. There was a great controversy in the late 1960s when the BBC refused to buy *Sesame Street*, not so much on ideological grounds as much on the basis of its style of pedagogy. The use of what were seen as 'advertising techniques' for drilling children in letter and number recognition was seen as somehow at odds with the more child-centred, play-oriented British tradition of pre-school education (see Buckingham et al., 1999).

In fact, however, *Sesame Street* has frequently worked with local producers around the world to insert local content. Alongside Big Bird, Elmo and Kermit, the programmes typically include locally produced documentary inserts that feature children in the country where the programme is screened. There has also been some research looking at how, for example, *Sesame Street* in Israel incorporated material about Israeli and Palestinian children, and the consequences of this in terms of their attitudes towards each other (Fisch, 2001).

Ironically, in recent years the BBC has been engaged in a very similar enterprise. Its ground-breaking pre-school series of the late 1990s, *Teletubbies*, was clearly produced with a global audience in mind; and indeed, it has become increasingly imperative for the BBC to earn revenue from overseas sales, even though it is primarily funded by compulsory taxation (the license fee). An investment on the scale of *Teletubbies* would not have been possible without assured overseas revenue, not just from programme sales but also from ancillary merchandising – and, as with the other texts we have discussed, the scale and diversity of the merchandising has been quite phenomenal (Buckingham, 2002b).

Like *Sesame Street*, *Teletubbies* also offers the facility for local broadcasters to insert local content. For example, despite resistance on the part of the Norwegian public broadcasters to buying it (on grounds that were not dissimilar to the BBC's concerns about *Sesame Street*), the programme is now screened in Norway and includes not just Norwegian voice-overs and dubbing but also documentary material featuring Norwegian children. Again, this could be seen as an example of glocalisation, a productive meeting of the global and the local. Nevertheless, there are questions to be raised about what is and is not culturally specific here. It may be that cultural specificity is not simply a matter of content, but also of form – or in educational terms, it is not just about the curriculum of the programme, but also about its pedagogy. *Teletubbies* has a very different style of pedagogy compared with *Sesame Street*; and while we would hesitate to label one essentially 'British' and the other essentially 'American', there clearly are cultural differences here that would be worth investigating more closely.

## Harry Potter goes global

The forms that this globalisation of media takes – and its consequences for children's sense of cultural identity – are diverse and variable. The notion of cultural imperialism does to some extent describe what is taking place here, at least at an economic level; but it fails to account for the diversity and complexity of how children use and interpret cultural texts. However, there are reasons to be cautious about the postmodern emphasis on hybridity and fragmentation: access to global markets is not equally open to all, and consumers are clearly not free to choose their cultural identities from an infinite range of global possibilities.

Yet, the global marketing of children's culture constantly throws up new paradoxes. The current worldwide success of Harry Potter is a striking case in point. Although it started life as a book (or a series of books), rather than a computer game or a television series, Harry Potter is another example of the kind of 'integrated marketing' we have described as characteristic of contemporary children's media. In addition to the books and the movies, it is possible to buy Harry Potter computer games, postcard and sticker books, calendars, posters, guidebooks, dolls, puzzles and card games; as well as watches, pens, wallets, coffee cups and even boxer shorts – commodities that (like the books) are clearly marketed to adults as well as children. The series has also spawned toys (such as magic wands and broomsticks) and play outfits that allow children – and, it would seem, adults as well – to act out detailed Harry Potter scenarios in the privacy of their own homes. As with Pokémon, the emphasis of much of this commercial activity is on *collecting*; and the continuity of the books and the films over a series of seven clearly promotes this, allowing new spin-off products to come on to the market at regular intervals.

Although the author of the books, J.K. Rowling, is British, distribution and licensing rights for Harry Potter products are owned by the major US-based conglomerate AOL Time Warner, which also produces the movies. As with all the other examples we have discussed in this chapter, AOL Time Warner have not been slow to find marketing partners for 'tie-in' deals, developing lucrative relationships with Lego, Mattel, Hasbro, Electronic Arts and many others. One key partner, Steve Jones, the Head of Strategy at Coca-Cola, exemplifies the global ambitions of this kind of marketing as follows:

> Both Harry Potter and Coca-Cola reach deep into the heart of local communities around the world to add a little bit of magic to everybody's lives ... Bringing the two together creates an opportunity for us to develop programmes that will not only touch people emotionally, but allow us to affect their lives in a tangible, meaningful way.
>
> (Quoted in Tomkowiak, 2003: 91).

Despite this rampant commercialism, children's enthusiastic consumption of the Harry Potter books has provided reassurance for many parents concerned by recurrent press reports about the apparent decline in children's reading (reports that are in fact highly overstated: see Neuman, 1995). Nevertheless, some critics have seen its success as symptomatic of the destruction of the traditional values of children's literature at the hands of marketers: Zipes (2001), for example, makes a very similar argument here to his earlier criticisms of Disney's versions of traditional fairy tales (for example, Zipes, 1995). Others regard the marketing of Harry Potter as indicative of a much broader 'commercialisation of childhood': it sustains the hegemony of commodity fetishism while masquerading as 'good, clean fun' (Turner-Vorbeck, 2003). However, such criticisms tend to underestimate the volatility and unpredictability of the children's market: like earlier 'crazes' such as the Ninja Turtles, Harry Potter was by no means an instant success (the initial print run of the first volume was allegedly a few hundred copies). Furthermore, such criticisms tend to present children (and, to a lesser extent, their parents) as passive, naïve consumers – mere victims of a manipulative, all-powerful corporate machine.

To what extent is Harry Potter culturally specific? For a British reader, there is a great deal here that is culturally familiar. Hogwarts, the school, and the Dursleys, Harry's foster family, both appear distinctly British; and they have many echoes in other British children's books, ranging from traditional boarding-school stories to the grotesque representations of family life in the work of Roald Dahl. At the same time, some critics have suggested that Harry Potter reflects some rather more contemporary concerns and anxieties in British culture, for example to do with education and indeed with consumerism itself (Blake, 2002). Others argue that the values of Harry Potter are far from timeless or universal: there has been widespread criticism, for example, of the gender stereotyping and class bias in the books, and of the exclusion of ethnic differences – in ways that some see as characteristic of old-fashioned British school stories (Heilman, 2003a). Meanwhile, some point to the highly problematic theme of 'racial' mixing in the books – the preoccupation with 'pure blood' versus 'mudblood' characters and the quasi-racial distinctions within the wizard community (Heilman and Gregory, 2003).

By contrast, others suggest that the books address fundamental dilemmas of childhood in ways that are universally applicable. The books are seen to deal with children's concerns about separation, about the initiation into adulthood, about terror and evil, as well as with more mundane anxieties about dealing with school and the peer group. Some argue that the books draw on a 'collective unconscious' of archetypes familiar from ancient myths and romances. Many critics are keen to point out – not always positively – how the books borrow or steal well-established themes and tropes from other children's books, ranging from fairy tales and classic hero narratives to more recent texts, from *The Chronicles of Narnia* to *Mary Poppins* and from *Tom Brown's Schooldays* to the Nancy Drew stories. While some regard this as evidence of the author's formulaic, second-hand approach, others see it as further evidence of the books' appeal to a trans-cultural, a-historical 'essence' of childhood. (Instances of such arguments can be found in the burgeoning – and very diverse – critical literature on Harry Potter: see, for example, Anatol, 2003; Gupta, 2003; Heilman, 2003b; Whited, 2004.)

As with Pokémon, Harry Potter has to be 'localised' for specific national audiences. In this case, of course, the books have to be translated into other languages; and in the process, all sorts of linguistic and cultural specificities have to be dealt with. Between its original publication in English (in June 1997) and the launch of the first film (in November 2001), *Harry Potter and the Philosopher's Stone* had been translated into 47 languages and was on sale in 115 countries. As Gillian Lathey (2005) describes, translators often face considerable difficulties, not just with wordplay, dialect and register, but also with specific cultural references (for example, to the customs of school life or eating habits). This 'localisation' is also reflected in the design of the book covers (see Lathey, 2005; Tomkowiak, 2003). While most of the covers draw on the US edition rather than the British one, there is considerable diversity both in the content and in the style of illustration. In some respects, then, the Harry Potter that is on sale in Korea or Egypt is not the same text as is on sale in Britain – although it would be interesting to look systematically at how far specific cultural references are still apparent in the films or in other products.

So how can we explain the global appeal of Harry Potter? Like the other phenomena we have discussed in this chapter, it is effectively a global brand, which is used to sell a whole range of media and merchandise to children around the world. Yet, to see this simply as evidence of the all-conquering power of marketing is to ignore much of what is most specific about it, and to underestimate the agency of children themselves. How, for example, do we explain the phenomenal success of Harry Potter in China? What is it that Chinese children, whose lives are very different in many ways from those of children in Britain, seem to recognise in Harry Potter? Does this success point to the existence of some kind of universal, global childhood – or is it that these texts are interpreted in such different ways in different cultures that they effectively become very different things? Does Harry Potter, for all the apparently old-fashioned nature of the story, somehow represent a *modernist* conception of childhood, which transcends cultural differences?

## Conclusion

Kenichi Ohmae (1995) may well be correct in arguing that global marketing is creating a common culture of childhood, which cuts across national differences. It is possible that this is helping children to communicate across cultures and making way for new forms of global understanding; yet in doing so, it may also be simply eradicating those differences and undermining the transmission of culture from one generation to the next. Even so, it would be a mistake to see this in terms of either/or choices: rather than the global simply replacing or destroying the local, it would seem that local and global cultures (and indeed transnational ones) can come to co-exist side by side, feeding into and influencing each other and providing children with a range of potential cultural identifications. Likewise, media can enable us to come to terms with the experience of change; but they can also provide a form of continuity, even stability, in a world that appears to be transforming at an ever more rapid pace.

What are the specific implications of this for migrant children? As Drotner (2001a) points out, there are many different types of 'otherness' potentially at stake here; and it would be a mistake to conceive either of the dominant 'host' culture or of the minority 'foreign' culture as somehow homogeneous and utterly distinct from each other. Ironically, such global material may provide just as much connection with these children's memories of their home country as the programming on specialist satellite channels. The particular combination of cultural specificity and universality ('otherness' and 'sameness') of a global production like *The Simpsons* may paradoxically unite Turkish children living in Germany both with their German peers and with their cousins back home in Turkey – and potentially with children in England or in Hong Kong or in Nigeria. Quite how they might interpret such a text – not least (in this instance) in the light of their own very different experiences of family life – and how they might discuss it with their friends and family is the kind of issue we shall be exploring in more detail in the following two chapters.

# 5
# Finding a Place: Migrant Children Using Media

In this chapter and the next, we move from broad overviews of previous studies to more detailed analyses of data drawn from our own empirical research. Our focus here is on the diverse ways in which migrant children use media in the context of their everyday lives and relationships. This chapter presents some findings from our CHICAM project, looking at these children's uses of media in different European national settings; while the next explores three individual case studies drawn from Liesbeth de Block's earlier research with migrant children in London.

Our central emphasis here is on how the experience of migration impacts on children's uses of media; and, conversely, how the use of media enables children to make sense of that experience. For most of the children in our research, the media had been a constant point of reference in lives that had otherwise been characterised by a high degree of change and disruption. Yet the media they encountered were also diverse; and they provided opportunities both for sustaining a sense of continuity with the past and for coming to terms with new cultural contexts. These forces of continuity and change may appear to pull in different directions; but they can also be held in tension – perhaps productive tension – in the fabric of children's daily lives.

## The context of CHICAM

As we have explained, CHICAM was a qualitative 'action research' project funded by the European Commission, which ran between 2001 and 2004. We set up media-making clubs in six European countries (Sweden, the Netherlands, Germany, Italy, Greece and the United Kingdom). In each club, a researcher and a media educator worked with recently arrived refugee and migrant children aged between 10 and 14

94

years to make visual representations of their lives and their experiences in their new locations. Using the Internet, a communications network was also established between the clubs to facilitate the sharing of the children's productions.

The clubs operated in parallel, although there were significant differences between them, for example in terms of the location, the range of children who were involved, and the approaches adopted by the media educators. In addition to working in the clubs, the researchers spent a considerable amount of time in the field sites, engaged in a range of informal activities. They visited the children's families, went out and about with the children in the cities and towns in which they lived, and sat in on school lessons and break times. 'In-between' settings – that is, the spaces between structured activities or institutional contexts – provided particularly valuable opportunities for gathering data; and we also conducted informal group and individual interviews with the children both during the production process, and when it was complete.

To say the least, this was not a neutral setting. As adult researchers, conducting a project in a school or a school-like environment, we could only gain very partial access to these children's lives. Clearly, what children say in such a context, or how they behave, cannot be taken as a reliable indicator of what might happen outside it. The researchers also presented themselves and defined the context of the clubs in quite different ways, and had very different kinds of relationships with the children. We would argue that our relatively long-term engagement with the children, and the variety of situations in which we observed and interacted with them, does provide us with a more in-depth picture than is often obtained in research on media audiences. Even so, data obtained in this way clearly cannot be taken at face value.

Our account in this chapter draws on reports written at various stages in the project by researchers in the different national settings. (The authors of these reports are identified in the acknowledgments at the start of this book.) In many cases, the reports are in the form of descriptive 'field notes', sometimes written shortly after the events they describe; although in others, they engage in more general reflection. Some of these were originally written in English, but others have been translated – as of course have the quotations from the children themselves. Inevitably, the reports themselves also reflect the cultural and political contexts and assumptions of their authors. Our experience of CHICAM confirmed the fact that the experience of migration – and how that experience is understood and defined – varies greatly, even between

European countries that are outwardly quite similar: differences that can be discerned at the level of policy – for example, between an emphasis on assimilation and a more 'multicultural' approach – can also reflect very different views of migrants, and of how they should be treated in everyday life.

These methodological issues are considered in more detail in Chapter 7, specifically in relation to the use of visual methods and the potential of participatory research with children. Our account in this chapter is relatively descriptive; and it brings together data from some very diverse cultural settings, often in a 'second-hand' form. Our aim here is to provide a broad overview, and to hazard some generalisations about migrant children's relationships with media: more specific experiences and issues are analysed in much greater detail in the chapters that follow.

## Continuity and difference

The children who joined our media clubs came from many different countries and spoke a correspondingly wide range of languages. Clearly, since refugees and migrants enter Europe from well-recognised international trouble zones, there were children from similar countries in several of the clubs. For example, in more than two of the clubs there were children from Somalia, The Democratic Republic of Congo, Colombia, Turkey, Iraq and Afghanistan. However, due to the location of some of the clubs, there was a predominance of one or another ethnic group in some cases. In Sweden, for example, the club was based in a small coastal town, and nearly all the children were from Kosovo; while in Greece, where the club was based at the Greek Council for Refugees, the majority were from Iraq and Turkey (mostly Kurdish).

Several of the children were refugees from conflict zones, and in some cases had arrived unaccompanied; while others were members of families that would be primarily defined as 'economic migrants'. Some were seeking asylum, having either arrived recently or having already experienced a long period of temporary permits or living in reception centres; whereas for others, who had been granted asylum or permission to remain, the situation was more secure, and their families were planning for their future lives in the new country. For some of these children, then, life was still unsafe and fragile, whereas for others it was already becoming more stable. Naturally, such different conditions affect how children establish bonds and ties with others (Black, 1994;

Virta and Westin, 1999); and yet, for all the children, the forming of friendships in the new location was a key imperative.

This was, therefore, a very diverse group. In addition to the differences between them, there were also often differences *within* particular immigrant groups in terms of social status and prestige. What they had in common was their 'otherness', their difference from the dominant culture of the host country; and that sense of difference could prove to be pervasive, manifested in a whole range of factors such as language, physical appearance, education, parental employment status, clothing, religious beliefs and practices, and shared codes of social behaviour. In some instances – for example, in the school in London – the wider community itself was extremely culturally diverse; while in others – such as the small town in Sweden – it was much more homogeneous, and the children were much more clearly marked as a 'minority'. Difference therefore *mattered* in different ways, and to different degrees, in different settings.

As we shall see, the media played several roles in these respects. There were some stark variations in terms of access to media both within and across the clubs, which in turn reflected variations in the children's economic and domestic circumstances. Broadly speaking, the children who were refugees, and had arrived relatively recently, were less likely to have access to new media such as the Internet and mobile phones; although there were also significant national differences in this respect. Even so, all the children who participated had constant exposure to a range of media, both local and international. Many brought with them vivid recollections of the media of their earlier childhood; and for many, it was possible to sustain aspects of this media culture in their new setting, through continuing exposure to both transnational and global media. Yet in coming to the new country, they were exposed to a different media environment and a different symbolic milieu. Experiences of media therefore formed a continuity with their past lives, with their countries and cultures of origin, while also introducing them to aspects of the new culture and society.

At the same time, the use of media is always socially mediated, negotiated and structured. It takes place within the context of family life and of peer group relationships; and while it helps to define those relationships, it is also defined by them. As we shall see, the use of media can serve as a means of sustaining or of undermining power-relationships within the family and the peer group, and of perpetuating forms of inclusion and exclusion that may prove to be particularly highly charged for migrant children.

## Family viewing

For the reasons we have explained, television was very much the dominant medium for these children. While some had access to multiple television sets in the home, parents tended to see 'family viewing' an important occasion for celebrating (or enforcing) family togetherness, and indeed for imposing particular parental values. In some cases, parents were quite restrictive of their children's access to television; and while this was partly a reflection of more general beliefs about the influence of the media, it was also informed by a view of television as a source of negative cultural and moral influences. For example, in the United Kingdom, Haamid's father was keen to talk to the researcher about the corrupting influence of Western media on the young, and was only persuaded to allow Haamid to participate in the club because it involved the use of computers. He found the editing side of the work acceptable, as Haamid would be developing his computer skills; and this may well have been one reason why Haamid himself was very interested in this aspect of the club activities.

Even so, the importance of television as a focus for family life was often symbolised by the arrangement of the television sets in the family home, and the fact that television was frequently a key priority in terms of family expenditure. The Swedish researchers emphasised this:

> The television set seems to be in the very centre of the family life. When one of the girls moved to a new apartment they bought a new television set worth 2000 Euro to be placed in the living room. Often, children have their own set in the bedroom as well, sometimes shared with one or two siblings. Access to cable (including pay-TV) and satellite television seems to be standard. However, they do not have access to cable and satellite television in all rooms equipped with a television set. The most well-equipped sets are placed in the living room.

Likewise, in most refugee households of the children in the Greek club, satellite TV was ranked as a necessity and was obtained even before other basic goods (such as a kitchen table). In many of the households we visited, the television was permanently switched on, and seemed to play the role of the family hearth, the focal point around which the family gathers. Most frequently tuned to programmes from the country of origin, it stood as a constant reminder and a permanent link: the language, the imagery, the dress codes, the current affairs, the overall cultural register that was communicated helped to maintain contact with the distant country of origin in the domestic space of the living room.

At the same time, there were also varying levels of negotiation and control over who would watch and what was watched. For example, one of the families in Italy had the main television and satellite links in the mother's bedroom, symbolising not only the importance of satellite links for the mother, but also who was in charge in the family. In general, our findings here confirm those of earlier research: the parents largely maintained control of the main TV set, which was used for viewing transnational channels, while the children resorted to (non-satellite equipped) sets in their bedrooms to watch national or global programmes (cf. Hargreaves, 2001c).

These family relationships also have an impact on the particular programmes children watch. Some television programmes formed an important part of the children's personal histories: most children had very strong memories of programmes they had watched with friends or family in their countries of origin. In addition to satellite and cable channels giving access to programmes in the family language, video also provided a means of contact with the home country. Video rentals from the local shop were occasionally supplemented by tapes sent from their country of origin, as we found in the case of the Italian children:

> A lot of them have collections of videotapes, and several spoke repeatedly with pride of the numbers of tapes they had. Only one club member, however, spoke openly about a backwards-and-forwards movement of videotapes with his home country. Parcels containing videotapes were continually arriving from Peru. Some were in Spanish, and others were in English with Spanish subtitles. Fernando's favourites were Kung Fu and other films with a lot of fighting and martial arts.

As this implies, the children potentially had access to very different types of material. In Chapter 3, we broadly categorised these as *transnational* (produced in their countries of origin), *national* (produced in the new host country) and *global* (produced for international consumption, often by US-based or Japanese companies). These categories are not exclusive: national programming includes many global products, especially programmes originating in the United States, as does programming on transnational channels; while global broadcasting is not entirely US-based, as we have indicated in Chapter 4. Even so, we can separate these out for the purposes of our discussion here.

## Transnational television and video

As we noted in Chapter 3, the viewing of transnational television can serve several purposes. It is not simply a matter of nostalgia, or of maintaining a fixed attachment to the past, as some have argued. It can also be a means of keeping in contact with the present, and with changing realities in the country of origin. In some families, it was also used specifically for maintaining children's fluency in the home language.

Maintaining continuity with their past lives was particularly important for many of the parents in our research. In some cases, it was not so much the connection with the country of origin itself that was important but the continuation of activities that the family used to enjoy before their migration. Of course, these kinds of nostalgic pleasures are by no means confined to migrant viewers, although they may take on a particular form in a transnational context. For example, the Dutch researchers described this phenomenon as follows:

> Satellite TV offers news programmes from the home country and some other material: melodramas and comedies (mainly watched by mothers and daughters) or family programmes watched by the whole family just as they did in their native country. For example, Masja's Armenian family all watched a Brazilian Telenovela through a Russian satellite channel, which is dubbed in Russian.

As in this case, such programmes did not necessarily have to be produced in the country of origin. Many families watched soap operas originating from regions other than their own, often in a third language – suggesting that the emotional connection to the programme was more important than following the details of the dialogue. Rodica, a Romanian girl living in Italy, for example, described how she and her sister regularly watched a Spanish soap opera, even though she could not entirely follow the language. As this suggests, and as we argued in Chapter 4, the global circulation of television is more complex than simply a matter of US domination or of linguistic minorities watching programmes in their own languages (Chalaby, 2005b); and it may be that genres like soap opera have a particular kind of cross-cultural accessibility in this respect (cf. Allen, 1994; Gillespie, 1995; Liebes and Katz, 1990).

Similarly, several of the children in the United Kingdom described family viewing of Hindi films, even where the family were not Hindi-speaking. These films appeared to provide common ground for children from very different ethnic and language communities, including Somali, Pakistani, Sri Lankan and Kenyan, as the following extract from our fieldnotes describes:

Some of the girls – those with an Asian or Islamic background – watched a lot of Hindi films on video. They also mentioned the Indian movie channel B4U. I was interested in how they understood them, as none of them spoke Hindi. Sahra said that she watched them dubbed into Somali. The others said that they could follow them very easily through the style, music and dancing. They also said they had learned some Hindi through watching but also that there were some crossovers between the languages. But it was the emotional resonance that appeared to be more important. Fatima [who came from Kenya] expressed this by saying that 'it's like a true story', unlike English films. Sahra said that they were strange because 'things happen for no reason – it's funny. It's not real life, but they can reflect real things, like war'. This sense of reality, along with the fact that they usually watched them with their mothers and other family members, made them a very important part of their lives. Some of the boys also said they watched for this reason. It was interesting that those girls, like Fatima, who felt more ambivalent about living in the United Kingdom expressed a higher level of enjoyment of these films. On the other hand, both Shakuntala and Sahra said they watched them for social reasons but didn't enjoy them much – though they could also have been saying this for my benefit because I represented the mainstream culture. Interestingly, Shakuntala [who came from Sri Lanka] was particularly embarrassed by Tamil films, and was more willing to accept the Hindi films, perhaps because they appeared to be more broad-based. This seemed to reflect her ability to differentiate between aspects of the two cultures she wanted to participate in, or be identified with.

Here again, it seems that the children's interest in these films overcomes their unfamiliarity with the language – and that this interest functions largely on a symbolic or emotional level, that has a particular resonance for them as migrants. Even where they do not reflect reality, the films are seen to hold a form of 'emotional realism' that transcends cultural differences (cf. Ang, 1985). Yet the children's engagement with the films – or at least their claims about this in discussion – also reflected their attempts to define their own cultural identities and to imagine their own futures.

## News from home

In other cases, however, transnational television was used for keeping in touch with current events and changes back home. As we have seen, satellite TV news often plays a particularly important role in this respect (cf. Journal of Ethnic and Migration Studies, 2006). Many families watched several sources of news, and the children were often very well informed about world events. It was argued by many that national news often gave a limited view of international events; and there was a preference for global news stations such as Al-Jazeera and CNN. This was particularly relevant to the refugee children, as was apparent in the Netherlands, for example:

> In refugee families, the role of TV is different than it is in migrant families. The satellite often is the only link between asylum seekers and their home countries, where many of them left family and friends. Depending on their specific situations, some of the refugee families had no contact with their family and friends for many years. During the war in Iraq, TV was very important to the children, too. The children told each other what they saw on television. Rana watched a Syrian network on satellite, and relates how the Iraqi government has been deposed. Masja adds that two palaces have been captured. All children in the club watch the Dutch Youth News. Kambooye [a refugee from Somalia] states that he watches news: 'So that you know what is happening in the world.'

In the case of major world events, satellite was used very intensively (for example, via live reportage from Morocco or Albania). To experience the fall of Saddam Hussein in 2003, families watched satellite TV (CNN or Al-Jazeera) for live reports: when the researchers visited one Iraqi family in the Netherlands, the family had turned on CNN and was witnessing events that were taking place not far from where they had once lived. Such live reports seemed to function as evidence of the places they had left, and in some cases also as a search tool for locating family members.

Even so, this use of TV news was often led by the parents, and created a particular kind of family dynamic. This was perhaps most explicit in the case of some of the boys in the Greek club, whose parents were Turkish-Kurdish political refugees:

> Elcin, and to a certain extent Rengin and Semset who belonged to the same sub-group within the club due to the close relations among their parents through their affiliation to a political party, are very much exposed to media from their country of origin. As their social life revolves mainly around the party office, their viewing patterns are those of the adults there, who constantly watch news reports and discussions about events in their country. They also spent hours watching taped documentaries about the revolt of their party comrades in Turkish prisons, as well as about some of them declaring their credo before embarking on fatal food-strikes. All these contained violent scenes, as well as a lot of propaganda. Television for them is a source of information (and indoctrination) and not of entertainment. As a result, the three children often did not take part in informal discussions about popular series on Greek TV along with the other kids in the club. Elcin in particular, although he was fascinated by the technical abilities and the potential to produce the things he was interested in, was quite snobbish about entertainment TV and claimed he never watched anything other than what interested him for information reasons. His attitude was very much influenced by the adult attitudes in his social environment, and by what was deemed acceptable and 'serious enough' by them.

As we shall see in more detail in the following chapter, children's exposure to international news via cable and satellite channels can provoke profound emotional responses of fear and insecurity; but it can also lead them to seek out alternative news sources, and to question the validity of what they watch (cf. Journal of Ethnic and Migration Studies, 2006).

## Generational viewing

This last example also points to another more general finding – that it is not only parents who exert influence over television viewing but also the wider community within which the family lives. Even so, this use of television can lead to some quite difficult debates between the generations, especially when it comes to different representations of family life. Among the Kosovan families in Sweden, this was particularly apparent in relation to a popular Albanian soap opera:

Several children have mentioned an Albanian programme within the genre of situation comedy or soap opera, called *Familie Modern*, which is very popular. On Sunday nights, families gather around the set to watch the everyday life of Familie Modern. Reports of episodes indicate that it is humorous and that it mirrors generational differences and illuminates how life used to be in Albania as compared to how it is now. Elderly people represent the olden ways and they joke about it in the series, whereas the younger family members strive towards a modern life.

Extract from interview with Hana:

*Hana*: It is really funny. It is about a family, who tries to be as modern as possible. And actually they have modern stuff in their house too. You know, in Albanian families, girls are not allowed to go to disco and stuff, but the girls in this series they go to disco and they are sleeping with guys. They can do anything they like. They can colour their hair every day, and the son in the family, he brings Danish, Swedish and English girls every night. Strange! They are like a Swedish family [in an ironic tone].

*Interviewer*: What do your parents think about the series?

*Hana*: They really think it is fun. The father is working, the mother is working, and then they have a grandmother, who is not modern. She is old-fashioned, as Albanians are in reality. She says: "You cannot do that and that. And what are you doing?" [affected voice]. She is saying this all the time and nobody listens to her. "Mind your own business and go to bed", they say. Then they do whatever they like, anyway.

An older sister of one of the CHICAM children spoke about the series with a smile and ironic tone, commenting that this series and television in general is much better now than it used to be. Albania has opened up towards the West, with less regulation and control of the media. From the interview with Hana (above), it appears that modern life in the series is more progressive or secularised than the Albanian way of upbringing in Sweden.

The viewing of *Familie Modern* therefore cued an explicit debate within the family about the differences between 'modern' and 'traditional' family values; although it seems from this account that the debate was by no means simply drawn on generational lines, and that there was a degree of irony and humour about the whole thing. This reflects the ambiguity and reflexivity about questions of cultural identity that was also apparent in these children's contributions to the production work in the media club: Hana was one of the girls who contributed to an ambivalent and very amusing *Big Brother*-style 'confession' about inter-racial friendships. (There are analogies here with Aksoy and Robins' (2000) analysis of Turkish migrants' use of television, discussed in Chapter 3.)

In summary, then, the use of transnational television reflects a range of motivations. It clearly can be a vehicle for nostalgia about life 'back home' – although in some cases this seems to relate more to the experience of family viewing than to the actual content of the programmes. However, it can also serve as a means of maintaining contact, not so much with a remembered past but with the changing realities of the present – and while news obviously plays an important role here, so too can fictional genres such as soap opera. In these respects, our research appears to confirm the findings of research with adult audiences, discussed in Chapter 3.

## National and global television

As we have seen, some parents felt that television and other media could threaten their cultural or religious values, and wanted to protect their children from it. This applied mainly, but not exclusively, to the national television stations of the new countries of residence, and to the global US-based satellite broadcasts. Nevertheless, there was little evidence in our research that families were watching what we referred to in Chapter 3 as 'ethnic minority' television: that is, television produced in the new country by more established migrant groups, or produced on their behalf by mainstream domestic channels.

Many parents explicitly recognised that national television was important in helping children (and themselves) to settle in and find out about the new country. While transnational television was used by some families for maintaining children's fluency in the home language, several actively encouraged their children to watch national television specifically to assist in their acquisition of the new language. In the United Kingdom, for example, Maria's stepfather did not allow her and her aunt to have access to Spanish channels via satellite TV, in order to force them to learn English. Meral in Germany described how she watched children's programmes with her younger brother specfically in order to learn German; while children in the Dutch club were encouraged by their parents to watch educational Dutch children's programmes and the national Youth News. In one example from Germany, this intervention had consequences for one boy's communication with his mother:

> Hakan's father liked his son to watch programmes in German and not in Turkish so as not to hinder the development of his (Hakan's) competence in the German language: "I must not, like, watch Turkish programmes but always German."
>
> On another occasion Hakan reported that when telephoning with his mother, who lives in Turkey, some Turkish words no longer occurred to him:
>
> *Hakan*: "I speak bit German because I have forget Turkish. I speak to my mother. I think always 'what I say, what I say?' I think German but I say to my mother German. My mother say 'what is that?' I think 'what is that, what is that in Turkish?', like that."

Several children described how they switched between different language channels. Mohammed in Sweden mentioned that his family had two satellite dishes and access to hundreds of Arabic-speaking channels, which his parents watched for news but also for entertainment programmes. Mohammed was particularly interested in how programme formats were adapted for different languages, and smilingly described how he had watched both the Swedish and Arabic versions of *Who Wants to be a Millionaire?* – noting that, while the formats were identical, the questions were rather different!

Much of children's viewing of mainstream television was very similar to that of their peers in other ethnic groups. In the United Kingdom, for example, the most popular programmes for most of the children were either the major soaps such as *EastEnders*, situation comedies such as *Friends*, family-based animations like *The Simpsons* or 'reality soaps' like *Big Brother*. Declared preferences were also age- and gender-related, but even within this there was a broad consensus. In many cases, the children's preferences reflected a mix of adult and more childish programmes that is broadly typical of their age group. Children also talked about needing to watch certain programmes in order to 'keep in' or to claim status with their peers at school. We found several instances where children claimed to have watched particularly high status or even taboo programmes or films that (it later emerged) they had not in fact seen. In the United Kingdom, as in most of the other clubs, we invited the children to create collages of their media enthusiasms, which often provided a vehicle for 'identity claims' of this kind:

Haamid's poster is dominated by a large picture of *The Hulk* but when I asked if he had ever seen it he said he hadn't and didn't want to. Yet the whole poster related to this figure. He chose four other pictures, three from *The Simpsons* and one of *Lara Croft*. In each of them he changed or added dialogue to relate it to *the Hulk* and the dialogue bubble he had made for him which said, 'I'm going to smash all these creature on earth, maybe in the sky as well'. He had competed with Claudio for the picture and won. His interest was not based on the film but on the social hype around the film.

Likewise, one of the Greek case studies highlights the importance of television in establishing status in the new place of residence:

> Balkys, a 13-year-old girl who did not attend school, filtered most of her social activity in her neighbourhood and her community through TV. Lacking other shared ground with her peers (due to not going to school) Balkys had developed a pattern of watching TV for many hours every day. She became familiar with the plots of most series, soaps and dramas, and followed them in such detail that the people around her started recognising her as an authority on the subject. As this was a current subject in most social interactions, Balkys became popular in her circle also in relation to this, and thus used TV as a means of social acceptance and socialisation.

As this example suggests, talk about television can serve important social functions (cf. Buckingham, 1993a). What you say about what you watch on television serves to define your identity, in terms of age and gender but also in terms of ethnicity and cultural origin. As we shall see in more detail in Chapter 6, television talk can also serve as a powerful means of inclusion within – or exclusion from – the peer group, which is particularly salient for migrant children. Talk about television is thus a complex – and often contested – space, in which claims and counter-claims about identity are staked out.

Thus, in some cases, children would not admit to watching particular programmes (such as children's programmes) for fear of losing face. Yet at the same time, there were some programmes and films that highlighted relationships across cultural differences and across distance that seemed to hold particular emotional resonance for these children. There were two such series in Greece at the time of our research:

Their favourites are two Greek series. One of these is a romantic comedy about a love affair across the continents ('You are my match'). The other is a series about the love story between a Greek woman married to a wealthy land-owner who falls in love with the Albanian worker who works in their fields ('Love came from far away'). In both of those, there is the element of distance, physical or otherwise, which both girls found exciting as it intensified the drama. Both series were very popular, and were often the subject of conversation at school, in the neighbourhood or in the club.

Even more overt forms of fantasy could provide a means of coming to terms with the experience of marginalisation or exclusion, as an example from Sweden illustrates:

Ibish and Mohammed had chosen movies from the video library that were rarely the ones voted for at the youth club in town. Both films were in the action genre, although they dealt with 'soft' themes: one was about a child who got a kind of grass which raised his efficiency so that he could be admitted to Harvard, while the other was about a short dark-skinned guy (as opposed to a tall black basketball player) who wins a pair of magic shoes which give him exceptional physical power. The choice of movies reflected the boys' own identities as immigrant boys. The most preferred film was about the little dark-skinned boy, who became a great hero.

Here again, it would seem that literal (or empirical) realism is not necessarily what is most important (cf. Ang, 1985). The children were using these media to work through – and potentially come to terms with – difficult issues in their own experience as migrants, even if the programmes or films did not purport to represent that experience directly.

## Music

Music played a similar role to television and video, both in maintaining particular cultural affiliations and in enabling the children to develop new ones. In this respect, it helped to cultivate forms of 'social capital' (cf. Putnam, 2000) – in some situations, providing a means of 'bridging' between culturally diverse groups, while in others, providing resources for 'bonding' within a group, and reasserting shared values.

Most of the children had eclectic tastes, which included music from their countries of origin as well as global popular music. Nearly all had personal CD or cassette players, and carried music with them wherever they went. They also accessed music channels on television, and (at least in our club sessions) used the web to find information about their favourite stars. Talk about music served similar functions to talk about television; although music was more easily separated from adult eyes and controls, and was therefore particularly important for the older children.

The use of music as a means of preserving ties to the home country seemed to be especially significant for children who belonged to persecuted minorities, such as the Albanians from Kosovo or the Kurds from Turkey and Iraq. When the Albanian girls in Sweden talked about their ethnic dances, they became lyrical; and their enthusiasm was evident when they performed in school at the annual 'multicultural days' (and recorded the event on videotape). As we shall see in Chapter 9, this use of national music and dance emerged very strongly in several of the videos the children produced: in one video from Sweden, Mohammed dances to Albanian music played from Ibish's mobile phone; while in another from Greece, a Kurdish girl recites a political verse in a very powerful voice while a boy accompanies her on the saz, a traditional stringed instrument. Meanwhile, in the Italian and German clubs, some of the children performed Latin American dances; and in the Netherlands they participated in a school musical, performing an Arabic-influenced dance they had devised themselves.

Tapes of music from the children's home country or region were frequently purchased from particular ethnic shops, and sent by friends and relatives in the mail. Yet this interest in music from their country of origin typically sat alongside an enthusiasm for global (and mainly US) popular music, as the Swedish researcher relates:

> Listening to music was important, and international music artists and their songs have cropped up in various contexts during club work. They talked about mainstream music as well as rap and hip-hop. Hana, for example, always switched on my car radio when I drove her home from the club. She tuned in various radio stations until she found music she liked and then she often joined in singing as well. All the children enjoyed it when Eminem was played in one of the Italian videos. But they also seemed to have a preference for ethnic music related to their own cultural background. The Albanian children played Albanian music on CD in my car and Ibish had

loaded his mobile with it. Hana said that she liked male Albanian singers better than female, the latter having a nasal high-pitched voice, whereas male singers have a darker voice, which fits her own voice better. In one of their videos, Hana is singing and switches between different music styles and artists. Her repertoire covers a range of music styles, from American pop music to Swedish lyrics to Albanian music. Mohammed likes rap music and Albanian music as well. The girls were very amused about the winning Turkish contribution (2003) in the Eurovision song contest. Shpresa emphasised that she liked the mixture of western style music with the Turkish style.

This international 'hybridising' of musical styles was also important for the children in Greece:

> Their music preferences were rather mixed, including both the music from the country of origin (traditional or modern, e.g. liberation or revolutionary songs from Kurdistan, pop songs from Turkey) as well as music from Greece and the West (pop, hip-hop, rap). The Turkish winner of the Eurovision contest, Sertab, became an idol within the club, due to her successful combination of western beat and oriental influences. The children loved the song, as it was familiar to them from both sides, and in a way, managed to constitute the sounds of their own background as 'trendy'. This was true, to a large extent, also in regard to various trendy Greek songs that also combined such diverse influences, bringing together different cultural contexts.

As we shall see in more detail in Chapter 9, rap was particularly important in this respect, especially for the boys. On one level, rap was implicitly perceived as the music of an oppressed group; although its popularity was clearly a function of the power of international marketing, and particularly of global satellite television channels. To some extent, the global popularity of US rap music could be seen as a clear instance of cultural imperialism: while Tupac and Eminem were recognised by very many of the older children, there was no mention (for example) of German, French or British rap artists. Yet the children also seemed to be appropriating the music and the style for their own purposes, as was apparent in the boys' use of hand gestures and their choice of ethnically marked nicknames. We will see some more developed examples of this in Chapter 9, where we explore the use of rap as part of a broader 'hybridising' and appropriation of global cultural forms (cf. Bennett, 2000).

## New media

We will be considering the use of new media in more detail in later chapters, but it is worth briefly noting some significant issues that arose here, particularly in terms of access. Across the six countries in our CHICAM research, there were marked national differences in access to the Internet. To some extent, these reflect national differences more broadly: for example, all the children in Sweden had computers at home and most had access to the Internet, while this was very rare in Greece, where access in general is lower. However, the migrant children in our clubs were significantly less likely to have internet access than their non-migrant peers, and this was particularly apparent for those who were refugees. For the children in Italy, for example, the Internet was alien territory:

> The children in the club had no internet access, either at home or in school. Almost everyone had seen the internet in action, but nobody knew how to surf around it. It excites their curiosity, they "know" how it works, talk about it to their school friends, and say they would like to have internet access. However, they think of it as something remote, and compare using it to other things they know more about.

These differences were also apparent within the clubs. In the Netherlands and the United Kingdom, for example, it was the refugee children who did not have computers at home, underlining their economic disadvantage when compared with the more established migrant families. Even where they had experience of using computers in school, they had not been encouraged to see computers as creative medium, but merely as a search tool; and as such, our use of computers for digital editing and for communication in the clubs was a completely novel experience for all of them.

Interestingly, when the children did begin to use the Internet for communication in our clubs, it was global commercial culture that provided the most productive common ground. Just as they were keen to surf the web for information about their other media enthusiasms, pop music and football – and, in one case, the Japanese multimedia 'craze' of *Yu-Gi-Oh* (a successor to Pokémon) – also proved to be the most effective means of promoting intercultural communication via our intranet chat facility. Yet for a variety of reasons, as we shall see in more detail in Chapter 9, the potential for communication with other children in distant countries was not generally regarded with much enthusiasm.

By contrast, mobile phones were particularly important, especially for the older children. In Italy, for example, none of the children had Internet access at home, but all of them had mobile phones which they used extensively, mainly to keep in contact with friends locally. This was also the case for most of the children in the United Kingdom, Germany and Sweden, although none of the children in Greece had their own phone. This was partly a matter of age differences (the children in Greece were mostly somewhat younger, those in Italy rather older than the average), and it reflects the way in which the mobile phone is becoming an indispensable component of young people's social networks (Katz and Aakhus, 2002).

While most of the children's uses were for local contacts, the mobile phone also offers the potential for communication where there are no existing landlines; and as we noted in Chapter 1, it may therefore be particularly important for migrants from some parts of the world. In the United Kingdom, one father who was a refugee from Sierra Leone explained that the mobile phone had revolutionised his ability to keep in contact with his family. Previously he could only contact family members very rarely; now it was on a weekly basis.

## Conclusion

As we have shown, migrant children's uses of media reflect different motivations and imperatives. In this chapter, we have roughly divided these media under three headings: transnational, national and global. However, it is clear that children may use each of these different forms of media for a wide range of purposes. Along with their parents, they use transnational media as a means of maintaining contact with the past, but also of informing themselves about contemporary developments, both in their country of origin and in the wider world. They use national and global media as a means of settling into the new location, but also of exploring other material from different parts of the world. Indeed, for these children, the sources of these different representations may not be especially significant: unlike their parents, they are growing up in a world in which globalised communications are a routine expectation, rather than a relatively novel development. For them, multi-channel satellite or cable television was the norm, and they rarely differentiated between these and national broadcasting, except when the programmes were very specific to their language and country of origin.

To some extent, our research does provide evidence of children using media to develop new, 'hybrid' cultural identities. They moved fluidly between the various media available to them, pursuing different media options in different settings, and aligning these with different facets of their personal histories and identities. The media offered them a wide range of symbolic resources with which to make sense of their own experience as migrants, and as children – not least through fantasy. To this extent, the media are certainly contributing to the development of hybrid 'new ethnicities'. However, there are at least three reasons why we should exercise some caution about these arguments.

First, it is important to stress that the bulk of the children's media use was oriented towards either national or global sources. While they watched transnational television and video, and engaged (often enthusiastically) in music and dance from their country of origin, their main orientation was towards the commercial media that largely dominate contemporary children's and youth cultures. This reflected their primary preoccupation, which was not to do with maintaining contact with the past, but with building friendships and participating in the here and now. This was also reflected in the importance of mobile phones, which was specifically related to making and maintaining local contacts and creating a more private space for peer group interaction away from their parents. By contrast, global communication with distant others via the Internet was a much less attractive proposition.

Secondly, the children's ethnicity or status as migrants was by no means the only factor determining their media uses and preferences. As we argued in Chapter 3, factors such as age, gender, geographical location and social class all intersect with ethnicity in complex ways, making it very difficult to generalise about particular 'ethnic' readings or media practices (cf. Hargreaves, 2001c; Tufte, 2001). In many respects, there were more similarities than differences between these children and their peers in other ethnic groups: as with this age group more generally, their position as children (or as children of a particular age) was a significant unifying factor.

Finally, it is important not to lose sight of the limitations and exclusions here. Access to satellite broadcasting is far from universal, and depends on economic and domestic circumstances. Many of the children came from countries or regions of the world that are not represented, or significantly under-represented, on global satellite networks. In both respects, the most excluded group were the refugees from the poorer regions of the world, particularly Africa. Likewise, access to the Internet is very unevenly distributed; and it depends largely on fluency in written English. In this respect, while some ethnic groups appear to be increasingly well served by media, others could be said to form a media underclass. In the rush to celebrate the diversity of global media, and its potential for fostering 'new ethnicities', it is important not to ignore these continuing structural inequalities.

As this implies, media can serve quite different purposes in different circumstances: sustaining continuities with the past, and offering new orientations to the future; affirming the specificities of the local, and providing real or imagined connections with the global; reasserting the shared values of the family or the peer group, and providing means of challenging them, or of building new relationships with outsiders. Media provide powerful opportunities both for inclusion and for exclusion. These seemingly contradictory functions are of course by no means confined to migrant children, although (as we have shown) they may take on a particular form in the context of migration. Nor are they mutually exclusive: media provide a diverse set of 'symbolic resources' that can be used to construct migrant identities which are not fixed and homogenous, but in constant movement and development. In the following chapter, we look much more closely at this process by means of three much more detailed case studies of individual children.

# 6
# Making Migrant Identities: Television in Children's Everyday Lives

In this chapter, we look more closely at a small number of individual children, exploring some of the ways in which they used and interpreted television in their everyday lives. The four children we consider in detail were aged 8 (two among them), 10 and 11, and they had all recently come to London from very different locations and circumstances around the world. Our focus here is specifically on television, which (at least for young children of this age) remains the medium that is most discussed and acted out in their everyday lives, and which forms their main means of access to world events. We explore how television was woven into the fabric of their lives, as they settled into their new locality and negotiated new relationships in school, in the playground, in their neighbourhoods and at home, while still remembering or maintaining contact with their places of origin. We also consider how particular types of television content – both children's programmes and 'adult' programmes such as news – resonated with their personal concerns and anxieties, and enabled them to address the emotional implications of their experiences.

Much of our focus here is on how children talk with their friends and family about television programmes they have watched; and of course, this kind of talk is not unique to migrant children. Television provides a shared basis for ritualised forms of play with language, music and action, as well as more distanced discussion. Talk about television takes different forms, both verbal and non-verbal, and demands diverse skills and emotional investments on the part of children. It relies on the detailed familiarity with story lines and forms to create an often unspoken knowledge base, in which minimal key words and references can come to define a person or group. Talk about television is thus a forum within which social behaviour is patrolled, identities are formed, and social inclusions and exclusions are defined (Buckingham, 1993a).

For migrant children, television can therefore become a key part of the way they engage with their new places of residence and maintain contact with places they have lived in before, and may in some cases return to again. This process is vital in the creation of the shared space within which social relations are negotiated – although, as we shall see, this can serve to exclude as well as to include.

The material here is drawn from Liesbeth de Block's doctoral research, conducted in London in 1999 and 2000 (and Liesbeth is the first person 'I' in this chapter). From a base in a primary school in a very deprived inner city neighbourhood, the research followed three friendship groups of refugee and migrant children over the course of one year (de Block, 2002, 2006). The research involved conversations recorded between the children, in-depth observations in school classrooms and playgrounds, at home and on journeys around London, and numerous individual and group interviews with the children and their parents. The children also created drawings, collage posters and videos, and both the production process and these texts themselves became part of the research.

## Jima

Jima was from Ethiopia and at the time of the fieldwork was 10 years old. He first came to the school where the research was based at the age of 6 years. He was unable to sit still for a second and spent most of the time running around grabbing things and people. Over the years he remained a 'live wire', and was often in trouble. He was both attention seeking and very charming. He had arrived in London with his father, Lema, and they were applying for asylum. Their case was rejected and they started on the appeal process. They were still waiting for an appeal hearing at the time of the research several years later (although they have since been granted indefinite leave to remain).

Jima and his father had recently been re-housed due to racist attacks at their previous flat. They appeared to be very isolated. Lema kept in limited telephone contact with his parental family in Addis Ababa and was distraught when he was not able to return for his mother's funeral. He suffered from an old back injury and was often so depressed that he could not function. Jima had a few very detailed memories of his family and where he used to live, but very little ongoing contact.

Jima was a member of a friendship group of four boys: Samuel from Kenya, who was also an asylum seeker, and twins Estava and David from Portugal and Angola, whose mother had brought them here to join extended family members. As with all friends, the boys fell out from time to time, but generally they spent a lot of time with each other both in school and out and about in the neighbourhood. There were always several other boys who moved in and out of the group, but these four appeared to stick together. Jima knew his way around the city and roamed far from home on the buses, often without his father's knowledge. Lema often worried that he had little control over his son.

When he talked about arriving in Britain and the process of making friends, Jima never mentioned learning the language. What he focused on was learning how children behaved – and particularly what they talked about. He said that he became interested in television when he realised how much people here watched and talked about it: 'I know that there are such things as TV and stuff and other programmes and stuff. People talk about them but usually I'm not interested in them. And as soon as I came to this country everybody talked about it more than they talk about it in my country. So then I started liking...you can talk to your friends about it.' His priority was clear: television was not a route to escape but an important aspect of his social life.

Jima aimed to develop a group of friends, so it was important that his interests allowed this. His favourite television programmes (*WWF*, *The Simpsons* and *South Park*) were all used to facilitate the sense of group togetherness that the boys needed for their friendship to work. Their TV talk involved the story lines, the characters and the 'behind the scenes' knowledge, but above all it meant knowing the details. Jima was the acknowledged expert on all this. *The Simpsons* and *South Park* also played with language and action in ways that suited the group's collective banter, whilst at the same time having long story lines that could be retold and applied to their local situation. Being the expert and being called on to demonstrate this knowledge gave Jima a status in the group that other activities did not. It allowed him access to the group and therefore to friendship and inclusion, and to some extent protected him from the isolation of his home life and legal situation. He was also adept at using TV references to promote a connection and sense of togetherness. Often, after initiating a topic, he would sit back and let the discussion roll, only intervening to keep it on track or to start it off in a new direction. For example, on seeing a busker in London's city centre, or a hot dog seller outside the British Museum on one of our trips around town, he went into long riffs retelling and adapting particular episodes of these programmes well known by the group.

Talk about wrestling programmes (*WWF – World Wrestling Foundation*) performed several functions for this group of boys. The programme itself is multi-layered, demanding different types and amounts of knowledge about stunts, stars, moves and international connections. In their discussions, the boys jostled for status by displaying their knowledge, challenging, confirming and reconfirming what they knew and enjoyed. The group often met to watch the show together, but if this was impossible, it was part of their commitment to the group that they would watch it at home. For one of the boys, this was difficult as his parents disapproved, but somehow he managed.

Through such talk, the boys often safely compared their different backgrounds and home situations. Estava, for example, described how he first watched wrestling as follows: 'When I just came to England I said um let me just watch Sky and I settled down and it was past nine o'clock 'cos I was bored and then I thought I would put the channel on. And I thought "hm, cool" and I stayed here watching it, all through it.' He earned a supportive compliment about his father from one of the others on these grounds: 'It's his Dad is the one who taught him to watch wrestling [laughter] . . . His dad is cool.'

The physicality of the show allowed the boys to play fight and have physical contact that was safe and couldn't be seen as crossing sexual boundaries, a topic they were always skirting around. This play fighting also created a grey area in the playground, where fighting was banned, and this appealed to their enjoyment of the subversive. A further element of this must have been that the excitement did not depend on mastery of the English language, which was still an issue for some of the group.

Each boy had his own moves, which were refined in practice with each other. Sometimes this was competitive, while at others it was about confirming group hierarchies and established identities. At the same time, it was often excessive and over-dramatic. The way the programme itself played with reality and fantasy allowed the boys to exaggerate, imagine, and play with their own realities and their own sense of power. As Barthes (1973) argues, wrestling is ultimate theatre, a type of pantomime, where the form is more important than the content. Fiske (1987), following Bahktin's notion of the carnivalesque, describes TV wrestling as parody, as an excessive and physical suspension of social order, inverting the rules of play. Central to the pleasures of the WWF shows in particular is the knowledge of the backstage dramas between the wrestlers, and between the wrestlers and their managers. These are also carefully orchestrated and leaked, adding to the drama of the fights. Such knowledge appears to offer viewers a feeling of 'empowerment' and involvement that heightens the pleasure of viewing (British Board of Film Classification, 2001).

All of this tallies with the ways in which these boys used wrestling in their TV talk. It allowed them to create and reconfirm a shared space of enjoyment, experience, knowledge, memory and play. Talk about past viewing created a collective history when little else was shared, remembering moves and stunts from way back, building shared knowledge of past fights and ongoing rivalries: 'It's a dummy, because remember what Generation X done to Owen Hart. They make a dummy of Triple H and then...' At the same time, as Ellen Seiter (2005) explains, TV wrestling allows a space for diverse ethnic identifications to be expressed, particularly given the diversity of the participants; and it also permits boys' struggles with masculinity to be dealt with through a safely parodic, theatrical form.

However, TV talk was not only used to facilitate social relations. Jima also used it to keep a barrier between his private and his public self: it became a kind of survival mechanism to enable him to cope with his difficult circumstances. It allowed him to hide his exclusion (as an asylum seeker), but also in some senses to confirm it. Jima was often trying to express the confusion in himself at this particular time, when all around him there was talk about the future, about moving on to secondary school and the new millennium. Yet for him it was dangerous to think ahead. In one interview, he talked about never thinking about the future: 'I'm not really thinking about the future...You get on with what's happening...Today is a new day and I get on with that...For me I just take it like each day I'd be, I'm not going to, whatever happens today I'm not going to talk about I wish this [would] happen tomorrow. I'm going to say this happened today, and this happened today and just get on with it...Yeah, most people talk about the future.' When he acknowledged his difference from his friends at the end of this extract, his voice was almost inaudible. This was clearly painful territory for him, and he rapidly bounced back with relief to the image of himself as the joker, the classic defence. This began to explain to some degree his social, behavioural and academic difficulties and the ways in which he felt excluded. Jima said that he was different from other children because he couldn't think ahead, couldn't plan, and couldn't even conceptualise a future, as he had no idea where it might be.

His use of television was very particular to these circumstances. This was apparent in two ways. In peer-group discussions, if things got too personal or too serious he would deflect the conversation by mentioning something funny that had happened on TV, effectively drawing his friends back into his created television world and to what they had in common. By contrast, in the classroom, where he was considered

*Picture 1*    Poster using Kenny in South Park to symbolise education

a problem both in terms of behaviour and learning, he used TV to subvert – to distract others from working, to avoid working himself, and to create the excitement and humour on which he thrived. With no future ahead, he saw no point in the learning in front of him. He lived in the moment, and at that moment he would rather have fun.

As part of the research they made a group video. I asked the group to decide five things that were important to them and one TV character that represented each of them. Jima chose Kenny from *South Park* to represent education, 'because he tries but he keeps getting killed'. This mirrored his own situation. He used what was available to him to engage in the process of education, but he was unable to overcome the exclusion he felt. Under the category of 'friends', the group chose one of the wrestlers, The Rock. In relation to Jima, this again made sense. He described The Rock as having 'loads of friends', yet he said he didn't know any of them; and likewise, he said that he too had no particular friends but also that he had many friends. Even though this was not what I observed in his main friendship group, it was a safer place for him to be. He spread himself thinly so that he did not need to develop any intimacy. He said that the thing he wanted to say about himself was that he liked jokes. It was very clear that he used TV references in the classic joker mode, to make social commentary, but also to hide his private self and to hide his intelligence.

Jima's use of television therefore allowed him to hold on to his identity as Ethiopian, as a refugee and as the 'excluded', the things over which he had no control; and yet it also enabled him to cope with the changing social landscape, and to create zones of inclusion. He used TV talk to create a familiar world outside the home that he could refer to and defend against the uncertainties of the future. This enabled him to make successful social connections, to affirm his 'expert' status within the peer group, and to learn about different types of social situations. But it also allowed him to defend himself against too much intrusion into his private space: he used TV humour to subvert what he found difficult, and to avoid dwelling on the differences between himself and his friends.

## Rhaxma

Rhaxma was 8 years old at the time of the research. She had been in the United Kingdom for 3 years. Her mother had been forced to leave Somalia when she was pregnant, and Rhaxma had been born in Italy. After a very difficult few years, during which Rhaxma was separated from her mother and looked after by foster parents, they had come to London and her mother had remarried. She now had three younger siblings and another on the way. Rhaxma was still coming to terms with these events. Perhaps as a result, she had an eating disorder that was a cause of much distress to her mother.

Rhaxma's family were very religious Muslims. She attended Qur'anic classes twice a week and this was clearly an important focus in her life. She was very conscious of codes of behaviour that were expected of her as a Muslim girl. She sometimes covered her ears if her friends said things she realised were inappropriate. Rhaxma fasted during Ramadan: although her mother said she didn't want her to, she said that the mosque wanted her to. However, she never spoke about her religion or mosque with her non-Muslim peers. She always wore her hijab and was one of only a very few Muslim children in the school to do so. Yet this was the only aspect of her home life that she made public. Even when her mother had a new baby, she told neither her friends nor her teachers.

Fatima, her mother, spoke remarkably good English for the time she had been in the United Kingdom and the lack of opportunity she had had to learn. She said she had learned English from the television; and she also spoke Somali, Italian and Arabic. At one time, because of the cost, the family had stopped receiving cable programmes that allowed them access to their own languages, and Fatima spoke about how she missed these programmes and felt more cut off without them. She was not specific about what she was cut off from, since there were no Somali programmes as such, but clearly this increased their feelings of isolation and their separation from what was familiar. As soon as they were financially able to restore the cable service, they did so.

Fatima also talked about the problem of Rhaxma seeing things on television that were in conflict with her religion. She said that she had told Rhaxma to look away from the screen when there was any kissing, and that she did this. She did not want her to know anything about sex until she started menstruating. However, she was aware of the contradictions. Rhaxma had a television in her bedroom and so all her viewing could not be monitored. She watched the dating game show *Blind Date* and other potentially 'unsuitable' programmes with her mother, and talked about these programmes with her friends. Her mother also discussed the problem of other parents taking a different approach and talking to their daughters much earlier about sex.

Rhaxma was highly sociable and gradually made contact with a wide range of children. She loved to talk about television and became almost hysterical when the topic was raised. When asked if she talked about television, she replied, 'a lot, a lot. ALL the time!' and followed this up with: 'sometimes when we are watching films we watch them and then we talk about it and we have fun talking about it, the funny bits', her voice getting higher and louder all the time. She played the joker and the crazy one in social relations and used TV talk to assist in this. In our interviews, she often referred to conversations she had had with other children about films and programmes, and it was acknowledged that this was what she talked about most frequently. It appeared that, like Jima, she had worked out that talking about television would provide her with an entry point to the peer group and a way of attracting attention.

Talking about television with her friends allowed Rhaxma some possibility of talking about her home life, but she also censored much of what she said. As for Jima, TV talk was also a way of avoiding having to talk about more private matters. As a girl, and as a Muslim girl living in a difficult area of the city, Rhaxma was allowed very little freedom beyond the home. Her television references and uses, therefore, did not form part of the ways in which she built a connection with the locality, but remained centred on close social relations and private fantasies. These were very much centred on what it meant to be a girl. TV talk acted as a way for her to explore and negotiate different ways of being a girl and of 'belonging' in her diverse world.

One of the preoccupations both for her and her group of friends was 'girl power'. Her favourite programme was *The Power Puff Girls* and her favourite fictional character was Cinderella. *The Power Puff Girls* is a ten-minute cartoon shown in the United Kingdom on Cartoon Network. The introduction to the show explains that these three five-year-old girls were created by Professor Utonium. The Professor was trying to make 'the perfect little girls' but as he was adding the ingredients, 'sugar, spice and everything nice', his lab assistant, the monkey Jo-Jo, jogged him and the magic Ingredient X was added by mistake. Jo-Jo was dismissed but he too had been changed. He became a megalo-maniac, called Mojo Jo-Jo, bent on seeking revenge on the Professor and the girls. The Professor became the girls' guardian and they live in his house/laboratory. He is a distant and authoritarian figure and they therefore lack any warm parental, especially maternal, figures in their lives. The girls are called Bubbles, Blossom and Buttercup, one blue, one red and one green. In most ways they are 'normal' little girls who go to nursery, play, argue, cry and giggle. However, they also have the capacity, through Ingredient X, to sort out power struggles between good and evil. The Sheriff in the local town has a hotline to them when he needs them to sort out a problem he cannot deal with.

The theme of the cartoon is parodic of *Charlie's Angels*, but the main difference is that these girls are non-sexual. Each one has distinct characteristics. Bubbles is sweet and emotional. She pretends to be stupid but is probably the most powerful of the group. Blossom, the red one, is clever, sensible and bossy. She is the leader. Buttercup is brave, often angry and the toughest fighter. She has 'ice breath' which can turn her opponents into ice. Rhaxma and her friends would sing the theme song at any opportunity:

> The Power Puff Girls
> Fighting crime
> Trying to save the world
> They are there just in time
> The Power Puff Girls
> POWER PUFF!

The narrative portrays the girls as powerful, able to be strong and assertive and not afraid to fight evil. In this sense, it could be seen as a source of empowerment for girls (Potts, 2001). At the same time, many of its references and story lines contain material aimed at adults: for example, in one episode Buttercup puts condoms in the Professor's pocket before he goes out on a date (ibid.).

Rhaxma stated that the reason she liked the programme was because 'they are heroes and they fight the "baddies"'. There is indeed a strong moral element in the story lines in which good overcomes evil, a fairy tale scenario. This matches Rhaxma's other more traditional media/fictional hero, Cinderella. Even so, there is a conflict here between the active power depicted in *The Power Puff Girls* and the more passive good of Cinderella.

There is a high level of adult rage in *The Power Puff Girls*. They roar, strike out and are irrational and unfair. In contrast, the Power Puff Girls are sweet but strong and powerful. They are in control of themselves and yet contained in the home/laboratory, even though this is not always safe. Similarly, in her life, Rhaxma had experienced a lot of difficult adult behaviour over which she had no control. She continued to have a difficult home life. Her mother needed her help, her stepfather was struggling to study and work, and there were three small children in the flat. She was expected to support her mother a great deal, looking after her siblings and helping out around the house.

Talk and play around *The Power Puff Girls* allowed Rhaxma to explore the possibility of being powerful over the adults in her life, who could behave irrationally. In the games she played with her friends in the playground, she often acted out being the victim, the baddie and the robber. Most games were based on television stories and characters, and were played over and over again, frequently taking quite ritualistic forms. Many became ongoing and developing narratives, played regularly with the same group. Rhaxma was beaten up, she suffered and yet again and again the games came to some kind of resolution. She escaped, she made friends, she was saved, she moved on to the next game in which she was restored as part of the group. She played with having a power that, in real life, she lacked. Her other favourite media characters were powerful girls who also had different ways of dealing with their problems. The Power Puff Girls were assertive, they relied on each other and they had special powers. Likewise, Disney's Mulan becomes strong, although in the eyes of Rhaxma's peers she becomes a boy when she cuts off her hair, thus breaking their rules about girl power (which require you to be strong but also pretty). Sabrina in *Sabrina the Teenage Witch* is a witch with special powers that make her strong. Cinderella is good, and because of this is discovered and transformed into a princess.

Rhaxma's drawings of her home may have revealed more than she would have intended. In one of them, she shows herself in a separate

*Picture 2*  Rhaxma's drawing of her bed room

room from her mother, who is watching Italian soaps on TV and looking after the newly born twins. Rhaxma is in the bedroom with her younger sister and brother. Her brother is screaming and Rhaxma is trying to block out the noise by putting her hands over her ears. At the same time, her favourite programme (*The Power Puff Girls*) is on TV and her body is tilted towards that rather than her siblings. All three of the Power Puff Girls are depicted, with Blossom (the clever and sensible one) in the centre. Rhaxma is depicted as quite alone in the midst of intense activity.

The themes of *The Power Puff Girls* clearly reflect the personal themes that Rhaxma was working through (cf. Bachmair, 1990): power (omnipotence and impotence), rage, destruction and reparation. These are set in the scenarios of good versus evil, child versus adult, girl versus boy. So, in another light, the rage of the adults can be seen as her own rage, her fury at her personal story and her exploitation; although at the same time, it is an aspect of her personal badness or evil. Coupled with this was her own eating disorder which, psychologically, could be seen as her own rage turned inwards on herself. The power of the Power Puff Girls is that of the 'good girl', conquering her own monstrous feelings and repairing the damage that she has caused. But she was left with several unresolved questions. Was she omnipotent or impotent? Had she herself caused the destruction? Did her birth cause the pain that both she and her mother experienced when they were separated in Italy? Could she repair it by being the good girl, by helping to look after her siblings and by being deeply religious now, despite the fact that (as she told me) she had eaten the wrong food as a toddler because she was looked after by non-Muslims?

Rhaxma's other media uses and preferences can also be considered in this way. When she watched Italian children's TV on cable with her mother, as she enjoyed doing, was she revisiting her past and taking comfort in familiarity? Or was she also revisiting a place of danger from within the safety of being now reunited with her mother? The role of siblings was also relevant here. Watching Italian TV with her mother excluded her siblings. It confirmed her own private history with her mother. Likewise, as Bettelheim (1979: 237) suggests, the Cinderella story can also seen as a story of sibling rivalry. Cinderella feels 'hopelessly outclassed' and degraded by her siblings, and rejected by her mother, and receives no credit for her hard work. Yet her triumph restores faith in the child's own ability to overcome these feelings. Likewise, Rhaxma chose the picture of Cinderella and the caption 'everyone can be a princess' for the collage poster she made; and in her playground games, she played the victim and the slave. She complained a lot about the babies crying, about the hard work she had to do at home and about getting into trouble when her younger sister destroyed her school books, but she believed that her 'good' behaviour would help her to prevail.

In *The Power Puff Girls* scenario, good and bad are split. An evil cat tries to take over the good professor. A bad man from the forest tries to destroy the town. The world is insecure, incomplete. In both *The Power Puff Girls* and *Sabrina, the Teenage Witch*, good is encapsulated and separate, a power you draw on to destroy the bad or to make something better. In psychological terms, this separation of the good from the bad is a less mature, less 'adult', mechanism for dealing with bad experiences. It is a way of keeping the good safe and separate from the bad that might manage to contaminate it. For Rhaxma, these programmes offered her a theatre in which she could play out her rages, her impotence and her strong feelings of good and evil.

A kind of hysteria often developed when Rhaxma talked about television, which may partly have been because talking about TV with an adult in school felt somehow 'wrong'. It was a private activity being brought into public space. Equally, it was also exciting because this private space was one in which her personal anxieties and pleasures were acted out. Talk gave them a release but it also felt exposing. Rhaxma was nervous about stating her favourite TV programmes. She became breathless and fearful, and only after encouragement did she list them. She then became more and more excited: we were entering her inner fantasy world, as well as her private social world.

Rhaxma acted out several very different girls in her everyday life: the helpful Muslim home girl, the good English schoolgirl, the loud English playground girl, the girl friend, the devout religious girl and so on. She often seemed unable to combine or resolve the different expectations of these different roles. She was expected by home, school and Qur'anic classes to work hard and concentrate in class. She was always proud when her work was praised and several times she boasted that in Qur'anic class she was ahead of many of her peers. Yet while succeeding in this, the conflict came when she was expected in school to initiate, participate and hold her own with her peers and the staff in a 'Western' style. In these situations, she often verged on over-excitement and attention-seeking rather than assertion. In the playground, she was often wild and hysterical. Sometimes this seemed to be because she needed a space in which to act out her demons, and express her anger; although what she was doing was perhaps no more than an exaggerated version of what all the other children were doing. Playgrounds are noisy places, with a lot of screaming and excitement. The soundtrack for *The Power Puff Girls* is also incredibly noisy, as are a lot of cartoons and children's programmes. The behaviour of the child audience in *Live and Kicking*, which she watched regularly, was the same. This loudness was presented to her as a way that children in the United Kingdom behaved, both at school and on TV, and was very different to what appeared to be expected at home.

By contrast, the Cinderella figure fits closest to the stereotyped Muslim girl. She is modest, quiet, home-based and hard working. This image also fulfilled Rhaxma's need to explore her emotions towards her new stepsiblings. Sabrina fitted well with the English schoolgirl model, being sensible and hard working but assertive and freedom-loving (not forgetting the special witch powers she has); and this also fitted with the ways in which her friendship group expected her to behave. Yet in this show, there is plenty that would conflict with other expectations. Sabrina has a great deal of social freedom. She has friends who are boys and she mixes freely. She messes up her room, in an episode that Rhaxma returned to frequently in our conversations. Meanwhile, Mulan represents another form of 'girl power', becoming actively engaged in her own freedom struggle; but interestingly, when raised by Rhaxma this role model was, to her surprise, rejected by her peers. The Power Puff Girls remain little girls, yet they are strong and good but recognisable and familiar in the small conflicts that they have with each other. They stay together and are essentially home-based, play different roles and model different types of 'girl'.

This is not to say that Rhaxma lived a schizophrenic life, jumping from one culture to another. However, she was negotiating her way through a complex puzzle of role models and expectations; and she used media to do this. Together, the different representations she preferred seemed to fulfil her need to play out her angers and overcome her demons. She claimed them all: unlike her friends who chose one or the other, Rhaxma stated clearly that she was going to draw them all. Although different from each other, they were one whole to her.

## Leyla and Selve

Leyla and Selve were 8 and 11 years old, respectively at the time of the research. They were Turkish Kurdish sisters, and their family (mother, father and younger brother) had been in the United Kingdom for a couple of years having travelled overland from Turkey. They had been re-housed from an area where there was a substantial Turkish/Kurdish community. Their mother spoke no English, had never been to school and was illiterate.

Leyla and Selve's experience of media was very different from that of Jima or Rhaxma. As we have noted, Turkey has a sophisticated media industry and there are also several Turkish and Kurdish channels based outside the country catering to a large and diverse Turkish diaspora. The girls therefore had access to a wide choice of channels and programmes that easily maintained a connection with their past lives. In addition, their family was part of a substantial Turkish Kurdish diasporic community in London.

When Leyla and Selve first came to the school, their mother did not want to have Turkish TV in their home: she argued that they were now living in the United Kingdom and had left Turkey behind. In her view, Turkey had offered them very little and they were making a new start. However, after a year they were regularly watching Turkish TV, albeit at a friend's house. Indeed, going to friends' houses to watch TV, particularly the news, became an important part of the whole family's social life. Eventually, their mother did get their own satellite dish, saying that she was afraid the children would forget their Turkish and she would no longer be able to communicate with them (a fear expressed by many of the Turkish mothers in the school). They also wanted to keep up to date with news events back home; and it was important for them to have access specifically to Kurdish television, which is broadcast out of Germany.

The decision to get access to Turkish and Kurdish television was therefore quite complex. Their mother was still having great problems learning English and was feeling increasingly isolated since the family had been re-housed; although she also felt isolated at home when her children watched English TV. The children never socialised with non-Turkish families or children outside school, yet they did not feel part of Turkey. Their feelings towards Turkish television were ambivalent, both because they were Kurdish and as such had been discriminated against in Turkey, but also because it showed them that life in Turkey was changing. Their shift of position therefore did not represent a simple rejection of assimilation into the new society, but a complex mix of nostalgia, needing to keep in touch with a changing 'back home', and having to deal with an increased diversity locally to which they were not accustomed. As we have seen in Chapter 3, there has been considerable debate about the extent to which Turkish transnational television limits the possibilities for integrating with non-Turkish peers, or alternatively facilitates the formation of new transnational Turkish identities (Aksoy and Robins, 2000). For this family, it clearly fulfilled several complementary roles: language teaching and continuity, combating cultural isolation, creating social connections in the new place among the diasporic community, and dealing with feelings of separation and change, of being away and not part of changes happening 'at home'.

This was also manifested in some of the family's home videos. The parents had hired a professional company to make a video to mark their son's circumcision ceremonies. It was a wonderful piece, linking their favourite places and images in their old and new homes. Mountains and waterfalls in Turkey were intercut with shots of Trafalgar Square and their favourite park in Wood Green, North London. Highly repetitive and stylised, it tried to make a connection between the past and the present as well as between the different countries. It combined nostalgia for old reference points with places that were gathering meaning in their new lives. Their son, entering manhood, was placed visually and metaphorically in the centre of the images as a symbol of a new future. The daughters did not feature at all. The media here facilitated an imaginative response to changed communities and places across great distances, but still kept many continuities and old differences alive (cf. Appadurai, 1996; Brah, 1996; Sreberny, 2000).

However, it was in news broadcasts of disasters or conflicts that these images became disturbed for the sisters. The familiar representations were replaced with ones that upset the equilibrium of the present but also at a profound level the equilibriums of the past. Thus, Leyla began to question her good memories of life in Turkey when images of the capture of the Kurdish leader Abdullah Öcalan in 1999, and shortly afterwards those of the earthquake, were shown on her screens.

On one of my visits in 1999 to Leyla and Selve's family, the atmosphere was clearly very fraught. I couldn't understand why the children kept telling me about men in masks with guns. I assumed it was a film they had been watching but I couldn't understand why, in that case, their mother was so agitated. It was only afterwards, when I got home and heard the news that Abdullah Öcalan had been captured by the Turkish government, that I began to understand. In several conversations with the girls over the following weeks, the great significance that Öcalan held for them became clear. They described it in the following way. They said that for me I believed in Jesus, and that for them they believed in Öcalan. His capture shook their personal security and it was after this that they kept asking me if I was 'a police'.

The Öcalan capture was followed by intense activity among the Kurdish community in London, in which their father was involved. They themselves had been on several demonstrations; and there was a very tense atmosphere at home and in their community. The girls had clearly been threatened by the capture which, although far away, had been so vividly depicted in their living rooms. Öcalan had not been in Turkey when he was captured, but in Kenya, which conveyed to them that wherever you are, you are not safe. There was a police presence at some of the events they attended, and they suddenly felt on the outside, unwelcome and unsafe.

Over the following few weeks, this developed for Leyla into a reworking of her memories of Turkey. Previously she had painted life there as a golden age of friendship and freedom, but now she described Turkey as a bad and dangerous place. This was confirmed when the earthquake followed so soon after the capture of Öcalan, and pictures of destruction were on the screens. She now described it as 'sad' and stated that she did not want to go there again. She was having a particularly difficult, lonely time at school, clearly partly affected by all these events. She seemed to feel that she had no home, no place of security. Selve too said that she was crying a lot at school, although she did have friends and was coping better than her sister. Leyla described having nightmares of being captured and chased, but she did not go to her mother for comfort but into her older sister's bed. As Richman (1998) describes, refugee children often do not want to add to their parents' worries and so keep their own fears to themselves.

Selve's attitudes hardened, and she was now quite openly anti-Muslim, making very derogatory remarks aimed at her Muslim peers. Her logic was that Öcalan had been captured by Muslims and therefore they were bad people. Her memory of what had been said on news broadcasts was very precise. She said that two women had been interviewed and had said that they didn't want Öcalan's 'sorry', but wanted him dead. She repeatedly asked about Muslims and what they believed, and finally she qualified her opinion by saying that Muslims from Rhaxma's country were all right – although she maintained her low opinion of Bangladeshis.

As with the Öcalan capture, the reporting of the earthquake which followed soon after (1999) shook the children's security and they began to rework their memories. Leyla said: 'Yeah, there isn't any water to drink. I don't know what's happened. It scary [she makes audible shivering noises] but in Turkey I've got loads of friends down there, loads, loads, loads. When I was about 5 years old or 4 in Turkey I wouldn't be any scared. If somebody comes I wouldn't be scared. At nights I play with my friends till about 10 o'clock I don't come inside till it's 11 o'clock. I come out in the morning I go outside at 10 o'clock and I still want to play but now I'm scared. It's scaredy now.'

Leyla and Selve were not alone in respect of the important role that news played in their lives. Jima was not only an expert on *The Simpsons*, but was also able to engage with other children in the dinner hall in discussion about international news events. When a new Kosovan classmate was struggling to talk about the bombings reported on the news the previous evening, Jima was able to relate this to his own situation and the war between Eritrea and Ethiopia. Several children described going to friends' houses to watch satellite news when important events were taking place. There was a strong sense that national television did not offer enough coverage and that they wanted access to different viewpoints (see Chapter 3).

As this implies, news events reported from and about the country of origin can have very direct effects on children's lives in their new country. Children who have direct experience of war, trauma and forced migration are affected by similar events elsewhere, and this will revive memories. Migrant children will often perceive world events as closely connected to their lives and see themselves not only as part of the local but in a very direct way part of the global. Yet such images can also create feelings of separation and isolation, which can of course be exacerbated by the kind of reception refugees and migrants receive in the media of the immigration country. Such responses were not acknowledged in the classroom, but the children needed to, and often managed to, find informal spaces in which to share these experiences and feelings.

This family's use of transnational media thus presents a complex picture of separation and connection. The media are used consciously to sustain old connections, but also to come to terms with separation and to build new forms of connection and identity. Transnational media do not simply maintain the old or hinder assimilation into the new: they also make possible new forms of belonging and diversity. Yet, as Aksoy and Robins (2000) explain, migrants watching different channels can experience an ambivalence and a consciousness of choices being made that non-migrants do not experience in the same way. For parents, the fear of losing your child in a society and culture foreign to you can be played out through the same technology that can bring you closer to your original home and can also facilitate the social success of your child. The complex emotions surrounding these conflicts are what Leyla and Selve, and their mother, were grappling with in their everyday engagements with television.

## Conclusion

The case studies we have presented in this chapter illustrate some of the diverse social and personal uses of television for migrant children. Television, and talk about television, can provide ways of creating a shared space with peers whose other experiences may be very different; but it can also serve as a means of shielding areas of pain and anxiety from the gaze of others. It can provide ways of working through personal conflicts, difficulties and desires; but it can also offer a means of escaping them into fantasies of power and control that may be denied in real life. It can keep alive memories of one's past life, and hence connections with others who may have shared that life; but it can also draw attention to new realities that may shatter those positive memories and the security they provide. In all these ways, it enables children to develop a working understanding of the complex interrelationships between the local and the global, and their own place within them.

In all three accounts, these children can be seen to be actively working to create a sense of 'home' and belonging, which is both about interpersonal relationships and about individual identity. Television provides multiple – and often quite ambivalent – meanings and pleasures that can be used to create this sense of belonging. For Rhaxma, Leyla and Selve, this meant simultaneous belonging to different places or cultures: they and their families built geographies of social relations, and (where possible or necessary) were able to extend or look beyond local boundaries (Massey, 1992). For Jima, cut off from Ethiopia and not knowing where his future lay, this was much more difficult. Even so, this sense of 'home' is clearly a matter not only of one's present geographical location, but also of where people *feel* they belong; and for many, this is no longer singular or fixed. As Morley (2000: 176) puts it, it is a matter of 'how the physical and symbolic networks become entwined around each other'. Talk about television thus provides a means of developing social relationships that are crucial to settling into a new place of residence; but it can also work towards defining a multiple 'sense of place' that moves beyond one's immediate circumstances.

# 7
## Speaking for Themselves?: Researching Youth Media Production

Our primary focus thus far has been on children as 'consumers' of media. In this chapter and the two that follow, we move on to look at their use of media for creative production and communication. Chapters 8 and 9 present further material from our CHICAM project, looking at the videos produced by the children, and how these formed the basis for intercultural communication between them. This chapter provides a more broad-ranging overview of the issues relating to children's creative production, looking at the use of media in the home, in educational settings and in the context of research. Our particular interest here is in the possibility of using media to 'give children a voice', and to promote intercultural communication: as we shall argue, achieving these aspirations is not as straightforward as it might at first appear. We will be referring briefly to our CHICAM research here; but we will also discuss an earlier project, VideoCulture, which similarly involved the production and exchange of videos by young people.

At least in principle, new media technologies offer significant opportunities for young people to engage in media production in their own right. The retail price of video camcorders, digital cameras and multimedia PCs has steadily fallen, as their capabilities have increased; and the Internet provides a means of communication and distribution that is no longer exclusively controlled by a small elite. In the process, it is argued, the boundaries between production and consumption, and between mass communication and interpersonal communication, are beginning to break down. More and more young people have home computers in their bedrooms that can be used to create music, to manipulate images or to edit video to a relatively professional standard. These technologies also permit a highly conscious, and potentially subversive, manipulation of commercially produced media texts, for example through sampling and 're-mixing' found material, alongside original creative production.

Of course, it is important not to exaggerate the scale of these developments. While children's access to new media is steadily increasing, there is also a growing polarisation between the 'technology rich' and the 'technology poor'. Furthermore, it seems that relatively few children have yet to exploit the *creative* potential of digital media – although the evidence on this issue is fairly sparse. The international contributors to Livingstone and Bovill's (2001) European survey, for example, make no mention of children's access to cameras, video camcorders or the production possibilities of multimedia computers. More recently, large-scale studies of the use of the Internet in Britain have found only a small minority of young people involved in more creative or participatory activities such as making websites (Facer et al., 2003; Livingstone and Bober, 2004). As Mark Warschauer (2003) points out, the potential for advanced multimedia production – which requires the latest computers and software, and high bandwidth – is actually quite inaccessible to all but the wealthy middle-classes. Although the sample of our CHICAM research was quite limited, it is reasonable to conclude that such opportunities and activities are least likely to be available to the most socially excluded groups, such as refugees; and of course this digital divide is writ large on a global scale.

Nevertheless, it cannot be denied that we are now moving towards a more participatory media environment (Jenkins, 2006). Young people in particular are likely to be increasingly involved in activities such as video production (not least via mobile phones), the creation of websites (for example, through 'social networking' sites like *MySpace*) and in using the various forms of 'social software' that are now emerging – including the growing range of photo and video sharing sites (such as *YouTube* and *Flickr*). Crucially, many of these media enable young people to find an audience for their creative expression, in ways that were previously very difficult, if not impossible. Such activities are not only taking place in the home, but also in 'informal' educational settings such as youth projects and community centres, as well as in the more formal context of schools. Before we turn to the use of such media in the context of research, it is worth briefly reviewing some of the issues that arise here.

## Media production in everyday life

Most of the research on children's media production has focused on activities in broadly educational settings. The question of how children might engage in more 'spontaneous' forms of media production – or at least, in activities that are not instigated or monitored by adults – largely remains to be explored. Ironically, most of the research here focuses on new media rather than on 'old' media such as video, radio or print. For example, in many Western countries, a significant proportion of households have portable video cameras (in the United Kingdom, the figure is now almost one-third, evenly distributed across social classes); yet very little is known about how these media are actually used in the home. Existing small-scale case studies (for example, Bloustien, 1998; Soep, 2005) suggest that video production can offer a valuable space for young people to perform, explore and play with identity; but there is a significant lack of research in this field generally.

When it comes to new media, it is clear that young people are increasingly using the Internet to communicate (via e-mail, instant messaging and chat). However, more developed creative production on the web is still a minority activity – although it is likely that the production of websites and blogs will become more widespread, particularly as the need for technical know-how declines (Herring et al., 2004). Sites like *MySpace*, for example, provide templates and 'cut-and-paste'-type options that make the creation of personal sites relatively straightforward – although of course this also sets limits on the creative possibilities. Much of the research on these issues is keen to celebrate the potential of the web as a means of building autonomous youth communities (Bortree, 2005; Davies, 2006; Driver, 2006; Scheidt, 2006; Stern, 2004). Here again, media production is seen as a focus for complex 'identity work' (and indeed 'identity play'); yet it also provides a means for young people to share personal concerns, and to generate dialogues, in ways that may be more difficult in other contexts. The opportunities these media present for *group* interaction, when compared with equivalent older technologies such as the telephone, cannot be denied; although it is also important to acknowledge the occasionally undemocratic and exclusionary nature of online communication.

These new media are also playing an increasingly important role in the lives of migrant communities – although, for many, access to them is still more likely to occur in public places (schools, internet cafes and libraries) than in homes (see Chapter 3). However, as Dayan (1998) suggests, research in this field also needs to consider the place of 'small' media in communication across the diaspora. Based on his research with Moroccan Jewish families, Dayan points to the importance of newsletters, audio and video-cassettes traded in local 'ethnic' shops, as well as the exchange of letters, photographs and telephone calls.

This was certainly borne out by our research with some of the families in the CHICAM project. Several of the children's families kept in touch with friends and family 'back home', not only through the exchange of media (commercially produced tapes and videos) and through telephone calls, but also by sending photographs and home videos back and forth. In many cases, photographs – displayed in albums and in the home – were used to keep memories of their family in their former locations alive, serving almost as concrete proof of the family's history; although clearly, they also represented family life in particular ways (cf. Spence and Holland, 1991). As Kambooye, a Somali boy in the Dutch club, exclaimed: 'you should only know how often we look at them!' These photographs also prompted the telling of family stories: although Kambooye had never met his grandfather or his great-grandfather, he knew many stories about them.

Many children had their own photograph albums and (at our suggestion) several made videos in the clubs based on these photographs, prompting discussions between the children about their different experiences of family life. For example, Hakan in the German club brought in photographs from Turkey that he kept in a metal box, which revived in him positive memories of a more harmonious family life. However, some children refused to make public this private use of media, pretending there were no photographs to be brought to the club (as with the Syrian Kurdish children in the Greek club), and their existence and importance only became clear when the researchers visited the families at home.

The reworking of pictures, absent or present, also helped to define – and redefine – the children's relationship with the past (cf. Hirsch, 1997; Lury, 1997). Not only photographs, but also other 'media' (such as drawings) and less obvious activities, such as travelling about the local area, helped to trigger memories about journeys and places where the children had lived, perhaps on their way from their homeland to the new country. When the Swedish researcher was driving Hana home one day, she started to talk about a journey to Kosovo, when the whole family was together. When drawing a childhood memory, Hana composed a picture of a couple seen from behind, sitting on a sofa and watching a blue-green sea or ocean: it was her family on a visit to Kosovo. A year later, in a series of photographs from her summer holiday with her mother in Kosovo, she returned to a similar composition, where her mother is sitting on a rock facing the sea.

In some cases, the use of photography helped to construct a family narrative in cases of disruption. After a couple of months in the Swedish club, Ibish brought in a set of well-thumbed pictures. They had been taken during a trip to Kosovo when the whole family visited the village they used to live in. Several pictures focused on the remains of their house, which was burnt down during the civil war. During the club activities, Ibish returned to his memories from the village on several occasions. He also made a drawing of the village and of the graveyard where his grandfather is buried. As this implies, these 'private' uses of media are largely about the preservation of memory, and could be seen to sanction a form of nostalgia; although for some children, they also provided disturbing and painful reminders of relationships and of a stability that they no longer possessed.

## Children making media in educational settings

These everyday uses of media provide an important means for children to represent their lives and experiences, and to communicate with others; yet they are largely confined to the private sphere of the family. In recent years, increasing numbers of educators, researchers and social activists have recognised the potential of media production, both as a means of developing children's understanding of how the media work and as a way of facilitating more public forms of communication. Media, it is argued, can be used to 'empower' children and enable their voices to be heard in the wider public sphere.

Among the countries involved in our CHICAM research, there were several examples of practical projects involving media production by young people, mostly outside formal educational institutions. Some of these projects are based around children's film festivals, such as the Thessaloniki International Festival in Greece. Some involve extra-curricular activities of various kinds, such as those involving video work with rural youth in Germany (Niesyto, 1991). Some involve working directly with the media, for example, in the case of the children's news agency Children's Express, which has offices in the United Kingdom and the United States. Others involve artists working in schools or in after-school settings, such as the Melina Project in Greece; while some, such as the 'Animation in School' project in Sweden, have sought to introduce teachers to low-tech media that can be easily used in the classroom, often with quite young children. There are many other such projects around the world, including innovative projects taking place in developing countries – again, often using relatively low-tech media such as radio and desktop publishing (see Asthana, 2006; von Feilitzen and Carlsson, 1999). UNICEF is particularly active in supporting participatory projects of this kind via its global 'MAGIC' initiative (*www.unicef.org/magic*) and its 'Voices of Youth' network (www.unicef.org/voy); and much of the emphasis here is on the role of media in promoting broader struggles to secure children's rights.

Some such projects have explicitly addressed migrant youth, or aspects of multiculturalism. For example, one of our partner organisations in CHICAM, MiraMedia, is a long-established project in the Netherlands that seeks to increase the participation of immigrant groups in the Dutch media. While its main focus is on training young adults, and on bringing pressure to bear on broadcasting companies, it is also involved in work with younger people, generally in 'informal' educational settings (several of these are part of pan-European initiatives such as 'More Colour in the Media' and 'Routes and Routes'). Meanwhile, in Germany, the 'Interkulturellen Jugendmedienprojekt' (Intercultural Youth Media Project) involves a virtual chat room in which children and adolescents of different nationalities meet in order to come in contact with – or confront – both their own and each other's cultural backgrounds. Likewise, in Australia, the Youth Internet Radio Project is developing communication among 'peripheral' young people, many of whom are Aborigines, living in remote rural locations (Notley and Tacchi, 2005).

Other such projects have a strongly international or intercultural dimension. For example, Faxcination is a project based in Vietnam that involves the collaborative production of animated cartoons by means of drawings faxed to a range of international locations. One-Minutes Junior is an international film festival, sponsored by UNICEF, showing one-minute films produced by children from around the world; while 'Euro-Arab Neighbourhood', sponsored by UNESCO in Germany, promotes the exchange of student-produced magazines between Europe and the Arab States. Global Action Project, based in New York, is a well-established video production project that has undertaken several international exchanges between groups of young video-makers, and worked in conflict zones such as Palestine and Northern Ireland.

Most accounts of such projects tend to be descriptive, even celebratory, and there has been little critical evaluation of their effectiveness. However, there are some more reflexive accounts written by practitioners (for example, Dewdney and Lister, 1988; Goodman, 2003); and recent surveys of informal youth production internationally have drawn attention to some of the difficulties that are encountered here (Asthana, 2006; Harvey et al., 2002; Tyner, 2003). Several of these are systemic: the precarious and uneven funding of such projects results in a lack of training for project workers, and a lack of continuity for participants. However, there are also more challenging questions here about the extent to which such projects are in fact 'empowering' for young people, what this might mean, and how it might be identified. Access to media means very different things for different social groups, in terms of what they do with the opportunity, how they are able to capitalise and build upon it, and in terms of potential outcomes; and there are bound to be significant differences in this respect between those who already possess social and educational capital and those who do not. Ultimately, the crucial question is what students might actually be *learning* from this kind of work, beyond merely acquiring technical skills: in providing young people with opportunities to represent their own perspectives and concerns, there is a risk of simply leaving them where they already are. As Selwood (1997: 333) has argued, such projects often seem to be regarded by policy-makers and funders as merely 'a form of temporary social service for young people who are disadvantaged or "excluded"': they may serve as a means of keeping such young people out of trouble, but they may achieve little more. (For a fuller discussion, see Buckingham, 2003: Chapter 12).

More sustained academic research on young people's media production mostly pertains to more formal educational settings. Thus, there is a tradition of research in art education that involves analysing children's visual productions, not least in terms of what they reveal about their experience of media (Neuss, 1999). This approach has also been taken up by researchers: for example, a recent cross-cultural study by Goetz et al. (2005) uses drawings by children to explore the role of media in their imaginative fantasy worlds. While many of the drawings use imagery from global media, the ways in which the children deploy it reflects both 'universal' shared preoccupations as well as some that are quite specific to the different national settings. Educational research also suggests that the use of visual methods provides a particularly valuable means of engaging with young people who are disaffected from traditional education; and that it is especially important for migrant children who may not be fluent in the language of the host country (Danielsson, 1998; Niesyto, 2000).

In the United Kingdom, where there is a strong tradition of media education in schools, there is a growing body of classroom-based research (for a review, see Buckingham, 2003). Yet this more formal media education typically prioritises conceptual learning *about* the media rather than the acquisition of production skills or creative 'self-expression'; and as such, production is usually seen as a means to an end, rather than an end in itself. Thus, the focus of much of the research has been on the relation between 'theory' (that is, media analysis) and 'practice' (that is, production); and there is a strong emphasis on the importance of students' critical reflection on the production process. Nevertheless, there is a growing recognition here that production should not be used merely as an illustration of predetermined theories; and that creativity and play – however difficult they may be to define – are also essential elements. (For a further discussion, see Buckingham, 2003; Buckingham et al., 2005; Sefton-Green, 1999, for accounts of projects taking place outside formal educational settings.)

These broadly educational activities therefore raise several questions about the status and value of media production by young people. While there is undoubtedly a great deal of exciting work going on in this field – not least with migrant children – there is often somewhat of a gap between rhetoric and reality. Ultimately, it would be naïve to assume that young people could simply use media as a means of 'self-expression' or a way of 'making their voices heard'. The media are not neutral tools; and young people will approach media production with a repertoire and a history of past media experiences that inevitably lead them in certain directions. Furthermore, they have to learn how to use media, just as they have to learn how to write. The media do not simply present their experiences or viewpoints: they re-present them using particular conventions, genres and forms of language that are by no means simply natural or spontaneous. As we shall see, this also has significant implications in terms of research.

## Media production as research

The use of visual media (photographs, drawings, film and video) is also increasingly popular in research with young people – and indeed in sociological and anthropological research more broadly (Banks, 2001; Pink, 2001a). In most cases, however, it is only the researchers who operate the cameras. Indeed, there has been a considerable amount of criticism, for example, in relation to ethnographic film, of the use of media to objectify 'others' of various kinds – although, in principle, this is no less the case with academic writing. However, in recent years there has been a growing emphasis on the potential of *collaborative* production, particularly among anthropologists working with indigenous or marginalised communities (Banks, 2001: 122–128; Pink, 2001b); and there are many connections between this kind of research and the long tradition of independent video or media activism (see Boyle, 1997; Dowmunt, 1993).

When it comes to working with children and young people, the use of this approach reflects a recognition of the importance of visual and audio-visual media in young people's lives: in this sense, it is a matter of the method of research following the object of the research (Niesyto, 2001). However, it can also be seen as an extension of the emphasis on *participation* that is characteristic of research in the 'New Sociology of Childhood' (Christensen and James, 1999). In principle, participation means that children move from being 'objects' of research to being 'subjects'. It entails an ongoing attempt to construct shared understandings and meanings between the researchers and the researched; consulting with participants about the nature and direction of the research; and attempting to access children's 'voices' in as unmediated a manner as possible.

The argument for using media production in research with children and young people is two-fold. On one level, media production can be seen to provide a form of 'empowerment': at least potentially, it enables children to depict their own experiences and to 'speak' on their own behalf. In this sense, it offers them the opportunity to represent themselves in their own right – and this argument carries particular weight when it comes to children who could be seen as socially and politically disempowered, such as migrants and refugees. Yet at the same time, media production also provides a different means for researchers to gain access to children's perspectives and experiences – to achieve a more privileged 'inside' view than might be possible using other methods. The use of visual methods in particular can potentially bypass the constraints and controls that apply to other means of communication. However, as we shall see, these two imperatives can potentially come into conflict, causing significant methodological and ethical dilemmas.

Thus, one of the aims of our CHICAM project – or at least one of the claims we made in our funding proposal! – was that video production would provide a means of enabling children's voices to be heard, not just by researchers, but also by policy-makers and other people in positions of power to affect the children's lives. The screening or distribution of the children's productions could potentially enable them to speak directly to these powerful audiences, without the mediation of adults. Yet at the same time, as researchers, we were also using video production as a *data-gathering technique* – one that we believed would have several advantages over traditional methods. The children with whom we were working had varying levels of fluency in the language of their new country of residence; and we were also hoping that they would communicate with children in other national settings. Working with visual media meant that they could use a variety of means to convey what they wished to express, without having to be totally reliant on

*Picture 3*  Preparing to film

verbal communication. Since the research also touched on emotional – and potentially traumatic – experiences, being able to approach such topics less directly, through forms of expression other than talk, was an advantage for both the researchers and the children. This 'therapeutic' use of visual media (generally in the form of drawing) is increasingly popular in organisations that work with refugee children, such as the Medical Foundation for the Care of Victims of Torture in the United Kingdom (see Eokter, 1998; Kalmanowitz and Lloyd, 1997).

Media also played a key part in motivating the children to participate. Acquiring the production and editing skills and having access to the equipment gave the children a considerable social status with their peers; and it also represented something lasting that they could 'take away' from the research. Many parents were also keen for their children to be involved, partly because they saw this as a way of their children acquiring technical skills (particularly in relation to computers) that would stand them in good stead in school and for future careers. We also found that the use of media production allowed important new opportunities for data-gathering. The processes of production (planning, shooting, editing and presentation) typically involve negotiation with

*Picture 4*   Learning to use the camera

others: producers have to debate and make decisions about what will be represented, why and how, and indeed what is *allowed* to be represented within the institutions in which they live and work. In our research, the times when the children were simply 'hanging out' and chatting while preparing to film, setting up equipment, editing and sharing ideas were all important opportunities for data collection.

Ultimately, however, there are circumstances in which these two imperatives might be seen to conflict. While claiming to 'give children a voice', this approach could equally be seen as a more devious means of satisfying the researcher's 'will to truth' – and as such, it does not necessarily resolve difficult questions about the power-relationships

*Picture 5* Out and about filming in Italy

between researchers and researched. Thus, involving children directly in the research process through their uses of media technology inevitably makes it more difficult for research to stick to a predetermined agenda or set of themes. In many respects, this is beneficial: it enables the children to highlight areas of concern or interest that may otherwise not have been addressed. Yet, as we shall see in more detail in our discussion of the CHICAM videos in Chapter 8, media also afforded opportunities for play that appeared (at least at first sight) to be quite irrelevant to our concerns as researchers. In some instances, these opportunities ultimately proved to be very fruitful – although it was not always possible to reconcile our different motivations and concerns.

Furthermore, unlike other forms of observational research, this approach also entails an *intervention*. The clubs we established for CHICAM and in the VideoCulture project (described in more detail below) were essentially artificial settings. The relationships formed and the work undertaken within the clubs were brought into existence for the purposes of our research. We would argue that the composition of the clubs and the ways in which the media work were carried out reflected the ways in which such clubs have operated elsewhere, and would operate if the clubs continued to be organised in these settings – yet this is certainly a debatable point. In both projects, researchers worked alongside media educators, who facilitated the production work; but in practice, it was often hard to maintain this distinction, and the researchers often could not avoid becoming very involved in assisting the children with their productions.

As we have noted above, children do not necessarily arrive in such a setting knowing how to use the technology. This is not simply a question of knowing which buttons to press, but also of being able to make meaningful (or comprehensible) 'statements' in a visual or audio-visual medium. Learning of this kind is self-evidently a long-term process; and different children will inevitably bring or develop different degrees of facility in this respect. Moreover, children are not necessarily possessed of a burning desire to communicate or to represent themselves – perhaps particularly in such adult-defined settings. Thus, while they were initially very enthusiastic about learning to use the technology, their interest was sometimes hard to maintain once they had acquired the basic skills and made their first productions. As we will discuss in more detail in Chapters 8 and 9, the questions of why and for whom they were making the videos became a key issue in the research. Ultimately, if we did enable the children to 'have their voices heard' by policy makers and others, it was only because we were subsequently able to edit their productions into a short and relatively polished final package; and even if we had enabled a more direct form of communication here, it is doubtful whether the children would have been particularly interested in pursuing it.

These points have several implications in terms of research methodology. It is clear, first, that we need to see the children's productions not as pristine reflections of what they really think or would like to communicate, but as highly contingent. What they produce depends crucially on the context in which the production occurs. This means that we need to take account of the institutional setting, the pedagogic approach of the media educators, and the ways in which the activities are defined and negotiated. What children produce also depends, crucially, on how they perceive their audience – if, indeed, they perceive there to be an audience at all. Ourselves as adult researchers, their peers in and beyond the club setting, or some more nebulous category of powerful people, are all potential audiences; but they may each be conceived in quite different ways by different children, and indeed by ourselves as researchers. Both CHICAM and VideoCulture involved the exchange of video productions with children in other national settings – but, as we shall see, the children were not necessarily especially concerned about these 'other' audiences, and the communication was by no means a straightforward process.

This means that we cannot see these visual productions as a form of 'self-expression' – at least if we take that to mean some kind of spontaneous outpouring of personal ideas and feelings. On the contrary, what the children produced was partly determined by the forms of 'media language' they had at their disposal. They did not simply seek outer forms for their inner feelings: for the most part, they used existing media forms and genres with which they were already familiar – although they also combined and mutated them in different ways. As might be expected (see Chapter 5), the children drew on the media cultures they knew from their home countries (for example, in traditional forms of music or storytelling), and on those of their new country of residence – and, more broadly, on the field of global media (for example, in adopting elements of existing media genres such as music videos, 'reality TV', documentaries or rap music).

As such, children's visual productions cannot stand alone as straightforward 'statements' of their lives and experiences – any more than we should take what they say in an interview at face value, as a straightforward reflection of what they really think or feel. In this case, we need to combine the analysis of the productions with other data – both

*Picture 6*   Using the LCD screen

*Picture 7*   Filming in process in the CHICAM club in Greece

observations of the production process and interviews and observations gathered in other settings. Despite the claims that are sometimes made on their behalf, we would argue that children's productions do not simply 'speak for themselves' and should be analysed in combination with other data.

## VideoCulture: media production and intercultural communication

In the final section of this chapter, we would like to explore these issues in more detail by drawing on material from a project that was in some respects a precursor of CHICAM. This was the VideoCulture project, directed by Horst Niesyto of the University of Ludwigsburg in Germany (for more details, see Buckingham, 2001a; Niesyto, 2003). Like CHICAM, VideoCulture sought to explore the potential of audio-visual media production as a means of intercultural communication. We set up and observed video production clubs in four national settings (the United Kingdom, Germany, Hungary and the Czech Republic), all of which took place in the context of after-school programmes or community arts projects. The young people involved (who were somewhat older than the CHICAM children, aged 14–17 years) produced short videotapes, either on a given theme or on another of their choice. 'Sampler' tapes of productions were then circulated among the clubs; and we interviewed the participants, both about their own productions and about their responses to the videos produced in the other countries. In a later phase, the videos were also seen and discussed by groups of young people in New York and Los Angeles (see Niesyto et al., 2003).

Over the 2 years of the fieldwork (1997–1999), a total of 36 finished video productions emerged. They addressed different topics and used different media forms and genres: some were broadly in a 'montage'-style familiar to most of the young people from music videos, while some used a narrative-based approach (although many combined the two). Inevitably, the quality and style of these films reflected the particular contexts in which they were produced, and the individuals or groups involved. In some cases, the media educators were keen to teach basic media conventions (such as continuity editing), while in others, a more associative, even 'poetic' approach was preferred. The videos also reflect the young people's different knowledge and experience of media genres, as well as broader social and cultural differences.

Interpreting the 'partner-videos' also depended upon the experiences and subjective tastes of the different audiences. 'Understanding' was not simply a matter of cognitive understanding of the content and the (suspected) intention: it also involved emotional or even intuitive processes, and connections to direct personal experiences. Several of the young people appeared to prefer 'open' productions to 'closed' ones: that is, if the 'message' was too unambiguous or too simple, and did not leave enough space for individual interpretation, it was often rejected. On the other hand, too much openness led to confusion; particularly when it came to intercultural communication, it was important for producers to use recognisable symbols and make reference to familiar areas of experience (Holzwarth and Maurer, 2001).

Thus, when young people in New York came to interpret some of the videos made in Europe, it was apparent that there were elements of 'teen life' that were shared and hence recognisable across cultures (this analysis was conducted by JoEllen Fiskerkeller from New York University: see Niesyto et al., 2003). Videos about the pleasures and difficulties of social interactions, about the 'boring' experience of school, about taking risks (for example, in relation to drugs or violence) or about remembering good times with friends at a party or on a shopping trip were all familiar, even when they were set in very different cultural circumstances – although comparisons with their own direct experience sometimes led these viewers to question the plausibility or accuracy of the scenarios. To some extent, this reflected one of the basic premises of the project: that young people would find a degree of resonance with the productions of other young people, which they might be less likely to experience in mainstream media (which are generally produced by adults *about* youth, rather than *by* young people themselves). Some suggested that adults could not communicate with youth as effectively as youth themselves, because, as one female participant explained, things are different for youth now, compared to when current adults were young. To some extent, they implied, young people might have more in common with other young people who live in other parts of the world and who speak different languages than they do with the adults in their own country, and even their own homes.

At the same time, these New York youth were also concerned about elements in the videos that were – or alternatively should have been – *different* from their experience. For example, they spoke about the different kinds of cars, buses and trams; and suggested that the car and the motor scooter in one Hungarian production looked like they were from 'the Third World'. On the other hand, however, they criticised the inclusion of well-known songs or video formats, arguing that the producers should have included music from their 'own' cultures, rather than material that was too much like that produced in the United States – thus reflecting an implicit critique of the homogenising influence of global media. In fact, most of these young people, or their parents or grandparents, had emigrated from other countries. Perhaps for this reason, they found points of connection in videos created by 'others': they appeared to recognise a 'we', even while they acknowledged that the films came from 'another place' (whether that place is perceived as geographical, social or emotional).

Two key issues emerged from this project that are relevant to the preceding discussion of visual research methods and to the two chapters that follow. The first of these is to do with how young people develop their sense of *audience*. To what extent did it make a difference to these young video-makers to know that their work would be seen by other young people, not just in their immediate community but also in other countries? And how did they in turn respond to each other's productions? Secondly, there is the question of *media language*. Although the young people involved were not necessarily migrants themselves, the project was working across different national settings. We therefore explicitly aimed to avoid or bypass verbal language; and while many of the productions used songs on the soundtrack, the young people were asked not to use talk or captions. One of our aims here was to discover whether there were forms of transcultural audio-visual language that might enable young people to communicate their emotions, experiences and fantasies in ways that moved beyond 'logocentric' verbal and written modes.

## Opposites attract: a VideoCulture case study

Two contrasting productions made by young people in London illustrate some of the complexities at stake here. The young people were given the theme 'opposites attract', although they were told that they could interpret this in any way they chose. The first production, simply entitled *Opposites Attract*, was in many respects a typical first exercise in video. It was made by Susanne, Robert and Sharon, three working-class young people from different ethnic backgrounds, and tells the story of a black boy and a white girl who meet at a video production course. Initially reluctant to communicate with each other, they eventually start to play around with the camera, and finally leave arm-in-arm as friends. In this film, there are clear sequences of establishing shots and close-ups, shot/reverse shot patterns and point-of-view shots. The images are accompanied by a fast drum-and-bass soundtrack. The producers expressed some frustration with the restriction on not using language or dialogue, as they felt this would be needed in order to convey 'a story'; although they never considered the possibility of interpreting the theme in a non-narrative form.

The second production, *Equilibrium*, is very different. Made in the montage-based style of a music video, it focuses on two characters, both white and in their teens: a girl dressed in a white sheet or a feather boa, and a boy dressed in a black cape with black mask-like shapes painted around his eyes. Rapidly cut sequences of images feature the couple kissing, close-ups of the girl's eye, the boy's face appearing through a black cloth, a rat licking a stud in the boy's tongue, and the girl's hand being drawn across her face, smearing her eye make-up down her cheek. Several images are reflected in mirrors (sometimes in negative); and the girl frequently looks directly into the camera. In some shots, the boy and the girl are seen lying down, arranged to form a yin/yang symbol. The tape is accompanied by an atmospheric techno soundtrack, which starts slowly and then speeds up; and the pace of the editing reflects this change of rhythm. *Equilibrium* was produced by Mia, a white, middle-class 16-year old. Like the others, she had not had any previous experience of video production; although she did have other experiences as a performer, and had recently acted in a commercial music video. Following the course, Mia went on to produce a number of short films, including some that were publicly screened.

In terms of 'film language', there are several striking differences between these two films. The group that made *Opposites Attract* set out to produce a narrative, with a beginning, middle and an end. In this respect, they achieved their goal. The characters have coherent motivations, and one event leads logically to the next. Their production employs the most obvious 'rules' or conventions of continuity editing; and there is never any doubt about where the viewer is positioned in time or space. By contrast, Mia set out to produce a non-narrative, montage-style film. Several recurrent images are intertwined, although there is no obvious logic about how they are juxtaposed or arranged. While there are 'characters' here, we are left to infer a good deal about what motivates them. The pace of the editing relates to the pace of the musical soundtrack, but there is no obvious use of continuity editing or any clear sequence of cause-and-effect.

Both films relate fairly explicitly to the given theme of 'opposites attract'. Yet where the opposites in the group production are primarily individual personalities, those in *Equilibrium* are much more abstract and self-consciously symbolic. Interestingly, the group film was interpreted by other young people who saw it as promoting a 'moral' or message – particularly in relation to racial harmony – although in fact this was not the overt intention. By contrast, *Equilibrium* specifically aims for an aesthetic response, rather than a singular 'meaning'. It requires a more intensive form of interpretative 'work' on the part of the reader; and it consciously promotes a degree of uncertainty.

These differences are partly a result of the films' use of different forms of 'film language'. Essentially, the group film uses Hollywood film language, while *Equilibrium* uses the montage-based style of music video – albeit, perhaps, with elements of the self-conscious visual symbolism of the art movie. These differences might be traced to the social and cultural differences between their producers. Mia clearly possessed a form of cultural capital that was unavailable to the other young people here. This was partly a matter of her middle-class background, and partly to do with her 'subcultural' experiences and identifications. The fact that she had been previously involved in production as a performer was also significant. In our interviews with her, Mia presented herself as an artist making a personal statement; although this was also made possible because she was able to work alone. By contrast, the fact that the *Opposites Attract* group had to negotiate their way to an agreed approach effectively militated against a more 'personal' style – even if this had been something they had wished to achieve in the first place.

Although the introduction to the project had included a brief explanation of the VideoCulture network, there was no explicit discussion among the group about how other young people from different cultures might view their films. It was only upon subsequent reflection that the question of audience became a significant concern – and this emerged particularly strongly when the group had the opportunity to watch and discuss some of the films produced by other young people involved in the project. At least initially, Robert and Sharon were reluctant to accept the suggestion – which had emerged strongly from some of the German students' feedback – that their film was conveying a 'message' about overcoming differences, whether of race or gender. Robert maintained that this social message had not been intentional on their part, and that the decision to use a black boy and a white girl was a simply a consequence of who was available. To this extent, therefore, the audience responses helped them to become aware of a gap between their intentions and the final results. By contrast, Mia had consciously seen the preparation and production stages of her film as personal and therapeutic – an attempt to express something she felt on an emotional level. As she put it, 'I don't really care that much if the audience totally misunderstands it or misinterprets it for themselves, 'cause I don't care – 'cause I did it for myself.' However, she also said that she had changed to a more distanced stance at the editing stage, and made her selections on the basis of which shots might have visual impact on the audience: 'By the time we were editing, I'd done all my film therapy. I was over that [laughs] and I just wanted to put across something that would stick in people's minds.'

Both in her presentation of her work, and in her reflections on the other young people's productions, Mia was able to access a quasi-academic – and broadly middle-class – discourse of aesthetic appreciation that was not available to the other young people. For example, she judged the other productions in terms of existing cultural movements ('surreal'); she searched for 'symbolism' and philosophical themes ('reality and perception'); she used a somewhat 'technical' terminology ('that violin harmony'); and she was able to assume a rational distance both from the productions themselves *and* from her own responses to them. Likewise, in relation to her own work, she was keen to present herself as an artist with 'vision' and 'imagination', claiming that her video was a 'personal' statement, which was 'clear and focused' from the very beginning. In fact, there are some grounds for questioning these claims, since at least some of what she produced was down to accidents in the editing.

Nevertheless, for all the young people, the experience of watching the other productions definitely influenced how they thought about their own – or at least what they were prepared to say about this. There was a kind of 'decentering' here: thinking about their own interpretations of other people's productions encouraged them to think about how other people would think about theirs. In particular, it led them to consider the relationship between intentions and results; to recognise that some of their intentions were not clear, or had changed as the work progressed; and that some of the outcomes did not correspond to their initial intentions, and may even have led to them being misinterpreted. The mere fact that there was a real audience out there somewhere – and indeed that they themselves were a real audience for somebody else's productions – seems to have helped them evaluate their own work in a more thoughtful and critical way.

As this implies, enabling young people to produce for a 'real' audience can encourage them to think through the choices they make in production, and their possible consequences; and being confronted with audience responses can motivate them to reflect more critically on the relationships between intentions and results. However, there may be limits in the extent to which they will be able or prepared to take account of *any* audience, however 'real'. They may have other concerns and motivations that run counter to rationalistic models of 'ideal communication'. In the context of the school classroom, 'real audiences' inevitably tend to be simulated, or at least very artificially constructed (Buckingham et al., 1995: Chapter 6); and even in the case of projects like VideoCulture or CHICAM, questions remain about how 'real' the audience is perceived to be – particularly if it is an unknown audience from another country that one never expects to meet face-to-face.

This case study also suggests that the issue of 'media language' is not simply a psychological question, which can be addressed through recourse to theories of perception and cognition (cf. Messaris, 1994). It is also a question about the social and historical institutionalisation of particular linguistic conventions and genres. At the risk of generalisation, it could be argued that the globalisation of the media industries has resulted in the dominance of two or three principal 'media languages': the 'classical' Hollywood style, with its reliance on continuity editing, realism and invisible narration; the montage-based style of MTV (and some advertising), which draws in turn on a history of *avant garde* film

aesthetics; and (perhaps) the style of the 'art movie', with its more ellipt-
ical approach to narration and its self-conscious use of visual symbolism.
Rather than expecting young people to spontaneously 'discover' a new
form of transcultural media language, we should not be surprised if they
use those that are already available to them. However, we also need to
situate these uses in terms of a sociology of taste cultures (cf. Bourdieu,
1984). Irrespective of the models they are offered by teachers, different
social groups may have different cultural competencies that will dispose
them towards different forms of media language, both as consumers and
as producers. Social class is not the only factor in play here, but it is
certainly a key one.

In terms of education, this would suggest that we should exercise
some caution here. *Equilibrium* was received with considerable enthusiasm by some of our fellow researchers, to an extent that we found
quite problematic. Mia appeared to conform to a particular fantasy of
what creative young people should be like: she was an artist, an *auteur*,
in the making. Both her production and her subsequent contributions
to interviews and discussion reflected a particularly middle-class (and
perhaps specifically 'Western') form of cultural capital. This is not in any
way to suggest that this perspective is invalid – or to dismiss it as 'just
middle-class'. It is, however, to suggest that it is partial; and that it is
a form of knowledge that not all young people will possess, or indeed
*want* (or feel they need) to possess. We would caution against the tempta-
tion merely to validate this kind of knowledge, or indeed to celebrate
it. On the contrary, we need to find ways of valuing the full range of
competencies, tastes and motivations that young people bring to media
production, rather than privileging those that are closest to our own.

## Conclusion: speaking for themselves?

In an important series of articles, Charles Husband has pointed to the
*right to communicate* as a vital dimension of multicultural societies, and as
a necessary element in the construction of a 'multi-ethnic public sphere'
(Husband, 1998, 2000). We support this argument. Indeed, we would
argue that communication rights of this kind should not be confined
to adults, but extended to children and young people as well. Both in
research itself, and in the wider public arena, we need to find more
effective ways of enabling children to represent their experiences and
concerns.

However, as we have shown in this chapter, gaining access to media
of communication, and learning to use them, are not straightforward

processes. Children – including migrant children – are already using many of these media in their everyday lives; and they are possibly more salient for them than they are for many adults. Yet we need to be wary of the idea that media communication is a spontaneous or natural process, or that it offers a simple way of enabling young people's voices to be heard. Young people have different types and degrees of cultural capital, and they are not necessarily any more 'fluent' in audio-visual communication than they are in verbal communication.

As we have suggested, 'finding an audience' can make an important difference to young people's learning; but communication across cultures is unlikely to be a transparent or straightforward matter. Different cultural traditions are likely to employ different forms and styles of representation, and meanings are therefore neither transparent nor instantly accessible to all. The experience of the VideoCulture project shows the need for communication that functions on an aesthetic level as well as on the level of explicit verbal meaning; it also shows some of the ambiguities and possibilities for misinterpretation that inevitably arise. All these issues will be addressed in more detail in the following chapters, where we look more closely at some of the CHICAM productions.

# 8
# Picture Me In: Migrant Children as Media Makers

In this chapter and the next, we return more directly to our CHICAM research, to consider the ways in which the children took up our invitation to create and exchange their own media productions. As we have explained, CHICAM was based around a network of media-making 'clubs' in six European countries. In each club, a researcher and a media educator worked with the children to create short productions, which were then shared via the Internet.

The principal aim of our research was to explore how these children would use the media – and particularly video – to represent and express their experiences as migrants and newcomers to their respective countries. We initially focused on three obvious areas in which children have important and varied experiences: friendship, school and family. At the same time, we were also interested in the media-making process in its own right. We were keen to understand how the children would develop their technical skills in camera and computer use; how they would use forms of representation – such as animation and music videos – that they were already familiar with; and how they might develop a sense of the different audiences that their productions might reach. As we have implied, none of these aspects is without complications and difficulties.

By the end of the project, the children had made approximately 50 'finished' video productions, as well as generating a large amount of other materials in the form of videotapes, drawings, photographs and posters. In this chapter, we discuss several of these productions in more detail, in the form of a narrative of our own. We look in turn at how the children developed production and communication skills in the early stages of the project; the ways in which they addressed or negotiated with our overt research themes; the elements of play and experimentation that began to emerge in their work; and some of the problems of

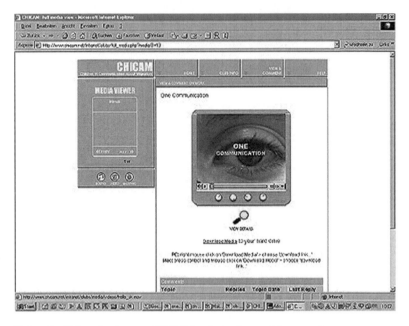

*Picture 8*    Video viewing on CHICAM website (www.chicam.org)

interpretation that we encountered. Along the way, we develop several of the themes introduced in Chapter 7, particularly the notion of the child's 'voice'.

## Learning the skills: the early stages

Most, but by no means all, of the children involved in the CHICAM clubs had some previous experience of photography or making videos. However, none had edited moving images or made photo stories before. This meant that a considerable amount of time had to be spent learning the skills. As we noted in Chapter 7, children's media productions inevitably reflect their existing media experiences as 'consumers'; and they are also bound to be affected by the ways in which they are taught and the expectations that are made of them (whether implicitly or explicitly). This is not simply a matter of learning the mechanical skills of operating the camera or the editing software; although acquiring these skills undoubtedly assists in 'freeing-up' the kind of experimentation that allows children to find different 'voices' and conceive of different audiences.

One starting point for most of the clubs was to make photo stories, filming and editing sequences of existing photos and adding commentary. Several of the children did this using family photos or drawings they had made. For example, during the pilot project in the United Kingdom, three girls used family photos and objects as a basis for interviewing each other about their countries of origin. The commentary describes each photo, saying where and when it was taken and why it was important to them. This was not a production the girls wished to share beyond the local club, seeing it as very personal. One girl showed photos of her father in Somalia before his death, another her home in Pakistan and the third brought in objects that symbolised her life in Russia. Despite their differences, the video allowed them to share and compare experiences. For example, Victoria said that she was the only one who felt she no longer had a home or a base, having left Russia several years before for Israel and then having to migrate again to live temporarily in the United Kingdom, not knowing where or when they would move next. The ideas of 'house' and 'home' developed into a very relevant discussion, as our field notes suggest:

> After making the photo essays, Victoria said: 'it's strange that everybody I know who comes from another country has a house in their country and I don't.' This was the beginning of an important exchange about migration experiences. Victoria brought in a teddy bear, some Russian dolls and spoons and a photo of herself when she was 4 years old. Each one had its own story which she was happy to tell. The photo reminded her of going to the dentist and she went into a long description of dental treatment in Russia and how scary it was. Getting the details correct seemed to be very important for the girls.

In several of the clubs, the researchers also used drawing as an initial 'way in' to the research themes. These drawings were often very revealing of the children's migration experiences. In the Netherlands, children who had lived in refugee reception centres drew and talked about the difficulties and emotional upsets that this entailed. In Greece, making family trees and drawings related to family provided an opportunity for different formations of family to be discussed (Christopoulou and de Leeuw, 2005); and the children here also initiated a session in which they drew their experiences of war. In the United Kingdom, we used drawing as a vehicle for discussing past experiences of schools in Guinea, Portugal and London. Haamid and Carlos talked as they drew and as we filmed. Again, it was the details that were important for both the boys. For Haamid, drawing the configuration of the buildings and the way in which people gathered in the central courtyard for assembly, showing exactly where his classroom was and the route he took to school and comparing this to his present situation, offered a way of talking about some of the difficulties he was currently experiencing. For Carlos, drawing the games he used to play in the playground provided an opportunity to talk about his current relationships with some of the other children, an area he was also finding very problematic.

These media productions facilitated this kind of discussion, although they were not oriented towards an external audience. However, after some months in the club, some productions of this kind were posted on the project intranet and addressed to a wider audience. Some children in Germany took stills cameras home and posted the resulting photo stories. Sharmake in the Dutch club made a photo story tracing his family's journey from Somalia, using photos of his grandfather (whom he had never met but knew through photos and stories) as well as contemporary photos of his family in the Netherlands.

Another starting point for learning the skills and starting to communicate between the clubs was for each club to make a 'hello' video introducing themselves and their locations to the others. These were posted on the project intranet. In this case, the audience was clear but unknown, and the productions reflected this. Each club drew on well-known symbols: the children in Rome filmed the Coliseum for their opening shot; those in London included a red double-decker bus, a letterbox and postcards of Tower Bridge; while the children in Sweden showed fishing in the nearby river. Most of the children introduced themselves saying how old they were and identifying their countries of origin. Yet even within these stereotypes, children in other clubs expressed some surprises. Where was the snow in Sweden? This video could not be from Germany, because some of the girls were wearing a hijab!

On the other hand, what sparked the children's interest and drew them together was the fact that Italy had used Eminem on the soundtrack (see Chapter 9) and that Sweden had offered them a packet of sweets. It was through a recognition of a shared global culture or simply through 'small' acts of connection – rather than as a result of any significant compulsion to express their experiences – that a basis for communication began to emerge. The role of the adult media educators was crucial here. Broadly speaking, the children were keen to use the occasion of media production as an opportunity to play with the possibilities of the technology, for its own sake or for their immediate peers. It was the educators who reminded them of the external audience and the need to take account of what they might have to know in order to make sense of, or to enjoy, their productions.

Meanwhile, several of the clubs looked at photographs taken by professional photographers that touched on aspects of the migration experience. For example, the UK club visited an exhibition of photo-graphs by Sebastian Salgado. In some cases, these images clearly had an emotional resonance with their own experiences, and this allowed them to look beyond the cultural specificity of the photos they viewed. For example, David was particularly interested in a photo of children riding between the carriages of a train. For him, the fact that one of them had no shoes reminded him of Angola; and this was an image to which he repeatedly returned. Likewise, the symbols employed by the children in their own productions were determined by their own cultural back-grounds, their values, beliefs, attitudes and experiences, including those of migration itself and the negotiations of inclusion and exclusion in their new countries of residence.

## Research-related stories

As the children's production skills developed and they settled into the club work, we began to address the research themes more directly, initially through discussions and interviews and subsequently through the children producing short videotapes. There are two productions in particular we would like to discuss here. They address different research areas, and both received very different responses from the other clubs.

The first, which is entitled *Ali and Vladimir*, was made in the Greek club and grew out of discussions about friendship. It is a well-structured, quite powerful dramatisation of a family story. A boy who has recently arrived in the city is lonely and without friends, while outside he can hear children playing. He cries as he looks at a photograph. Later he is nearly run down by a car as he tries to cross the road. He is rescued by two boys and they make friends; he then invites them home and his mother prepares them something to eat. The next sequence involves his father: he loses his job and the family are forced to move. They say tearful farewells to their friends and exchange mementoes. The film does not use dialogue, but there are brief titles in English to lead us through each scene and explain what is happening.

The theme for this production emerged through discussion of the issue of friendship and was then formalised into an agreed story and acted out by the children. In this case, at a fairly early stage in the project, it was filmed and edited by the media educator, with the guidance of the children. The video tells a very common migration story; and for our purposes as directors of the project, it provided quite an effective way of presenting the difficulties and disruptions that many refugee and migrant children experience. It was well received by the other researchers and by other adults who have seen it; and we included an excerpt from it in the DVD that we produced specifically targeting policy-makers at the end of the project. Nevertheless, there is a confusion here about the audience the children were aiming at and a conflict between research and production needs that is a central dilemma in many projects of this nature. The video tells a powerful, authentic story that fits into our concerns; but it also talks of one type of experience, in a way that largely confirms well-rehearsed stereotypes. As the project proceeded, it became clear that this was not necessarily what the children wanted to do. The Swedish report discusses the reception of this film in terms of narrative structure, but there is also a strong sense that these apparently 'universal' experiences did not necessarily correspond to how the children saw their own lives:

> there were some productions that were very ambitious in terms of visual language, plot and story structure, but still required a little too much from the viewer. The Greek production *Ali and Vladimir* was not grasped by the Swedish viewers. When we asked them what the story was about, they had no idea about the plot. I told them that it was about a family who had to leave the country, because the father had lost his job, but the children looked a bit confused. The topic was familiar for the children, as they have experienced severe moments of separation themselves. But they had no use for this experience when interpreting the film.

The reception in the United Kingdom was similarly distant. In viewing these early productions, the children were looking for information about the other places and children involved in the research. Here again, the film did not speak of their lives in the present or connect visually or aurally with any shared culture: it felt too distant, too much like somebody else's narrative. The main comments were criticisms of the way the girl who played the mother wore her hijab or of exactly how the food was served – both questioning the film's authenticity. On the other hand, the film did provoke some specific discussion about the significance of taking your new friends home and the different customs involved in this. One girl started talking about how she never invited her 'English' friends home, and they did not invite her either; and it seemed that this was partly because she was not sure of the right etiquette. Of course, it might well have been that the film did indeed touch their experiences, but that they did not want to talk about this, on the grounds that doing so would be too exposing. However, we would argue that the 'voice' of the video was ultimately that of an adult, and as a result it spoke more easily to an adult rather than a youth audience. By contrast, this was not what the children in the other clubs were expecting or seeking.

The second production we would like to consider here was made in the UK club. Again, it arose out of discussions in the club sessions, in this case about school, but also out of a conversation about school detentions that had been running among the children over several weeks. The school where the club was located was in a neighbourhood where many of the members did not feel safe. There were stories circulating about several children who had been mugged on their way home from school. Being put in detention meant that you would be going home after the main crowd leaving school, which they felt protected them to some extent. There also appeared to be some misunderstanding about why you were put in detention. Most of the children had not experienced this type of punishment in their previous schools. As a way of discussing this further, we asked some of the children to prepare a short film about the reasons for detention. Three of them took on the task and developed a short story that they then acted out, filmed and edited (with some assistance from the media educator).

The resulting video is entitled *The Register*. Registration time (roll call) is disrupted by two boys starting a fight about some stolen money. The teacher intervenes and says that both of them will go to detention unless the money is returned. The boys' angry responses clearly show that they feel the punishment is unfair. The production is somewhat rough around the edges – there are problems with sound and wobbly camerawork – but the main incident is fairly clearly portrayed. The fight itself continues for too long, not least because the participants were clearly enjoying it! It was in the course of this production that one of the girls in the club, Brigitta, first understood the role of editing. Initially, she had wanted to film the whole sequence in one shot. Through explanation and demonstration, she came to realise the purpose of editing – both in terms of the brevity needed and in terms of how you could build a story visually. This production was shown to the others in the UK club and posted on the project intranet.

The central concern here was with fighting in school and its consequences. This was an issue to which some of the children in the other clubs related very directly and one which went beyond their identities as migrants. It was a very straightforward story, obviously filmed by the children themselves, and it provoked discussions in the other clubs about fighting, bullying and racism. Like *Ali and Vladimir*, it was a simple drama, with a straightforward aim or 'message'. However, its primary address was not to an adult audience of 'policy-makers' – to whom it would probably have seemed insignificant and 'childish' – but to other children. In this sense, while addressing one of our research themes, it also showed signs of the emergence of a more independent voice.

## A space for play

Over the period of the project, each of the clubs developed a certain 'house style', which derived at least partly from the media educators and their own preferred ways of working. However, the children also began to experiment themselves and to develop their own voices. Their ideas and expectations about working with media were sometimes quite different from those of the educators and the researchers. While we tended to think in terms of more or less 'finished' products, in a closed form, they expected to be able to experiment in a more spontaneous and open-ended way. In some cases, this was a matter of playing with the technology – for example, with the 'tricks' that could be achieved through editing – while in others it was about acting and performance. Thus, alongside the productions that related directly to our research themes, there were several that took a much more playful form.

The pleasure and amusement to be gained from performing in front of the camera was not something that simply 'wore off' as the project proceeded. We eventually decided to utilise this, and some clubs set up a private space screened off from the other club activities where children could simply go and talk to the camera or play-act in front of it. This was facilitated to some degree by the LCD screen on the cameras that could be flipped round, allowing them to easily watch what they were filming. Thus, in one Swedish video modelled on the *Big Brother* 'diary room', one girl talked about difficulties she was having with her friends. In the Dutch club, a boy played wild games with a kind of blanket over his head. The freedom that was allowed here spilled over into other videos made in the more public spaces of the clubs. For example, one video made in Greece showed two boys wearing head scarves shouting about Osama bin Laden, wielding a tripod as a gun and subsequently rolling

*Picture 9*   Playing to the camera in the Dutch club

on the floor 'dying'. Since both the boys' families had been affected by armed conflict, there was clearly a personal resonance to this play; but here they were bouncing around and laughing, thoroughly enjoying subverting the seriousness with which such issues are often represented. Most of these videos were made for viewing within their own clubs, and only a few found their way onto the intranet – although this in itself raises interesting issues about how the children chose to represent themselves for a wider audience.

Of course, such visual explorations of the self were often surrounded by uncertainties, particularly for the older children. In many of the photos the children took of themselves, they were very conscious of the contexts in which the photos were taken and what backgrounds they chose, anticipating the opinion of the audience who would be viewing them. Here, the Swedish researchers describe one such occasion, where this uncertainty mingled with a more playful element of performance:

Hana and Shpresa posed in front of Fredrik [the media educator] for the group photography. Both are very self-critical and are checking in the camera how they look. They pose together, they are hugging and are really anxious to show up their very best appearance. They are fixing their hair, but suddenly they are children making mimes and gestures. Hana shoots a picture of Shpresa where she is lying on all fours like a model.When experimenting, they go out in the spacious corridor. Here they feel free to experiment without adult intervention or control. This is their secret room, after the school day. Yet their control and approval of the picture seems to be compulsory.

Meanwhile, there was often another kind of play being carried out here – that is, play with the camera and the other technology itself. For example, in the United Kingdom one boy worked on his own production, using toys he had brought from home (a blue car and 'action man' figures). He used the camera to film the car in close-up crashing through a line of pens so that it appeared to be a full size car in an action movie. He also played with his action men climbing up a picture of a skyscraper, again in close-up. Meanwhile, he narrated the commentary to himself, as young children often do while playing, voicing the thoughts of the figure and mimicking a TV commentary on the crash and the figure trying to get into the building. Here the camera was not a tool for communicating any message, but rather another toy to add to his collection: it allowed him to play with familiar media images, and to some degree place himself within them, creating his own fantasy world.

In Greece, one of the boys asked if he could take the camera onto the roof of the building. He went on his own and filmed the rooftops of Athens, with the traffic noise in the background. The only words spoken are at the end when he says 'I want the camera to do something!' When he had finished, he returned the camera, said nothing about what he had been doing and showed no interest in seeing the tape. It may have been simply the experience of filming that counted; or perhaps he was disappointed in the possibilities the camera offered. However, the camera had enabled him to explore a new aspect of the city in which he had recently arrived; and it is not incidental that he was living at the time with his family in one basement room, a fact gleaned from interviews and a family visit.

Several clubs capitalised on this more playful use of media by using animation, particularly claymation, to tell simple stories. This was a popular genre in the children's television viewing, associated both with humour and social comment (for example, in the case of *The Simpsons*); and it is also a highly visual form, reducing the need for verbal communication. In this context, it also offered the possibility of telling personal

*Picture 10*  Playing football in *On the Beach:* claymation

stories at a distance, with less danger of exposure. For example, one of the first productions by the children in Greece was an animation (in this case made from cutout drawings) that featured begging as part of the narrative. This was at a time when so-called 'economic' migrants were being accused of street begging in many major European cities and allowed the children to talk about how this affected them.

In general, the claymation films were well received by the other clubs, mainly because of their humour and simple narratives. The one we would like to discuss here is called *On the Beach*. It was made in the German club by Mustafa, who was originally from Tunisia. The video opens with pictures of Tunisia filmed from postcards brought back from a recent holiday with his family. They show pictures of the beach, palm trees and buildings. You can hear the sea swishing in the background. Then three boys are seen playing football on the beach, which is made with sand that Mustafa had also brought back from his holiday. Suddenly, two of the boys run away in fear, leaving the third puzzled until a monster comes up behind him and knocks him down. The monster in close-up looms over him, but the boy gets up and knocks the monster down in turn. The conflict is then resolved and the two play football together. Children in the other clubs enjoyed this film a great deal and were keen to know how it had been made.

The discussion on the intranet was full of questions:

| Author | Comment |
|---|---|
| **Worldkids** | **About the animation** |
| Netherlands | The animation was very good. |
| 13/06/03 | We liked the use of clay. |
| | We liked the sounds. |
| | Because of the pictures the beach looked like a real beach. |
| | Here are some questions about your animation. |
| | – How much time did you spend to prepare and to make the animation? |
| | – Whom does the pictures belong to? |
| | – Who made the shooting? |
| | – How have you create the sand? |
| **MUSTAFA** | **HALLO** |
| Germany | ALSO ICH HAb drei schtunden von dem film gebraucht das war lange zeit. |
| 14/06/03 | die foto geheuren mir das habe ich in TUNISIEN gemacht. |
| | der film habe ich selber gemacht. |
| | der sand habe ich von TUNISIEN GEBRACGT |
| | MUSTAFA |
| **MUSTAFA** | **(TRANSLATION)** |
| Germany | HALLO |
| 14/06/03 | Well it took me three hours to make the film |
| | It was a long time. |
| | The pictures are mine, I took them in TUNISIA. |
| | I made the film myself. |
| | I brought the sand from TUNISIA. |
| | MUSTAFA |

Unlike some of the other online exchanges, this was quite effective because of the concrete nature of the questions. However, what is most interesting here is how Mustafa invokes Tunisia (in capital letters) and

*Picture 11*   Claymation: playing football

identifies so strongly with it. He was a boy who found concentration difficult; and the recognition of his efforts by the Dutch club was clearly important. The success of his production meant that he could publicly and proudly identify with his origins.

At the same time, by allowing him a degree of distance, and through its association with humour, the form of animation also allowed him to risk exposure. As we have noted, telling stories through a 'third person', such as puppets, drawn animations or, as in this case, claymation, is a method increasingly used in therapeutic work to help young people come to terms with traumatic or highly personal experiences (Eokter, 1998; Kalmanowitz and Lloyd, 1997). In this case, the film is not merely a simple, funny story of difficulties overcome: making it also had a wider significance for Mustafa. The place of football is not incidental in this respect. For all the boys, football was a topic that allowed them to establish common ground between the clubs: in several of the videos, they wear football shirts, quite consciously marking their support for well-known teams in other countries (in *Ali and Vladimir*, for example,

*Picture 12*   Preparing figures for a claymation

one of the boys wears a Beckham shirt). Football is of course a key part of the global commercial culture we discussed in Chapter 4, and so it was not surprising to find that it was also a topic of discussion on the project intranet. In Mustafa's film, the game is a mark of contact and friendship, both between the three boys but also between the monster and the boy. Standing up to the monster and making friends with him could be interpreted as a story of emotional problems overcome, and in the context of this film as a representation of leaving old friends and meeting new ones through the shared experience of football. In combination with Mustafa's use of pictures and objects from Tunisia, this makes it possible to read his film as a personal exploration of migration and of his relationship with his country of origin.

## Questions of interpretation

As this implies, the meanings of these productions – particularly for the children who made them – are not necessarily straightforward or open

*Picture 13*   Beckham T-shirt worn in Ali and Vladimir in Greece

to easy inspection. It is largely for this reason that productions cannot be viewed in isolation, and need to be read in relation to other data drawn from observations and interviews. A further example bears this out. *Brigitta's Colours and Sounds* was made in the UK club by a 12-year-old girl from Lithuania. She had previously worked on *The Register*, discussed above, although this production was made on her own. Along with the other children, Brigitta took a camera home, but she returned saying that there was nothing to film. This may partly have reflected her anxiety about revealing too much about her home to a public audience – particularly since the family were in the country precariously and might have to leave at any time. We discussed the possibilities with her and agreed that she would only film things in close-up. She returned with some footage of various objects at home that she said were significant for her: a Winnie the Pooh clock her grandparents had sent her from Lithuania, a toy belonging to her brother, a poster and the wallpaper in her bedroom. We then discussed this and she added drawings of a cooking pot, a bag and a pencil. Meanwhile, she had been complaining that everything was so grey (which appears to be a common feeling for those who migrate to the United Kingdom!) and she had gone round the school building filming any surfaces with colour and texture. The media educator suggested putting these together as an editing exercise, developing her skills from *The Register*. She did this and subsequently added sound, which she improvised using various percussion instruments. She was really pleased with the final result, which she took home to show her parents.

One of the interesting things about this production is that, unlike most of the others, it appears not to derive from Brigitte's media consumption, but to have developed only as a result of the discussions and her own experiments in the club. This is hard to know and may well be a false assumption since in situations of migration children can have many varied experiences of media and cultural expression. Even so, on the face of it, it is quite an avant-garde piece, a kind of poetic photo-essay that is difficult for outsiders to interpret. It is a compilation of symbols and sensual and visual expressions that are highly meaningful for the author, and for those who know her well, although it barely attempts to speak to a wider audience. Yet together with the other data that we gathered about Brigitta, it can be interpreted as a reflection of her personal experience of migration – an experience in which objects and physical sensations of place often play a crucial role.

A further example here illustrates some of the difficulties that this can cause, particularly in the context of projects that involve dialogues and exchanges across national and cultural differences, as CHICAM did. Obviously, some types of productions lent themselves more easily to this exchange than others. Where the exchange did not work, this was due to a variety of factors: some productions were simply more 'personal' than others, while in other cases the stories were just too difficult to understand without access to the language. In some instances, however, productions could only be understood within a specific national context. One such film made in the Netherlands was a production called *Sinterklaas*, based on the Dutch version of the St Nicholas story. The group had chosen to make this production since this was a festival currently being celebrated in their schools and neighbourhoods, which some of them did not understand.

However, there was an additional issue here. Not only was the story itself difficult to understand outside the Dutch context, but it is also controversial within the Netherlands. Sinterklaas traditionally wears a red bishop's costume and is accompanied by one or several mischievous black boys (Zwarte Pieten – 'Black Petes'), who wear Moorish dress. During the Middle Ages, the Zwarte Pieten were associated with the devil, although over the years they have also taken on a racial connotation. There have been several debates in the Netherlands about how to depict this element of the story. In some cases, the fact that Pete is black and a slave is changed, while in others people insist that since this is an old story it should remain intact: some also suggest that the boys' faces are merely black with soot from climbing the chimneys to deliver presents. The arrival of Sinterklaas is announced on television and radio, shops are filled with figures from the story alongside special sweets, cakes and gifts. People make special gifts for family and friends.

Because one of the black boys in the club did not wish to play Zwarte Piet, the story was adapted. Rather than following the traditional narrative, the group added in a thief who comes to steal the gifts Sinterklaas brings. This was also seen as making the story more exciting. However, since the boy playing the thief was black, this change brought its own problems for the audience (if not for the players), particularly in the UK club. This was not helped by the fact that the slave boy who was substituted was wearing a black plastic mask, in order to stick more closely to the original story – although this looked more like a minstrel mask. This was the children's own solution to the racial issue, but to an outside audience it simply compounded it. To some extent, then, the problem was that the story was simply too obscure and nationally specific; but it also included representations that were seen by some of the other children (and indeed the researchers) as offensive and racist. While this is perhaps an unusually spectacular example, it does nevertheless point to some of the broader difficulties of interpretation that can arise in these kinds of cross-national exchanges.

## Speaking positions

CHICAM set out to enable the children to explore and represent their own experiences, specifically as migrants or as refugees. While this was a worthy aim, and one we would still wish to defend, it was significantly more problematic than might at first appear. Many of the children had good reasons to want to preserve their own privacy and that of their families. Some of these were perhaps typical of children of their age, although others were quite specifically to do with their status as refugees or migrants. Several of the children's families had left their country of origin under threat of violence and their permission to remain in the receiving country had only been granted temporarily or was still being pursued. This precarious status made them – and their families – justifiably suspicious of public visibility. This was a particularly important concern when it came to 'publishing' the children's productions on the Internet. On the one hand, we wanted to make the children's productions available to a wider audience; and we also wanted the children themselves to enjoy the self-esteem that this could provide. But we did not wish to do so at the cost of undermining or jeopardising their safety and their right to privacy.

More generally, the children's position as migrants – as members of minority groups who were often stigmatised or abused by members of the host society – created a more general form of insecurity. From what position was it possible for them to speak? The constitution of our clubs – which were generally only open to those who were defined as 'migrants' – in some ways compounded this marginal position; and, of course, part of our interest as researchers was precisely in encouraging the children to offer us perspectives and representations that were specific to their position as migrants. In a sense, we could not avoid constructing the children as *representatives* of the broader category of 'migrant' – even though this was only one facet of their identities. The danger here was of 'othering' – and, in the process, of exoticising or merely patronising – some essentialised 'migrant' experience, albeit in the interests of making it publicly visible.

Moreover, the children did not necessarily want to be seen primarily as migrants or to speak from that position – and some attempted quite strongly to disavow it. Some of the children in the Italian club even spoke of *'those* poor refugees' in the other clubs, clearly dissociating themselves from such a label. A boy in the United Kingdom suddenly decided to leave because he belatedly discovered that the club was 'for refugees' – although he himself was a refugee and had been told at the outset and several times over the preceding months what the aims and membership of the club were. It was clear that some of the children at least had internalised the generally pejorative view of migrants (and more specifically of asylum seekers) that was prevalent within the wider society. 'Speaking as a migrant' was therefore the very last thing many of them would have wanted to do. For these reasons, our aim of enabling the children to represent and express perspectives that were specific to the migrant experience was quite problematic.

Indeed, in retrospect, some of our early activities could be accused of inviting the children to stereotype themselves. This was true to some extent of the 'hello' videos, discussed above, and of the instances where children were asked to bring in 'something from your country', an object or a photograph that reminded them of their country of origin. In many cases, what they brought in were simply tourist souvenirs or objects

*Picture 14*   Young film makers in Italy

that carried little meaning for them. In general, these kinds of activities were undertaken in the early meetings of the clubs, where the children were more keen to figure out and to meet what they imagined were the expectations of the adults.

By contrast, some of the later productions produced much more nuanced and sophisticated reflections on these issues. For example, in one Italian video, *PiazzaVittorio*, the children interviewed people on the street in a high immigration area and asked them to define their identities. Many definitions emerged from this context: from very close ties with the country of origin to a larger cultural identity (being African) or a mixture (being 'half and half'). This more investigative approach also took the focus away from the children, placing them in a position of power (as interviewers), and prevented them from being seen as merely the bearers of some singular national culture.

Furthermore, when we look at the 'incidental' footage filmed during the clubs, when the children were not consciously making a film, it is striking to see how interested they are both in the physical appearance and 'body language' of their friends and in the symbols they wear – such as the images on T-shirts, clothing and jewellery. This spontaneous material somehow says more about questions of identity and how it is lived out than some of the more formal productions where the children were explicitly asked to address these issues.

## Conclusion

Research is always a learning process for researchers themselves, as much as it can sometimes be for their subjects. In this case, we learnt a great deal about the difficulties both of participatory research and of intercultural dialogues. There will always be compromises between the agendas of researchers and those of the people whose experiences they seek to research. We did not begin this project with any naïve belief that giving children access to media production would somehow magically 'empower' them, or enable their voices to be heard – although we emerged from it even more convinced of the difficulty and complexity of such an approach.

Nevertheless, we continue to believe that this creative, participatory use of media provides exciting possibilities – both for us as researchers and for the young people whom we study – that are less easily available using other methods. It does to some extent begin to equalise the power relationships between us and permit young people to represent themselves in their own terms. For migrant children, who are typically rendered invisible both in research and in the public media, this has a particular and perhaps unique significance.

# 9
# Rapping All Over the World: Music, Media and Intercultural Communication

Music can provide a powerful means of representing identity, and of asserting cultural difference. Yet it also increasingly crosses boundaries, offering the potential for transnational communication and new forms of global culture. This applies particularly to children and young people – both to their consumption of music and to what they produce. The expanding array of new media technologies offers many different opportunities for young people to make and exchange music, through file-sharing, sampling, re-mixing and creating their own sounds. Youth cultures may have local references and influences, but they are also increasingly global, allowing young people from very different parts of the world to recognise, identify with and utilise similar styles of music, and the varieties of fashion, graphics and dance that are associated with them. Contemporary popular music often incorporates a range of styles, bringing them together to create new 'hybrid' forms. For children who have experienced migration, separation and new settlement, and who are coming to terms with different cultural influences, the role of music can therefore be particularly significant.

Of course, developments in music also reflect broader social, economic and political changes. Governments, commercial companies and nationalist movements frequently play a key role in the local and global circulation of musical forms. Music has long been used to create a national identity through national anthems or the promotion of particular forms of popular music – and the exclusion of others. The concern that a given national identity will become corrupted can lead to minority or 'alien' forms of music being sidelined or repressed. For example, in Bulgaria today *chalga* (a popular music form which draws on traditional gypsy music) is effectively censored because of the government's concern to build a Western orientation and deny the historical links with Turkey and the 'East'. As Levy (2004: 51) states, sometimes 'in contesting what is acceptable to the elite it is often music from far away that is more acceptable than minority music locally'. She notes the similarities with other examples of musical repression, particularly of 'black' music such as the blues and early jazz in the United States. To give a different example, rock music in the former Soviet Union met with suspicion and censorship, and was seen to be undermining youth morality and threatening the political system, because it originated in the capitalist United States. Yet in the United States itself, it was also feared and seen as a threat to community and family values, not least because its origins were associated with 'black' music.

In all these examples, the role of migration and global media are central. Musical forms travel, taking with them some of the sentiments that created them, but also being adapted for new purposes and contexts. For example, reggae is closely identified with Jamaica, yet its power as a form of protest has spread much more widely, and been reworked to address specific local concerns elsewhere. Closely aligned to Rastafari-anism and a desire for reparation for the oppression of slavery, reggae was taken up and adapted in the United Kingdom in the late 1970s by young people (both black and white) protesting at the exclusion of black youth from British national culture, in the so-called 'Two-Tone' move-ment – although paradoxically it was also a favoured form among racist skinhead groups (Jones, 1988). In a different way, Brazilian music reflects its rich but difficult colonial and slave history, incorporating influences from both Africa and Europe; and it is now celebrated internationally as a demonstration of rich cultural diversity. As Whiteley et al. (2004: 3) suggest, music can help to express forms of community identity that are strongly rooted in specific locations; but it can also help to articulate more symbolic ideas of community that transcend space and time.

Rap and hip-hop – which will be the particular focus of attention in this chapter – have been widely seen as an example of these new global-ised musical cultures. Hip-hop is an expressive musical and performance form that developed from the meeting of different cultures; but it is also being adapted throughout the world to reflect and give voice to the local conditions and concerns of young people. Most accounts of the history of rap (for example, Chang, 2005; Toop, 1998) stress its didactic nature, the ways in which early rap in particular focused on educating its audience about black history, leaders and resistance – what is some-times termed 'message' rap. However, rap was also born out of gang life and the posturing of gang leaders – 'gangsta' rap. Both traditions speak from local neighbourhood conditions, depicting particular places and events, 'representing' the 'hood and its inhabitants. Rappers' identity is very much connected to their posse (gang members and followers) and their need to speak of their local experiences (Forman, 2000), 'keeping it real' and not 'selling out' to commercial success (Huq, 2006:113). Rap videos are often set and located in specific neighbourhoods: Keyes (2002) describes how video producers go to great lengths to create a sense of the artist's locality and belonging.

However, rap is also increasingly used in very different settings, both to assert other local identities and to claim identification with a global youth culture (sometimes significantly termed the 'hip-hop nation'). This carries particular significance for migrant youth. For example, Solomon (2005) traces the flow of rap and hip-hop between Turkey and Germany in an ongoing diasporic dialogue which relies on the Internet to avoid Turkish government censorship. Likewise, Sernhede (2002) describes how rap music has become a kind of symbol for the feeling of social exclusion among immigrant boys from Latin America and the Balkans living in ghettos and segregated areas in Sweden. In France, which has a very vibrant hip-hop scene, a high proportion of rappers come from West African, North African, Arab and Mediterranean migrant origins (Mitchell, 1998, Huq, 2006). Other accounts (Bennett, 2000; Mitchell, 2001) testify to the ways in which rap is being appropriated in different ways in different settings around the globe. The mixing of local and international languages creates what Mitchell (2001) calls 'resistance vernaculars' that speak to local audiences while still maintaining a global connection. For example, Strelitz (2004) explores the ways in which American rap spoke to young black youth in South Africa under apartheid.

The fact that hip-hop has its roots in different musical and performance traditions (Jamaican toasting, Puerto Rican dance styles and so on) and is therefore, even in its origins, a hybrid form may mean that it lends itself more easily to the development of international variations. As a form that encompasses fashion, language, dance, graffiti, video and technology, it provides rich resources with which meaning can be inscribed and negotiated, and specific forms of 'subcultural capital' (Thornton, 1995) that allow it to represent different locales and identities. The idea of 'mix' or 'bricolage' is central to hip-hop (Simpson, 1996). The 'mix' creates a loose structure, in which new and 'borrowed' elements can be changed and rearranged over and over again. The creation of new mixes may involve elements of imitation, although the imitation itself acquires a new meaning as a result of the person who appropriates it, and the context in which it occurs. In this respect, the global distribution and creation of rap could be seen as a telling example of the process of 'glocalisation' (Robertson, 1995), discussed in Chapter 1.

However, this argument can become over-romanticised. Obviously, much hip-hop style has become a fashion accessory and is promoted for commercial rather than 'counter-cultural' reasons. Much of the 'bling-bling' rhetoric of contemporary gangsta rap seems a very long way from the oppression of the ghetto – although in some respects it could be seen precisely to flaunt its denial of stereotypes of black poverty. The music is also very reliant on technology, both in the way it is produced but also in reaching its audience; and as such, it can be quite dependent on access to economic capital. Solomon's study (2005), for example, stresses the fact that the youth he studied in Istanbul were middle-class kids who had become involved in rap partly because of their interest in computers and because they had access to the necessary technology.

Furthermore, the process of 'glocalisation' can be far from smooth or easy. On the contrary, it may be 'fraught with tensions and contradictions as young people try to reconcile issues of musical and stylistic authenticity with those of locality, identity and everyday life' (Bennett, 2000). For example, there is a significant debate in many European countries about the authenticity (or lack of it) that is at stake in rapping in languages other than English; while in the UK hip-hop scene, there is an ongoing disagreement over the use of American or British accents.

How young people relate to music, and how they use and adapt it, therefore raises several interesting questions in the context of our own research. What musical forms do young migrants and refugees draw on when making their own productions? What role does this play in communicating the experiences of migration? And how are such productions received and interpreted by other young people? In this chapter, we look more closely at the role of music in some of the CHICAM productions.

## The place of music

As we have noted (Chapter 5), music was very important to all the children in the CHICAM clubs. In terms both of maintaining existing cultural identifications and of exploring new cultures, music played a similar role to television; although in some respects, it was seen more as the children's 'own' culture, that was somehow distinct and separate from that of adults. Commercial 'Western' pop music was a shared enthusiasm throughout the clubs: the children talked a great deal about pop celebrities, sang and discussed their music, watched MTV videos and searched the web for information about them, often downloading songs and lyrics. Favourites were contested, and it was clear that they were symbolic of different styles, fashions and social groups or 'tribes'. Nevertheless, knowing about and listening to this form of music gave the children a means of entry into the wider peer group.

By contrast, much of the music that the children had grown up with, and that was played at home, was excluded from the public gaze. Many of the children hid their more diverse musical tastes and only spoke of them selectively with their close friends, with friends from the same country, or with us in private. For example, the children in the UK club were reluctant to play music from their countries or regions of origin in public, although some allowed the researcher to listen to it on their walkman or personal radio (none of them yet had an MP3 player). Despite the importance of music in their lives, most of the early videos did not include it except where this was initiated by the media educators. One exception to this was the German 'hello' video, which features a girl from the Dominican Republic teaching another girl salsa dancing. As a more 'accepted' international form, this was safe to include and in fact was regarded by the other children as having high status.

However, towards the end of the project, a video was made in the Greek club that sparked an excited response by the Turkish and Kosovan children in the other clubs. The video is a rendition of a poem by Nazim Hikmet, accompanied by the playing of the saz, a traditional Turkish instrument. Hikmet is now widely acclaimed as one of the leading modern Turkish poets; although throughout his life, he was involved in radical politics, was imprisoned by the government and stripped of his Turkish citizenship, and spent many years travelling and in exile. His work was only widely distributed in Turkey after his death in 1963, although much of it continues to be suppressed.

Elcin, a 12-year-old Turkish Kurdish boy, had wanted to shoot this for a long time and seized the opportunity to do it one afternoon when he and two of the girls from the club were at the cultural centre where they spent much of their out of school time. He went straight into a small music room and placed the camera right in front of him, slightly lower than eye level, checking the shot through the reversible LCD screen. The video is a still, continuous shot of himself playing the saz while Rengin speaks the poem in a mounting and powerful crescendo. At the end of the song, Elcin gets up and you see him turning off the camera. It is the live performance he is interested in, not the special effects or dance moves of commercial music videos.

*Picture 15*   Elcin and Rengin (+saz) performing

The saz is a type of long-necked lute widely used in folk music across Turkey and the wider region. It was familiar to several of the children in the clubs and associated closely with their families and places of origin. Traditionally it is played by travelling musicians and often used in political protest music. Elcin was a regular performer at political meetings of the Kurdish communist party, of which his parents were active members. In his choice of the poem, he is following in the path of a musician, Zulfu Livaneli, known in the 1980s for his musical renditions of Hikmet's radical poetry. Hikmet was clearly an important political and cultural figure for Elcin and for his family.

Interestingly, however, the poem in this video is recited in Greek rather than in Turkish – which might itself be seen as a rather paradoxical political shift. Because of this, the Turkish children in the other clubs could not understand the words, although they understood and related to the form of the piece at an emotional and aesthetic level (and quite possibly, since many were children of Kurdish/Turkish parentage, at a political level as well). The posting of the video on the project intranet gave them 'permission' to communicate in the project intranet in Turkish. The video was watched enthusiastically in the German club, where there was a majority of Turkish/Kurdish children. It was ranked first in the club's 'film jury' evaluation, and the following comment was placed on the intranet:

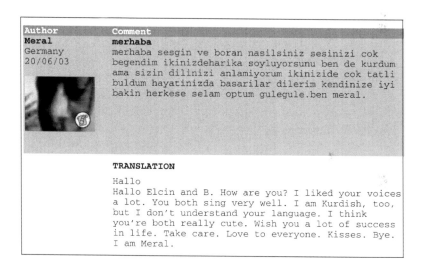

| Author | Comment |
| --- | --- |
| **Meral**<br>Germany<br>20/06/03 | **merhaba**<br>merhaba sesgin ve boran nasilsiniz sesinizi cok begendim ikinizdeharika soyluyorsunu ben de kurdum ama sizin dilinizi anlamiyorum ikinizide cok tatli buldum hayatinizda basarilar dilerim kendinize iyi bakin herkese selam optum gulegule.ben meral. |

TRANSLATION

Hallo
Hallo Elcin and B. How are you? I liked your voices a lot. You both sing very well. I am Kurdish, too, but I don't understand your language. I think you're both really cute. Wish you a lot of success in life. Take care. Love to everyone. Kisses. Bye. I am Meral.

In this instance, a 'local' musical form is used to create transnational or diasporic communication – albeit in a translated form. Although the video did not adopt an MTV format, it was very enthusiastically received. Interestingly, this was despite the fact that the majority of the children could not understand the words: it was the form of the poem and the music, and to some degree the passion and directness of the performance, that came across. Similar points could be made about the raps that we discuss next: here again, it was the form and the delivery that facilitated the initial connection, while the words themselves played a secondary role.

## The Place to Be

Most studies of rap culture have concentrated on older adolescents; although in our research, it was clear that this was a significant genre for most of the children in all the CHICAM clubs. It was quite difficult, particularly in the early stages of the project, to engage the children in the online discussions and exchanges; but the first real spark of interest came as a result of the Italian 'hello' video that used Eminem as a soundtrack. Several months later, a music video production from the UK club called 'The Place to Be' was posted on the intranet that again provoked some interesting responses.

David, the author of 'The Place to Be', was a 14-year-old boy from Angola who had been living in the United Kingdom for 2 years. He had arrived as an unaccompanied asylum seeker and was living with extended family members in East London. He never spoke about his parents or his life in Angola, other than to refer to the plane journey on his own and his desire to focus on the future and adapt to his new circumstances. From the start, he saw himself as a performer and was reluctant to take part in the production side of the media work. However, one afternoon, working alone with the researcher he began to play with making a sound track for a group production the club was completing. He began (with some encouragement) to use objects in the room to create different sound effects and lay them straight onto the soundtrack. The afternoon ended with him conducting the others in creating overlaid voice patterns that again were immediately edited in. This experience encouraged him to participate more fully in the subsequent sessions. Sound was clearly his entry point to media production.

David was also an ardent fan of the rapper Tupac Shakur, and spent a lot of time in the club searching for Tupac websites. Since his death, Tupac has taken on a mythic quality for many fans. His history as a talented youngster who had to struggle with relocation, family separation and violence is part of the rap tradition (White,1997). His lyrics are a mix of romanticism and violence, speaking of his love for his mother, family and friends, and of the injustices of society; while at the same time he was being indicted for violent crimes, and his death came about as a result of warfare between East and West coast gangs in the United States in 1996. David was very interested in the fan debate about whether Tupac was alive or dead. He also wrote poetry at home and said that this was his way of dealing with issues that worried him. Yet although he wrote privately, he didn't talk about this publicly.

'The Place to Be' arose from a group discussion about the club members' experiences of schools. Many of the topics raised by the group gave a fairly negative view of their present school life. In the group, David was the only one who dissented from this. Despite what he and his teachers had told us about his difficulties in school, he insisted on portraying it in a positive light. The researcher asked him to write a rap about school and suggested that he direct the filming and edit the piece himself. He rose to the occasion and arrived at the club the following week with a script:

THE PLACE TO BE
School fantastic the teachers are cool
I am a teen but don't take me as a fool
My mission is to study hard, be brave
Never fall apart
And dress smart
I came here to learn
Always look at where I'm gonna turn
Listen to the teacher if u wanna have a future
Try not to be an abuser
Cos if you're not qualified u a loser
Try to keep your head up
Never give up
Cos in the future u gonna pay your own bill
Starting tomorrow realise that school is for real
Cos if u turn into a gang dealing
Look at the pain u might feel
School school the place to be school
Be a man
I am trying to help you my friend
We all go through hard times
So let me hold your hand
I won't say this again


This is a very positive take on school, teachers and educational aspirations. David states that he came to the United Kingdom to learn and to improve his circumstances. He takes, and is encouraging others to take, responsibility for their lives. He states that he is young (a teenager) but not irresponsible. But he also makes it clear that he lives with the street temptations of drugs and gangs, that are difficult to resist. The rap clearly arises from his experience as an asylum seeker and black youth coming to this country to make a new future and living in the East End of London with its drug and gun problems. At the time that David produced 'The Place To Be', there had been an ongoing public debate in the United Kingdom about the influence of rap on violent crime. There had been calls by several artists to repudiate guns and violence, and this had been voiced in popular raps. David's rap can be seen in this didactic, 'message' rap tradition, as a call to recognise the dangers and to aspire to better values.

It is also important to examine the visual style of the video, since this is central to the message and the form. David performed and directed the filming. He chose the locations in the school, the camera movements and angles. He chose his clothes and also completed the editing on his own. In all the shots he dominates the scene. It is almost as if he is alone in the school. There are no teachers, no other authority figures. He parades in the main hall and across the stage. He uses the equipment in the gymnasium. He wears a red jacket, rejecting the usual school uniform. In every way he is in charge. In the edit he uses reversals so that he jumps backwards up onto the platform. Slow motion is used when he makes a prayer-like movement as he raps about 'trying to help u my friend'.

David was very proud of his work, but he was initially reluctant for other students to see it. He was continually struggling with the tension between his 'street image', in which he needed to oppose authority, and the belief that he must try to conform and have an education, to fulfil his aspirations and his reason for being in the United Kingdom. Similarly,

*Picture 16*   Last shot of The Place to Be: David's rap

*Picture 17*   David's rap: The Place to Be

he draws on the form of rap both because it allows him to identify with his hero, Tupac Shakur, and his political messages of oppression and rebellion and because it is a form he can play with and adapt to his own lived experience and his own expression of hope in his new locality. Rap also offers him status in his local environment as a form that his peers have adopted. He is therefore using the form to negotiate a sense of place and identity, while also making a more generalised statement about education and migrant aspiration.

David chose to use a form that is representative of his identity in different ways (as young, as black, as a boy and as a refugee), and one that speaks across cultures. Yet he chose not to draw on Angolan music. This may reflect his sense that the other members of the club would not be particularly interested in finding out about his culture of origin. Both his and their primary interest was in connecting with where they were now, and with the global and local youth cultures that were visible and accessible to them, and would enable them to find acceptance in their present community. David was careful to control what he said and refused to rap 'free style', fearing that what might come out would be inappropriate to the context in which it was being performed. He controlled and adapted the form to the immediate context of the club and its educational setting. The rap form, although generally viewed as symbolic of subcultural alienation, in this context acted as a means of communication and inclusion: indeed, it offers a relatively conventional message. Yet interestingly, this is not how it was received by the members of the other clubs, who focused on what the rap form symbolised and not on the message the text of the rap contained.

## The reception of the rap

David's rap video was fast-moving and tightly edited, showing elaborate and expressive body language. The children in the other clubs appreciated both the performance and the style of music. It inspired several of them to write comments in response on the intranet, and to make video productions in a similar style. We would like to track some of the exchanges that took place around 'The Place to Be', and the response raps from the Netherlands and Sweden in particular.

'The Place to Be' was posted on the project intranet quite late, about a month before the fieldwork finished. Around the same time, David placed a question on the General Discussion Room (the intranet's open discussion forum) about Tupac Shakur. David wanted to initiate a discussion about whether Tupac was alive or dead, but the question also indicated that he really wanted to find out how many serious followers of rap were there in the other clubs. To his disappointment, it was a long time before there were responses to his video or to his query about Tupac. This coincided with David beginning to drift from the club. With the better summer weather coming, he wanted to do sports after school or hang out with his friends. He felt he knew all there was to know about video now that he had made a production he was clearly proud of and that was highly rated by the rest of the club and by his friends. However, he did return to the club a few weeks later when the researcher said that there had been some replies to the rap.

The initial responses were as follows. The club from Germany said: *'Hi, as you know I love your video and it's really good'*. David was pleased with this first positive response, but when he opened the following Italian reply he was shocked at the title and refused to reply:

*Fuck World*
your rap is very beautiful, but we don't like the music.
I like the video but not the end
By
ARfis

(The comment about the music may relate to the fact that there is a fire alarm sounding in the background of the rap, which the children may have taken as accompanying music.) Meanwhile, the following comment arrived from the Netherlands:

> We were surprised that you can jump backwards off the ground on the table. Did you do that with the computer? We liked the way you walked around in the school and that you were allowed to stand on the tables.

Here again, David felt he had been misinterpreted: he was not walking on the tables, but on the stage; and the word 'allowed' also indicated a misunderstanding of what he was doing, which was a demonstration of his control of the situation. As a result, he felt that the other clubs were not worth replying to. The media educators tried to explain that this rudeness (as he had interpreted it) was not intentional and that they were trying to be 'cool' but had got it wrong. However, David did not agree. Despite the fact that the other messages were all positive, he refused to reply at all. His reaction was probably compounded by the lack of response to his query about Tupac. In Thornton's terminology, the other club members had demonstrated a lack of 'subcultural capital' (1995), and so for David they had failed the test that would qualify them for entry into his group.

David had expected commentaries on the substantive message about education. This lack of response may partly have been due to the language barrier, although the text was also posted on the intranet and translated to the other children by the researchers. Yet even if David was disappointed because the other children did not catch his text, they were impressed by his physical and rapping skills. The video spoke to the children in the other clubs, but on a different level: body language, visuals and rap music were enough to evoke interest. In the Netherlands, this encouraged two boys (one Somali and one from the Democratic Republic of the Congo) to finish a production they had started long before as a personal project. In the video, one child raps in Dutch while the other accompanies, beat boxing. The research report from the Netherlands describes the local connections here:

> Among the boys, the hip-hop artists are especially popular, because they are drawn to their 'tough-guy' image. Najib likes the music of the rapper Tupac. He writes in his media collage: 'I am a rapper, too'. He goes by the name of 'Abdel' when he raps. Together with Beaugarçon, who provides the beatbox, he performs a rap on camera. Just like Najib, Beaugarçon likes the American rappers, and he flashes hand signals during the rap on camera. One of these is the 'W' for 'Westside' (thumb extended, ring- and middle-finger crossed), a symbol that stands for the American West Coast. Beaugarçon says 'I learned this on television'. He is from West-Roosendaal, which is his reason for imitating this particular sign. He does not use it often, because he is afraid he might get into fights with other boys from Roosendaal who may be 'supporting' other rappers.

As we have noted, there are important questions about which language is used when rapping (Bennett, 2000; Mitchell, 2001). Here the boys have chosen to adapt the form into their new shared language (Dutch). They are demonstrating an understanding of the form but also of the local street culture for themselves and their local friends. Their concern is therefore less about imitation of an African-American style, and even less about their new audience in the other clubs, none of whom would understand what they are rapping about or the local meaning of the hand gestures.

The other rap response came from Sweden, and it is this one that we would like to examine more closely. In the Swedish club, two boys took a video camera directly after they had watched the UK video and went outside the school building and started to improvise. Such improvisations normally took place either in the school corridor or outside, rather than in the club itself. Both boys were from refugee families, but had been living in Sweden for some time. Mohammed, who belonged to a refugee family of Palestinian descent, was the performer, the artist and dancer; whereas Ibish, an Albanian boy from Kosovo, was the film crew, standing behind the camera and offering encouragement. The two boys were used to working together, and they were good friends outside the club.

Mohammed's video begins with an imitation of the rap 'In Da Club' from the 50 Cent album 'Get Rich or Die Tryin'. The song had been a hit on the radio as well as on the web. We will not present the entire lyrics, but some selected verses, which give a flavour of the content of this rap:

> Go, go, go, go
> Go, go, go, shawty
> It's your birthday
> We gon' party like it's yo birthday
> We gon' sip Bacardi like it's your birthday
> And you know we don't give a fuck
> It'not your birthday!
> Go, go, go, go
> Move it lil' lady
> [...]
> [Chorus]
> You can find me in the club, bottle full of bub
> Look mami I got the X if you into taking drugs
> I'm into having sex, I ain't into making love
> So come give me a hug if you into getting rubbed
> [...]
> [Verse 1]
> When I pull out up front, you see the Benz on dubs
> When I roll 20 deep, it's 20 knives in the club
> Niggas hear I fuck with Dre, now they wanna show me love
> When you sell like Eminem, and the hoes they wanna fuck
> [...]

Mohammed recited the lyrics almost verbatim in his performance. His enthusiasm is partly an effect of the provocative content of the lyrics (to do with money, sex, drugs, booze and so on), and of performing in public what is 'forbidden'. Mohammed's performance here mimics the US style and (unlike the Dutch video) uses English. The gestures and body language are all within the genre, but he is clearly parodying as well. He is able to adapt and play with the form; and as the video moves on, he ironically raps in front of a very un-American small car, belonging to the CHICAM researcher, referring to it as a 'limo'. (In most hip-hop videos, the large cars depicted are a symbol of wealth, power and sexual appeal.)

The following section of the video takes up melodies and lyrics from current commercial pop songs. Finally, the two boys step inside the school, and Mohammed performs to a tune that has influences from Arabic music. Of course, this music style has been adopted

*Picture 18*   Mohammed rapping by the researcher's 'limo'

by mainstream musicians globally and can be downloaded from the Internet. Here Ibish's mobile phone provides the background music, and Mohammed finishes off his performance with a dance influenced by Arabic culture. The boys are clearly very proud of being able to master different musical styles and being able to switch between them. In this very moment, they have appropriated the schoolyard and the empty school and treat these spaces like a huge theatre scene, very much like David did in his rap. In both his rapping body style and his dancing, one can imagine Mohammed practicing in front of the mirror at home in private. Yet here he has the opportunity to perform, to make visual his adaptations of his favourite global and local musical styles. This rap differs from David's in the sense that it contains a mix of Arabic music and mainstream global music, reminding the audience of the ethnic origin of the rapper.

Simpson (1996) argues that rap consciously promotes derivative borrowing. Such intertextual references to other artists and phenomena

*Picture 19* Mohammed rapping

in the society are certainly apparent in Mohammed's performance. He performs with a joking face. He is re-contextualising his sources, and thereby giving them a new meaning. He moves rap from the US urban ghetto into a schoolyard in a rural Swedish town. By combining the original text from 50 Cent with his improvised text as well as main-stream music, his performance gives a fresh and somewhat 'benign' impression. The subversive and anti-social content of the original text loses its meaning. Yet at the end, when he performs an Arabic dance, global forms are combined with traditional ones, in a clear example of embodied 'hybrid' culture (cf. Garcia Canclini, 2005). The same holds for David, with his inspiration from Tupac as a base for his own text, whose overt message is far from subversive.

Both videos present a mix of cultural influences that are combined together to form new expressions. David had a conscious political message in his mind, which he wanted to communicate to children in the other CHICAM clubs. Their responses failed to catch the message presented in the verbal mode, but they had enough understanding of visual language and music to respond anyway. Even so, both videos (as well as the Dutch rap) in different ways repudiated the subversive and anti-social character of the popular 'gangsta' rap form.

## Conclusion

In seeking to communicate with each other, both within and between the clubs, the children implicitly realised that verbal language would be a constant obstacle and that body language and music were likely to be more effective. They were also keen to present themselves as participants in a shared youth culture, rather than as 'schoolchildren' or only as 'migrants'. Yet even where they made use of global forms such as popular music, this communication was not always as controllable or successful as the researchers and educators might have wished – as the diverse and contradictory discussions and responses around David's video clearly show.

What do these productions tell us about these children's attempts to make sense of their experiences as migrants? To some extent, they could be seen precisely as a means of avoiding communication about these experiences. Both David and Mohammed's raps could be dismissed as derivative or inauthentic, a pick-and-mix of African-American styles that neither represents themselves nor where they are now living, and that was chosen simply in order to make them appear 'cool'. Even Elcin's performance could be seen as merely a rehearsal of a traditional form, of the kind he produced to order at his parents' political meetings.

By contrast, we have argued that all these videos can be read as narratives about migration – albeit in very different ways. Elcin's rendition of the poem reflects his and his family's experiences of exile, and the continued emotional 'pull' of traditional forms from his country of origin. David's video uses a global 'message' rap form to speak of his educational aspirations and his hope for a better life, despite the dangers of his local neighbourhood. Mohammed is less interested in the spoken message, and more concerned to reflect the range of cultural influences in his life, both in music and dance, and to move fluently and playfully between them. In creating these texts, the children drew on different musical traditions as a way of addressing current global cultural connections, as well as coming to terms with the changing cultural circumstances in which they were now living. While rap and poetry clearly played an important role here, much of what was expressed and communicated remained – perhaps necessarily – unspoken.

# 10
## Conclusion

In this book, we have explored some of the many connections and relationships between four key areas of concern: childhood, media, migration and globalisation. Self-evidently, we have provided only a partial view. Our arguments emerge from empirical research projects that have been conducted in quite particular circumstances, and from debates that have taken on a specific form in our particular national and historical context. Although we have tried to draw on examples from other settings, our research primarily reflects our location in the United Kingdom and in Europe – in relatively wealthy, industrialised nations. Childhood, media, migration and globalisation are obviously seen and experienced differently in different political, economic and cultural settings. We hope that our account will at least play a part alongside other, equally located studies in contributing to the broader global debate about these issues. In this brief conclusion, we would like to summarise the key points of our argument and offer some indication of the implications of our work for those who work directly with children and young people, for policy-makers and for other researchers.

Exploring the overlaps between these different areas of study has drawn attention to what we would see as some of the limitations and absences in each of them. Research on migration – and indeed the official statistics – have not thus far paid much attention to the specific situations and experiences of children. Work in the sociology of childhood has tended to neglect the central role of the media in children's lives; while media research still tends to focus on the psychological, rather than the social and cultural, dimensions of children's experiences. Studies of globalisation rightly place a central emphasis on the media; but many of them tend to explore the phenomenon 'from above', in terms of broad structural forces, rather than 'from below', through a focus on the everyday experiences of individuals and social groups – such as migrants and children. Combining these different areas of concern thus hopefully allows us to bring a fresh perspective to bear on each of them and to provide a more specific focus to discussions of questions of culture and identity that are often framed in quite abstract terms.

In addressing our key themes, we have sought to pay due attention to the power of social, political and economic structures, while simultaneously recognising the significance of human agency. Thus, we have represented children as social actors and as creators of meanings in their own right; but we have also argued that they act only within social and institutional constraints. Likewise, we have challenged the prevalent view of migrants merely as passive victims, emphasising their ability to assert control and to define the terms of their own experiences; yet we have also drawn attention to the structural inequalities and the broader social and historical forces that inevitably frame and shape those experiences. Equally, we have argued that the media provide powerful 'symbolic resources' with which people actively make sense of their social worlds; yet we have argued that the media also construct and define those worlds in particular – and inevitably partial – ways. Thus, while we have emphasised the diversity of migrant children's experiences, we have not intended to imply that those experiences should be understood in merely individual terms, or indeed that individuals are free to choose or define their own identities at will.

We have argued that children are often central players in the process of migration. Children frequently motivate the decision to migrate in the first place, and they are in the 'front line' as migrant families negotiate their relationship to their new situation. As this implies, migration can have a significant, and unsettling, impact on power relationships within the family. For parents, children are likely to become the focus for fears and aspirations for the future, and for the tension between cultural continuity and change. Many of these concerns may come to focus on the experience of education, which can offer the promise of a better life, but which can also reconfirm existing inequalities. Meanwhile, the experience of migration is cut across by differences of social class and of gender. The children of wealthy, cosmopolitan migrants have very different forms of cultural capital when compared with refugees; and girls may well be more restricted in their access to the wider social world when compared with boys.

The media play a central role in children's experience of migration. Children in migrant families are likely to experience a mixed 'diet' of media, including local, national, transnational and global media. These media are bound to provide them with some quite mixed messages, and some very diverse symbolic resources with which to build their own identities. For migrant families, the media can serve as a powerful means of sustaining connections with their countries of origin. However, this cannot be seen merely as a matter of nostalgia, or of a regressive longing for the past: it is also about keeping in contact with changing realities in the present. At the same time – and particularly for children – the media serve as a means of learning about, and participating in, the new cultures to which they have come. The media can provide a key means of access to the peer group, offering a shared ground for relationships that transcend other differences. However, their role in this latter respect is far from neutral: the media serve as means of exclusion as well as inclusion and may offer representations that stigmatise or marginalise particular cultures. Yet here again, there is often considerable diversity: experiences of these different forms of media depend very much on where you have come from, on where you arrive and on how you imagine your future.

Media produced for global consumption cannot be seen merely as transmitters of fixed cultural or ideological values. Economic power does not simply 'translate' into cultural or ideological domination. We have argued against the view of media as mere agents of cultural imperialism – although we have also cautioned against a more celebratory account of the 'global village', which would see the media as an unproblem-atic vehicle for dialogue between cultures. As we have shown, children use and appropriate media in diverse ways, in light of their needs and circumstances, and in relation to the dynamics of the family and the peer group. The media offer them multiple representations of 'otherness' and 'sameness', which cannot be reduced simply to a binary opposition between 'us' and 'them'. The global production and circulation of media, and the ways in which children use and interpret them, are therefore contributing to a continuing reconfiguration of relations between the global and the local.

Our empirical research illustrates some of the diverse – and often surprising – ways in which this occurs, as children use and combine media from different cultures, both in order to provide 'windows on the world' (for instance in the case of news) and as the basis for imagina-tion and fantasy. The specific case studies we have discussed offer some indication of the complex ways in which individual children use media forms, images and narratives in their attempts to make sense of their experiences and to construct their own identities. Jima, Rhaxma, Leyla and Selve (Chapter 6), or David and Mohamed (Chapter 9) are actively appropriating the media that surround them, in order to find a place among their peers, to explore their own tensions and dilemmas, to understand the seemingly arbitrary events that affect their family lives and to express their own positive 'take' on the world.

Our primary focus here has been on the 'old' medium of television – which remains the most significant medium for younger children in particular. However, we have also sought to draw attention to the possibilities of new media, especially in terms of creative participation. As we have argued, digital media provide significant new opportunities for young people to become producers of media, rather than just 'consumers'. Potentially, they can enable young people to 'find a voice' and to represent their experiences in their own terms. Yet in exploring these possibilities in our research, we have found that access to media technology is only the starting point in a much longer process of learning. What children do – and indeed what they *want* to do – with these media depends very much on their social circumstances and on the social contexts in which they gain that access. Likewise, in seeking to exploit the potential of these media for intercultural communication, we have found that a great deal depends upon young people's motivation to communicate and on how they conceive of the audience for what they produce.

Thus, while we remain optimistic about the potential of these media, we do not see them as straightforwardly 'empowering'. Nor indeed do we believe that children should be seen as 'global citizens of the digital age', as much of the rhetoric on these issues tends to suggest. Our research shows that children can use the global and transnational possibilities of media, provided they are motivated to do so and their circumstances allow it. But in many respects, even migrant children are primarily oriented towards the here and now; and they are more inclined to adapt media to their local needs and purposes, taking what they find and reworking it in their attempts to create their own sense of home and belonging.

Our research has several implications for both policy and practice. We share Charles Husband's view that the *right to communicate* should be seen as a vital dimension of modern, multicultural societies (Husband, 1998, 2000). The media can play a vital role in facilitating communication between migrants and the new cultures to which they have come, as well as sustaining global and transnational connections. But if this potential is to be fulfilled, we must have educational and cultural policies that will explicitly support it. In the context of education, we need to move beyond the view of schools as only national institutions and to acknowledge that the majority (if not all) students are now subject to global economic influences, images and cultures. We can no longer take a nationalistic view on citizenship and participation nor encourage a view of study and work as independent from the rest of the world. This has immediate implications for those schools that do have a substantial group of immigrant students but in many senses it applies even more to those schools which remain more monocultural. While the lens of migration studies is focused on the migrants, there is an onus on education and educators to assist those who have not migrated to be able to live in a globalising world.

While there is a need for the ethos of schools to adapt to global possibilities and influences there are also particular areas of the curriculum that need to be reorientated. For example, we need to move on from a view of digital technology as a means of simply delivering 'information' and the narrow, skills-based training that tends to dominate the ICT curriculum. Young people require new forms of literacy – or what some have termed 'multi-literacies' (Cope and Kalantzis, 2000) – that are appropriate to the increasingly multicultural, media-saturated societies in which they are growing up. We have to enable children to exploit the creative and communicative potential of these new media, as well as developing a more critical form of media literacy that is capable of questioning and challenging dominant representations. We need specific initiatives that will enable excluded groups to sustain a positive sense of their own cultural identities, but we also need to find ways of using media to facilitate communication and dialogue across cultures; and in order to do this, we will require the specialist forms of professional development for teachers that can support such activities. While the school curriculum remains a vitally important location for such work, we also believe that it can fruitfully be carried out in the more informal, leisure-oriented settings we have described in this book.

In terms of the media themselves, there is a continuing need to ensure equality of access and representation for marginalised groups. Refugee children in particular are one of the groups most likely to find themselves on the wrong side of the continuing digital divide; and this in turn is likely to exacerbate their exclusion from the culture of the peer group, from educational opportunities and from the wider public sphere. Children have rights, not merely to be protected or provided for, but also to participate in the media, not least as producers in their own right (Buckingham, 2000a). New media have considerable potential in terms of enabling children to find an audience and to have their voices heard; but this crucially depends on the provision of open public platforms for distribution. We are seeing the popularity of such moves with the expansion of social networking and file-sharing sites such as MySpace and YouTube. Here again, there is a need for specific local initiatives that use new media to address the particular needs of migrant and refugee children.

As researchers, we have sought to use the media not simply as a topic of study, but also as a method in itself. We have sought to enable children – in this case, migrant and refugee children – to represent themselves and their experiences, rather than simply speaking on their behalf. We see this as an important extension of the more participatory approach that is now emerging in childhood studies and in media research. Inevitably, in the context of this book, these children have remained largely 'objects' of our research, rather than subjects in their own right – although resources such as our CHICAM website (*www.chicam.net* and *www.chicam.org*) provide more direct access to the children's images and voices. Even so, we have cautioned against a romanticised view of this process: as researchers increasingly make use of visual media, we believe there is a need for much more rigorous discussion of the methodological and ethical issues such media inevitably raise.

The early years of the twenty-first century have brought the concerns of this book into sharp, even painful, focus. The escalation of regional and global conflict seems to have polarised attitudes and made communication across cultures even more fraught with misunderstandings and difficulties. Yet the development of new media technologies is creating unprecedented opportunities for self-expression and global dialogue – perhaps particularly for young people. We seem to be in a state of precarious transition, in which the risk of mutual incomprehension and hostility is escalating at an alarming rate. Children, and particularly migrant children, are often the focus for these tensions and concerns – yet they rarely have the opportunity to represent themselves. As researchers and educators, we can play a small part in enabling them to be both seen and heard.

# Bibliography

Adelman, H. (1999) 'Modernity, globalization, refugees and displacement', in Ager, A. (ed.) *Refugees: Perspectives on the Experience of Forced Migration*, London: Cassell.

Aksoy, A. and Robins, K. (2000) 'Thinking across spaces: transnational television from Turkey', *European Journal of Cultural Studies* 3 (3): 343–365.

Aksoy, A. and Robins, K. (2003) 'Banal transnationalism: the difference that television makes', pp. 89–104 in Karim, K. (ed.) *The Media of Diaspora*, London: Routledge.

Allen, R.C. (ed.) (1994) *To Be Continued . . . Soap Opera Around the World*, London: Routledge.

Allison, A. (2000) 'A challenge to Hollywood: Japanese character goods hit the US', *Japanese Studies* 20 (1): 67–88.

Anatol, G.L. (ed.) (2003) *Reading Harry Potter: Critical Essays*, New York: Praeger.

Anderson, B. (1983) *Imagined Communities: Reflections on the Origins and Spread of Nationalism*, London: Verso.

Anderson, B. (1991) (revised edition) *Imagined Communities: Reflections on the Origins and Spread of nationalism*, London: Verso.

Anderson, B. (ed.) (1998) 'Long distance nationalism', *The spectre of Comparisons: Nationalism, Southeast Asia and the World*, London: Verso.

Ang, I. (1985) *Watching Dallas*, London: Methuen.

Appadurai, A. (1990) 'Disjuncture and difference in the global cultural economy', in Featherstone, M. (ed.) *Global Culture: Nationalism, Globalization and Modernity*, London: Sage Publications.

Appadurai, A. (1996) *Modernity at Large: Cultural Dimensions of Globalization*, Minneapolis, MN: University of Minnesota Press.

Asis, M. (2002) 'From the life stories of Filipino women: personal and family agendas in migration', *Asian and Pacific Migration Journal* 11: 67–94.

Asthana, S. (2006) *Innovative Practices of Youth Participation in Media*, Paris: UNESCO.

Bachmair, B. (1990) 'Everyday life as action and as reality – action theory outlines of everyday life' in Charlton, M. and Bachmair, B. (eds) *Communication Research and Broadcasting No. 9*, Munich: KG Saur.

Back, L. (1996) *New Ethnicities and Urban Culture: Racisms and Multiculture in Young Lives*, London: UCL Press.

Banaji, S. (2006) *Reading 'Bollywood': The Young Audience and Hindi Films*, Basingstoke: Palgrave.

Banaji, S. and Al-Ghabban, A. (2006) ' "Neutrality comes from inside us": British-Asian and Indian perspectives on television news after 11 September', *Journal of Ethnic and Migration Studies* 32 (6): 1005–1026.

Banks, M. (2001) *Visual Methods in Social Research*, London: Sage.

Barker, C. (1997a) *Global Television: an Introduction*, Oxford: Blackwell.

Barker, C. (1997b) 'Television and the reflexive project of the self: soaps, teenage talk and hybrid identities', *British Journal of Sociology* 48 (4): 611–628.

Barker, M. (1990) *Comics: Ideology, Power and the Critics*, Manchester: Manchester University Press.

Barker, C. (1998) ' "Cindy's a slut": moral identities and moral responsibility in the "soap talk" of British Asian girls', *Sociology* 32 (1): 65–81.

Barthes, R. (1973) *Mythologies*, London: Paladin.

Bauman, Z. (1995) 'Searching for the centre that holds', pp. 140–154, in Featherstone, M., Lash, S. and Robertson, R. (eds) *Global Modernities*, London: Sage.

Bauman, Z. (1998) *Globalization: the Human Consequences*, New York: Colombia University Press.

Bennett, A. (2000) *Popular Music and Youth Culture*, London: Palgrave Macmillan.

Besozzi, E. (1993) *Elementi di Sociologia dell'educazione*, Rome: La Nuova Italia Scientifica.

Bettelheim, B. (1979) *The Uses of Enchantment: the Meaning and Importance of Fairy Tales*, Harmondsworth: Penguin.

Bhattacharya, N. (2004) 'A "basement" cinephilia: Indian diaspora women watch Bollywood', *South Asian Popular Culture* 2 (2): 161–183.

Black, R. (1994) 'Livelihoods under stress: a case study of refugee vulnerability in Greece', *Journal of Refugee Studies* 7 (4): 360.

Blake, A. (2002) *The Irresistible Rise of Harry Potter: Kid-Lit in a Globalised World*, London: Verso.

Block, D. (2004) 'Globalisation, transnational communication and the Internet', *International Journal of Multicultural Societies* 6 (1): 13–28.

de Block, L. (2002) *Television as a Shared Space in the Intercultural Lives of Primary Aged Children*. Unpublished doctoral dissertation, Institute of Education, University of London.

de Block, L. (2006) 'Talking television across cultures: negotiating inclusion and exclusion', pp. 169–184 in Adams, L. and Kirova, A. (eds) *Global Migration and Education: Schools, Children and Families*, Mahwah, NJ: Lawrence Erlbaum.

Bloustein, G. (1998) ' "It's different to a mirror 'cos it talks to you": teenage girls, video cameras and identity', pp. 115–133 in Howard, S. (ed.) *Wired-Up: Young People and the Electronic Media*, London: UCL Press.

Bortree, D. (2005) 'Presentation of the self on the web: an ethnographic study of teenage girls' weblogs', *Education, Communication and Information* 5 (1): 25–39.

Bourdieu, P. (1984) *Distinction: A Social Critique of the Judgment of Taste*, London: Routledge.

Bourdieu, P. (1986) 'The forms of capital', in Richardson, J. (ed.) *Handbook of Theory and Research for the Sociology of Education*, New York: Greenwood Press.

Boyden, J. (1997) (second edition) 'Childhood and policy makers: a comparative perspective on the globalization of childhood', in James, A. and Prout A. (eds) *Constructing and Reconstructing Childhood: Contemporary Issues in the Sociological Study of Childhood*, London: Falmer Press.

Boyden, J, and de Berry, J (eds) (2004) *Children and Youth on the Front Line: Ethnography, Armed Conflict and Displacement*, New York: Berghahn Books.

Boyle, D. (1997) *Subject to Change: Guerrilla Television Revisited*, New York: Oxford University Press.

Brah, A. (1996) *Cartographies of Diaspora: Contesting Identities*, London: Routledge.

British Board of Film Classification (2001) *Wrestling: How Audiences Perceive TV and Video Wrestling*, London: BBFC.

Bromley, H. (2004) 'Localizing Pokémon through narrative play', pp. 211–225 in Tobin, J. (ed.) *Pikachu's Global Adventure: The Rise and Fall of Pokémon*, Durham, NC: Duke University Press.

Brougere, G. (2004) 'How much is a Pokémon worth: Pokémon in France', pp. 187–208 in Tobin, J. (ed.) *Pikachu's Global Adventure: The Rise and Fall of Pokémon*, Durham, NC: Duke University Press.

Buckingham, D. (1993a) *Children Talking Television: The Making of Television Literacy*, London: Falmer Press.

Buckingham, D. (ed.) (1993b) *Reading Audiences: Young People and the Media*, Manchester: Manchester University Press.

Buckingham, D. (1996) *Moving Images: Understanding Children's Emotional Responses to Television*, Manchester: Manchester University Press.

Buckingham, D. (2000a) *After the Death of Childhood: Growing Up in the Age of Electronic Media*, Cambridge: Polity.

Buckingham, D. (2000b) *The Making of Citizens: Young People, News and Politics*, London: Routledge.

Buckingham, D. (ed.) (2001a) 'Special issue: Videoculture', *Journal of Educational Media* 26 (3).

Buckingham, D. (2001b) 'Disney dialectics: debating the politics of children's media culture', pp. 269–296 in Wasko, J., Phillips, M. and Meehan, E. (eds) *Dazzled by Disney?*, London: Leicester University Press.

Buckingham, D. (ed.) (2002a) 'The child and the screen', pp. 1–14 *Small Screens: Television for Children*, London: Leicester University Press.

Buckingham, D. (ed.) (2002b) 'Child-centred television? Teletubbies and the educational imperative', pp. 38–60 (2003) *Media Education: Literacy, Learning and Contemporary Culture*, Cambridge: Polity.

Buckingham, D. (2003) *Media Education: Literacy, Learning and Contemporary Culture*, Cambridge: Polity.

Buckingham, D. (2004) *Young People and Media*. Briefing paper for the United Nations Workshop on Global Media-Driven Youth Culture, New York.

Buckingham, D. (2007) 'Selling childhood/children and consumer culture', *Journal of Children and Media* 1 (1): pp. 15–24.

Buckingham, D. with Banaji, S., Burn, A., Carr, D., Cranmer, S. and Willett, R. (2005) *The Media Literacy of Children and Young People: A Review of the Academic Research*, London: Ofcom.

Buckingham, D. and Bragg, S. (2004) *Young People, Sex and the Media: The Facts of Life?*, Basingstoke: Palgrave Macmillan.

Buckingham, D. and Sefton-Green, J. (1994) *Cultural Studies Goes to School: Reading and Teaching Popular Media*, London: Taylor and Francis.

Buckingham, D., Grahame, J. and Sefton-Green, J. (1995) *Making Media: Practical Production in Media Education*, London: English and Media Centre.

Buckingham, D., Davies, H., Jones, K. and Kelley, P. (1999) *Children's Television In Britain: History, Discourse and Policy*, London: British Film Institute.

Burman, E. (1994) *Deconstructing Developmental Psychology*, London: Routledge.

Burton-Carvajal, J. (1994) ' "Surprise package": looking southward with Disney', pp. 131–147 in Smoodin, E. (ed.) *Disney Discourse: Producing the Magic Kingdom*, New York: Routledge.

Campion, M.J. (2005) *Look Who's Talking: Cultural Diversity, Public Service Broadcasting and the National Conversation*, Oxford: Nuffield College.

Cartwright, L. and Goldfarb, B. (1994) 'Cultural contagion: on Disney's health education films for Latin America', pp. 169–180 in Smoodin, E. (ed.) *Disney Discourse: Producing the Magic Kingdom*, New York: Routledge.

Castles, S. and Davidson, A. (2000) *Citizenship and Migration: Globalisation and the Politics of Belonging*, London: Palgrave Macmillan.

Castles, S. and Miller, M. (2003) (third edition) *The Age of Migration: International Population Movements in the Modern World*, London: Palgrave Macmillan.

Chadna, K. and Kavoori, A. (2001) 'Media imperialism revisited: some findings from the Asian case', *Media Culture and Society* 22 (4): 415–432.

Chalaby, J. (2005a) 'The quiet invention of a new medium: twenty years of transnational television in Europe', pp. 43–65 in Chalaby, J. (ed.) *Transnational Television Worldwide*, London: I.B. Tauris.

Chalaby, J. (ed.) (2005b) *Transnational Television Worldwide*, London: I.B. Tauris.

Chamberlain and Leydesdorff (2004) see Yeoh, Huang and Lam.

Chang, J. (2005) *Can't Stop, Won't Stop: A History of the Hip-Hop Generation*, London: Ebury Press.

CHICAM (2002) (WP1) *Global Kids, Global Media: a Review of Research Relating to Children, Media and Migration in Europe*. Available at www.chicam.net and www.chicam.org.

CHICAM (2004) *Home is Where the Heart Is: Family Relations of Migrant Children in Media Clubs in Six European Countries*. Available at www.chicam.net and www.chicam.org.

*Children in Aliens Processing System – Summary Report* (2001) Swedish Migration Board. *www.chilout.org*.

Christensen, P. and James, A. (1999) *Research with Children: Perspectives and Practices*, London: Routledge.

Christopoulou, N. and de Leeuw, S. (2005) 'Children making media: constructions of home and belonging', pp. 113–136 *Childhood and Migration: From Experience to Agency*, New Brunswick, NJ: Transaction Publishers.

Cinar, D (1994) *From Aliens to Citizens*, Vienna: Institut für Höhere Studien.

Cohen, R. (1997) *Global Diasporas: An Introduction*, London: UCL Press.

Cohen, P. (1999) 'Through a glass darkly: intellectuals on race', *New Ethnicities, Old Racisms*, London and New York: Zed Books.

CON RED Project (2005) *Routes of Small Dreams: Unaccompanied Migrant Minors in Europe: Comparative Report*, Barcelona: Fundacio Pere Tarres.

Cope, B. and Kalantzis, M. (eds) (2000) *Multiliteracies: Literacy Learning and the Design of Social Futures*, London: Routledge.

Cottle, S. (2000) 'A rock and a hard place: making ethnic minority television', pp. 100–117 *Ethnic Minorities and the Media*, Buckingham, UK: Open University Press.

Cowen, T. (2002) *Creative Destruction: How Globalisation is Changing the World's Cultures*, Princeton, NJ: Princeton University Press.

Crawley, H. (2004) *Working with Children and Young People Subject to Immigration Control: Guidelines for Best Practice*, London: Immigration Law Practitioners' Association (ILPA).

Crawley, H. and Lester, T. (2005) *'No Place for a Child': Children in UK Immigration Detention: Impacts, Alternatives and Safeguards*, London: Save the Children.

Cunningham, S. (2001) 'Popular media as public "sphericules" for diasporic communities', *International Journal of Cultural Studies* 4 (2): 131–147.

Cunningham, S. and Sinclair, J. (eds) (2001) *Floating Lives: The Media and Asian Diasporas*, Lanham: Rowman and Littlefield.

Daniels, T. and Gerson, J. (eds) (1989) *The Colour Black*, London: British Film Institute.

Danielsson, H. (1998) *Video som språk och kommunikation* (PhD dissertation), Stockholm: Stockholm University (Department of Education).

Davies, L. (2006) ' "Hello newbie! **big welcome hugs** hope u like it here as much as i do! ☺": an exploration of teenagers' informal on-line learning', pp. 211–228 in Buckingham, D. and Willett, R. (eds) *Digital Generations: Children, Young People and New Media*, Mahwah, NJ: Erlbaum.

Dayan, D. (1998) 'Particularistic media and diasporic communications', pp. 103–113 in Liebes, T. and Curran, J. (eds) *Media, Ritual and Identity*, London: Routledge.

De Santis, H. (2003) 'Mi programa es su programa: tele/visions of a Spanish-language diaspora in North America', pp. 63–75 in Karim, K. (ed.) *Media of Diasporas*, London: Routledge.

Dewdney, A. and Lister, M. (1988) *Youth, Culture and Photography*, London: Macmillan.

Dijk, T. van (2000) 'New(s) racism: a discourse analytical approach', pp. 33–49 in Cottle, S. (ed.) *Ethnic Minorities and the Media*, Buckingham: Open University Press.

Dorfman, A. and Mattelart, A. (1975) *How to Read Donald Duck: Imperialist Ideology in the Disney Comics*, New York: International General.

Dowmunt, T. (ed.) (1993) *Channels of Resistance: Global Television and Local Empowerment*, London: British Film Institute.

Driver, S. (2006) 'Virtually queer youth communities of girls and birls: dialogical spaces of identity work and desiring exchange', pp. 229–248 in Buckingham, D. and Willett, R. (eds) *Digital Generations: Children, Young People and New Media*, Mahwah, NJ: Erlbaum.

Drotner, K. (2001a) ' "Donald Seems So Danish": Disney and the formation of cultural identity', pp. 102–120 in Wasko, J., Phillips, M. and Meehan, E. (eds) *Dazzled by Disney?*, London: Leicester University Press.

Drotner, K. (2001b) 'Global media through youthful eyes', pp. 283–306 in Livingstone, S. and Bovill, M. (eds) (2001) *Children and their Changing Media Environment*, Mahwah, NJ: Lawrence Erlbaum.

Durham, M.G. (2004) 'Constructing the "new ethnicities": media, sexuality and diaspora identity in the lives of South Asian immigrant girls', *Critical Studies in Media Communication* 21 (2): 140–161.

ECRE Country Report 2003: Greece. Retrieved 10.2.07 from http://www.ecre.org/country03/10. %20Greece.pdf.

Eokter, E. (1998) *Art Therapists, Refugees and Migrants: Reading Across Borders*, London: Jessica Kingsley Publishers.

Facer, K., Furlong, J., Furlong, R. and Sutherland, R. (2003) *Screenplay: Children and Computing in the Home*, London: Routledge.

Fanon, F. (1968) *Black Skin, White Masks*, London: MacGibbon and Kee.

Featherstone, M. (1995) *Undoing Culture*, London: Sage.

Featherstone, M. and Lash, S. (1995) 'Globalization, modernity and the spatialization of social theory', pp. 1–24 in Featherstone, M., Lash, S. and Robertson, R. (eds) *Global Modernities*, London: Sage.

Feld, S. and Keil, C. (1992) *Music Grooves: Essays and Dialogues*, Chicago, IL: University of Chicago Press.

Fisch, S. (2001) *G is for Growing: Thirty Years of Research on Children and 'Sesame Street'*, Mahwah, NJ: Erlbaum.

Fiske, J. (1987) *Television Culture*, London: Methuen.

Fog Olwig, K. (2000) 'Modernity at large: cultural dimensions of globalization: a book review', *Theory, Culture and Society* 17 (1): 176–179.

Fog Olwig, K (2002) 'A wedding in the family: home making in a global kin network', *Global Networks* 2 (3): 205–218.

Forman, M. (2000) ' "Represent": race, space and place in rap music', *Popular Music* 19 (1), 65–90.

Forgacs, D. (1992) 'Disney animation and the business of childhood', *Screen* 33 (4): 361–374.

Frachon, C. and Vergaftig, M. (eds) (1995) *European Television: Immigrants and Ethnic Minorities*, London: John Libbey.

Fritsche, Y. (2000) Modernes Leben: Gewandelt, vernetzt und verkabelt', pp. 181–219 in Shell, D. (ed.) *Jugend 2000* Shell Jugendstudie, Band 1, Opladen: Leske+Budrich.

Garcia Canclini, N. (2005) *Hybrid Cultures: Strategies for Entering and Leaving Modernity*, Minnesota, MN: University of Minnesota Press.

Gardner, K. and Grillo, R. (2002) 'Transnational households and ritual: an overview', *Global Networks* 2 (3): 179–190.

Gauntlett, D. (1997) *Video Critical: Children, the Environment and Media Power*, Luton: John Libbey.

Georgiou, M. (2002) *Diasporic Communities On-Line: A Bottom-Up Experience of Transnationalism* (paper issued by the European Media Technology and Everyday Life Network), London: London School of Economics. Retrieved 3 March 2006 from http://www.lse.ac.uk/collections/EMTEL/ Minorities/minorities_docs.html.

Giddens, A. (1990) *The Consequences of Modernity*, Stanford, CA: Stanford University Press.

Giddens, A. (1991) *Modernity and Self-Identity*, Cambridge: Polity.

Gillespie, M. (1995) *Television, Ethnicity and Cultural Change*, London: Routledge.

Gillespie, M. (2000) 'Transnational communications and diaspora communities', pp. 164–178 in Cottle, S. (ed.) *Ethnic Minorities and the Media*, Buckingham: Open University Press.

Gilroy, P. (ed.) (1993a) 'A dialogue with bell hooks', *Small Acts: Thoughts on the Politics of Black Cultures*, London: Serpent's Tail.

Gilroy, P. (ed.) (1993b) 'On the beach: David A. Bailey' *Small Acts: Thoughts on the Politics of Black Cultures*, London: Serpent's Tail.

Giroux, H. (2001) *The Mouse that Roared: Disney and the End of Innocence*, New York: Rowman and Littlefield.

Goetz, M., Lemish, D., Aidman, A. and Moon, H. (2005) *Media and the Make-Believe Worlds of Children*, Mahwah, NJ: Erlbaum.

Goodman, S. (2003) *Teaching Youth Media*, New York: Teachers' College Press.

Granato, M. (2001) Freizeitgestaltung und Mediennutzung bei Kindern türkischer Herkunft. Eine Untersuchung des Presse- und Informationsamtes der Bundesregierung (BPA) zur 'Mediennutzung und Integration der türkischen Bevölkerung in Deutschland' und der 'Mediennutzung und Integration türkischer Kinder 2000 in Deutschland', Bonn: BPA.

Griffiths, M. (2002) 'Pink worlds and blue worlds: a portrait of infinite polarity', pp. 159–184 in Buckingham, D. (ed.) *Small Screens: Television for Children*, London: Leicester University Press.

Guarnizo, L. and Smith, M. (eds) (1998) 'The locations of transnationalism', pp. 3–34 *Transnationalism from Below, Comparative Urban and Community Research Vol 6*, Piscataway, NJ: Transaction Publishers.

Gupta, S. (2003) *Re-reading Harry Potter*, Basingstoke: Palgrave Macmillan.

d'Haenens, L., Beentjes, H. and Bink, S. (2000) 'The media experience of ethnic minorities in The Netherlands: a qualitative study', *Communications* 25 (3): 325–341.

d'Haenens, L., Kokhuis, M., Summeren, C. van and Beentjes, H. (2001) *Ownership and Use of 'Old' and 'New' Media Among Ethnic Minority Youth in the Netherlands: The Role of the Ethno-Cultural Position* (Research report commissioned by NOW), Nijmegen: University of Nijmegen (Department of Communication).

Hall, S. (1991) 'Old and new identities, old and new ethnicities', in King, A. (ed.), *Culture, Globalization and the World System*, London: MacMillan.

Hall, S. (1992) 'The question of cultural identity', pp. 273–325 in Hall, S., Held, D. and McGrew, T. (eds) *Modernity and its Futures*, London: Sage.

Hall, S. (1993) 'Culture, community, nation', *Cultural Studies* 7 (3): 349–363.

Hall, S. (1996) 'Who needs "identity"?', pp. 1–17, in Hall, S. and du Gay, P. (eds) *Questions of Cultural Identity*, London: Sage Publications.

Halloran, J.D., Bhatt, A. and Gray, P. (1995) *Ethnic Minorities and Television: A Study of Use, Reactions and Preferences*, Leicester: University of Leicester (Centre for Mass Communication Research).

Hannerz, U. (1996) *Transnational Connections: People, Culture, Places*, London: Routledge.

Harding, J. (2000) *The Uninvited: Refugees at the Rich Man's Gate*, London: Profile Books.

Hargreaves, A.G. (2001a) 'Maghrebis and television broadcasting in France', pp. 190–201 in Dacyl, J.W. and Westin, C. (eds) *Cultural Diversity and the Media*, Stockholm, Sweden: CEIFO.

Hargreaves, A.G. (2001b) 'Media effects and ethnic relations in Britain and France', pp. 23–36 in Wood, N. and King, R. (eds) *Media and Migration: Constructions of Mobility and Difference*, London: Routledge.

Hargreaves, A.G. (2001c) 'Diasporic audiences and satellite television: case studies in France and Germany', pp. 139–156 in Ross, K. with Playdon, P. (eds) *Black Marks: Minority Ethnic Audiences and Media*, Aldershot: Ashgate.

Hargreaves, A. and Madjoub, D. (1997) 'Satellite television viewing among ethnic minorities in France', *European Journal of Communication* 12 (4): 459–477.

Harindranath, R. (2000) 'Ethnicity, national culture(s) and the interpretation of television', pp. 149–163 in Cottle, S. (ed.) *Ethnic Minorities and the Media*, Buckingham: Open University Press.

Harvey, D. (1989) *The Condition of Postmodernity*, Oxford: Basil Blackwell.

Harvey, I., Skinner, M. and Parker, D. (2002) *Being Seen, Being Heard: Young People and Moving Image Production*, London: National Youth Agency/British Film Institute.

Hassanpour, A. (2003) 'Diaspora, homeland and communication technologies', pp. 76–87 in Karim, K. (ed.) *The Media of Diaspora*, London: Routledge.

Heilman, E. (ed.) (2003a) 'Blue wizards and pink witches: representations of gender identity and power', pp. 221–240 *Harry Potter's World: Multidisciplinary Critical Perspectives*, London: RoutledgeFalmer.

Heilman, E. (ed.) (2003b) *Harry Potter's World: Multidisciplinary Critical Perspectives*, London: RoutledgeFalmer.

Heilman, E. and Gregory, A. (2003) 'Images of the privileged insider and outcast outsider', pp. 241–260 in Heilman, E. (ed.) *Harry Potter's World: Multidisciplinary Critical Perspectives*, London: RoutledgeFalmer.

Held, D. and McGrew, A. (2000) 'The great globalization debate: an introduction', pp. 1–47 in *The Global Transformations Reader: An Introduction to the Globalization Debate*, Malden: Polity.

Hendershot, H. (2004) *Nickelodeon Nation: The History, Politics and Economics of America's Only TV Channel for Kids*, New York: New York University Press.

Herring, S., Kouper, I., Scheidt, L. and Wright, E. (2004) 'Women and children last: the discourse construction of weblogs', in Gurak, L., Antonijevic, S., Johnson, L., Ratliff, C. and Reyman, J. (eds) *Into the Blogosphere: Rhetoric, Community, and Culture of Weblogs*, http://blog.lib.umn.edu/ blogosphere/women_and_children.html.

Higonnet, A. (1998) *Pictures of Innocence: The History and Crisis of Ideal Childhood*, London: Thames and Hudson.

Hirsch, M. (1997) *Family Frames: Photography, Narrative and Postmemory*, Cambridge, MA: Harvard University Press.

Hirst, P. and Thompson, G. (1996) *Globalisation in Question*, Cambridge: Polity.

Hoffman, E. (1989) *Lost in Translation: A Life in a New Language*, London: Heineman.

Holland, P. (2004) *Picturing Childhood: The Myth of the Child in Popular Imagery*, London: I.B. Tauris.

Holzapfel, R. (1999) 'Kinder aus asylsuchenden und Flüchtlingsfamilien: Lebenssituation und Sozialisation. Unter Berücksichtigung der Lage unbegleiteter minderjähriger Kinderflüchtlinge', pp. 53–233 in Dietz, B. and Holzapfel, R (eds) *Kinder aus Familien mit Migrationshintergrund. Kinder in Aussiedlerfamilien und Asylbewerberfamilien – allein stehende Kinderflüchtlinge*, Materialien zum Zehnten Kinder- und Jugendbericht, Band 2, München: Deutsches Jugendinstitut, Opladen: Leske+Budrich, S.

Holzwarth, P. and Maurer, B. (2001) 'Aesthetic creativity, reflexivity and play with meaning: a VideoCulture case study', *Journal of Educational Media* 26 (3): 185–202.

Home Office (2005) *Asylum Statistics United Kingdom 2004*. Retrieved 10 February 2007 from http://www.homeoffice.gov.uk/rds/pdfs05/hosb1305.pdf.

Huq, R. (2005) *Beyond Subculture: Pop, Youth and Identity in a Postcolonial World*, New York: Routledge.

Husband, C. (ed.) (1994) *A Richer Vision: The Development of Ethnic Minority Media in Western Democracies*, Paris: UNESCO.

Husband, C. (1998) 'Globalisation, media infrastructures and identities in a diasporic community', *Javnost* 5 (4): 19–33.

Husband, C. (2000) 'Media and the public sphere in multi-ethnic societies', pp. 199–214 in Cottle, S. (ed.) *Ethnic Minorities and the Media*, Buckingham: Open University Press.

Hussein, A. (1994) 'Market forces and the marginalization of black film and video production in the United Kingdom', pp. 127–142 in Husband, C. (ed.) *A Richer*

*Vision: The Development of Ethnic Minority Media in Western Democracies*, Paris: UNESCO.

Hutnyk, J. (2000) *Critique of Exotica: Music, Politics and the Culture Industry*, London: Verso.

International Federation Terre des Hommes (April 2005) Contribution and comments to the Green Paper on *A EU Approach to Managing Economic Migration* (COM(2004) 811 final) European Office, Brussels.

International Organisation for Migration (2005) *World Migration 2005*, Geneva: IOM.

Iwabushi, K. (2004) 'How "Japanese" is Pokémon?', pp. 53–79 in Tobin, J. (ed.) *Pikachu's Global Adventure: The Rise and Fall of Pokémon*, Durham, NC: Duke University Press.

Jakubowicz, A. (2001) 'Australian dreamings: cultural diversity and audience desire in a multinational and polyethnic state', pp. 195–214 in Ross, K. with Playdon, P. (eds) *Black Marks: Minority Ethnic Audiences and Media*, Aldershot: Ashgate.

James, A., Jenks, C. and Prout, A. (1998) *Theorizing Childhood*, Cambridge: Polity.

Jenkins, H. (2006) *Convergence Culture*, New York: New York University Press.

Jones, S. (1998) *Black Culture, White Youth: The Reggae Tradition from JA to UK*, London: Macmillan.

Journal of Ethnic and Migration Studies (2006) *After September 11: TV News and Transnational Audiences*, special issue, 32 (6).

Kalmanowitz, D. and Lloyd, B. (1997) *The Portable studio: Art Therapy and Political Conflict: Initiatives in Former Yugoslavia and South Africa*, London: Health Education Authority.

Kamp, U. (ed.) (1989) *Der Offene Kanal: Erfolge und Strukturen*, Bonn: Bundeszentrale für Politische Bildung, Schriftenreihe Band 283.

Karim, K. (2003) *The Media of Diaspora: Mapping the Globe*, London: Routledge.

Katsuno, H. and Maret, J. (2004) 'Localizing the Pokémon TV series for the US market', pp. 80–107 in Tobin, J. (ed.) *Pikachu's Global Adventure: The Rise and Fall of Pokémon*, Durham, NC: Duke University Press.

Katz, J. and Aakhus, M. (eds) (2002) *Perpetual Contact: Mobile Communication, Private Talk, Public Performance*, Cambridge: Cambridge University Press.

Kaufman, N., Rizzini, I., Wilson, K. and Bush, M. (2002) 'The impact of global economic, political and social transformations on the lives of children: a framework for analysis', in Kaufman, N. and Rizzini, I. (eds) *Globalisation and Children: Exploring Potentials for Enhancing Opportunities in the Lives of Children and Youth*, New York: Kluwer Academic/Plenum publisher.

Kaye, R. (2001) 'Blaming the victim: an analysis of press representation of refugees and asylum seekers in the United Kingdom in the 1990s', pp. 53–70 in King, R. and Wood, N. (eds) *Media and Migration: Constructions of Mobility and Difference*, London and New York: Routledge.

King, R. and Wood, N. (2001) *Media and Migration: Constructions of Mobility and Difference*, London and New York. Routledge.

Keyes, C. (2002) *Rap Music and Street Consciousness*, Chicago: University of Illinois Press.

Kline, S. (1993) *Out of the Garden: Toys and Children's Culture in the Age of TV Marketing*, London: Verso.

Knorr, J. (ed.) (2005) 'When German children come home' in *Children and Migration, Max Plank Foundation*.

Lathey, G. (2005) 'The travels of Harry: international marketing and the translation of J.K. Rowling's Harry Potter books', *The Lion and the Unicorn* 29 (2): 141–151.

Lemish, D. and Bloch, L.-R. (2004) 'Pokémon in Israel', pp. 165–186 in Tobin, J. (ed.) *Pikachu's Global Adventure: The Rise and Fall of Pokémon*, Durham, NC: Duke University Press.

Levitt, P., De Wind, J. and Vertovec, S. (2003) 'International perspectives on transnational migration: an introduction', *International Migration Review* 37 (3): 565–575.

Levy, C. (2004) 'Who is the other in the Balkans? Local ethnic music as a different source of identities in Bulgaria', in Whiteley, S., Bennett, A. and Hawkins, S. (eds) *Music Space and Place: Popular Music and Cultural Identity*, Aldershot: Ashgate Publishing Co.

Liebes, T. and Katz, E. (1990) *The Export of Meaning*, Oxford: Oxford University Press.

Livingstone, S. (1998) 'Mediated childhoods; a comparative approach to young people's changing media environment in Europe', *European Journal of Communication* 13 (4): 435–456.

Livingstone, S. and Bober, M. (2004) *UK Children Go Online: Surveying the Experiences of Young People and Their Parents*, London: London School of Economics and Political Science.

Livingstone, S. and Bovill, M. (eds) (2001) *Children and Their Changing Media Environment*, Mahwah, NJ: Lawrence Erlbaum.

Lull, J. (2000) *Media, Communication, Culture: A Global Approach*, Cambridge: Polity.

Lury, C. (1997) *Prosthetic Culture: Photography, Memory and Identity*, London: Routledge.

Lustyik, K. (2003) *The Transformation of Children's Television from Communism to Global Capitalism in Hungary* (PhD thesis), Boulder, CO: University of Colorado.

Mahler, S. (1998) 'Theoretical and empirical contributions towards a research agenda for transnationalism', pp. 64–100 in Smith, M. and Guarnizo, L. (eds) *Transnationalism From Below*, Comparative Urban and Community Research V6–1998, New Brunswick: Transaction Publishers.

Mahler, S. (1999) 'Engendering transnational migration: a case study of Salvadorans' *American Behavioral Scientist* 42 (4): 690–719.

Mahler, S. and Pessar, P. (2001) 'Gendered geographies of power: analysing gender across transnational spaces', *Identities* 7 (4): 441–459.

Mandaville, P. (2003) 'Communication and diasporic Islam: a virtual ummah?', pp. 135–147 in Karim, K. (ed.) *The Media of Diaspora*, London: Routledge.

Massey, D. (1991) 'A global sense of place', *Marxism Today* June.

Massey, D. (1992) 'A place called home?', *New Formations* 17: 3–15.

Massey, D. (1994) *Space Place and Gender*, Minneapolis, MN: University of Minnesota Press.

Massey, D. (1999) 'Imagining globalization: power-geometries of time space', in Brah, A., Hickman, M. and Mac an Ghaill, M. (eds) *Global Futures: Migration, Environment and Globalization*, Basingstoke: MacMillan.

Mattelart, A. and Waksman, D. (1978) ' "Plaza Sezamo" and an alibi for the author's real intentions', *Screen Education* 27: 56–62.

Mauri, L. et al. (1999) *Così Vicini, Così Lontani: Per Una Comunicazione Multiculturale*, Rome: RAI-ERI.

McChesney, R. (2002) 'Media globalisation: consequences for the rights of children', pp. 33–42 in von Feilitzen, C. and Carlsson, U. (eds) *Children, Young People and Media Globalisation*, Göteborg: UNESCO International Clearinghouse on Children, Youth and Media.

McGray, D. (2002) 'Japan's gross national cool', *Foreign Policy* May–June.

McQuillan, M. and Byrne, E. (1999) *Deconstructing Disney*, London: Pluto.

Mercer, K. (1989) 'General introduction', pp. 1–12 in Daniels, T. and Gerson, J. (eds) *The Colour Black*, London: British Film Institute.

Messaris, P. (1994) *Visual 'Literacy': Image, Mind and Reality*, Boulder, CO: Westview.

Milikowski, M. (2001) 'Learning about Turkishness by satellite: private satisfactions and public benefits', pp. 125–138 in Ross, K. with Playdon, P. (eds) *Black Marks: Minority Ethnic Audiences and Media*, Aldershot: Ashgate.

Miller, D. (ed.) (1997) 'Coca-cola: a black sweet drink from Trinidad', pp. 169–188 *Material Cultures*, London: University College London Press.

Mitchell, T. (1998) *Australian hip hop as a 'glocal' subculture*. Paper presented at The Ultimo Series Seminar, University of Technology, Syndey. 18 March 1998.

Mitchell, T. (ed.) (2001) *Global Noise: Rap and Hip Hop Outside the USA*, Middletown: Wesleyan University Press.

Mitra, A. (1997) 'Virtual community: looking for India on the Internet', pp. 55–79 in Jones, S. (ed.) *Virtual Culture: Identity and Communication in Cyber Society*, London: Sage.

Morley, D. (2000) *Home Territories: Media, Mobility and Identity*, New York: Routledge.

Morley, D. and Robins, K. (1995) *Spaces of Identity: Global Media, Electronic Landscapes and Cultural Boundaries*, New York: Routledge.

Morss, J. (1996) *Growing Critical: Alternatives to Developmental Psychology*, London: Routledge.

Mullan, B. (1996) *Not a Pretty Picture: Ethnic Minority Views of Television*, Aldershot: Avebury.

Murad, Z. (2002) Refugee children: a world beyond pain, *NIPA Karachi* 8 (2).

Murdock, G. (1990) 'Redrawing the map of the communications industries: concentration and ownership in the era of privatisation', in Ferguson, M. (ed.) *Public Communications: the New Imperatives*, Beverly Hills, CA: Sage Publications.

Naficy, H. (1993) *The Making of Exile Cultures: Iranian Television in Los Angeles*, Minneapolis, MN: University of Minnesota Press.

Naficy, H. (2003) 'Narrowcasting in diaspora: Middle Eastern television in Los Angeles', pp. 51–62 in Karim, K. (ed.) *The Media of Diaspora: Mapping the Globe*, London: Routledge.

Nederveen Pieterse, J (2000) 'Shaping globalization', pp. 1–19 in Nederveen Pieterse, J. (ed.) *Global Futures*, London: Zed Books.

Nederveen Pieterse, J. (2004) *Globalization and Culture: Global Melange*, Lanham: Rowman and Littlefield.

Neuman, S.B. (1995) *Literacy in the Television Age*, New Jersey: Ablex.

Neuss, N. (1999) *Symbolische Verarbeitung von Fernseherlebnissen in Kinderzeichnungen*, München: KoPäd.

Niesyto, H. (1991) Erfahrungsproduktion mit Medien: Selbstbilder, Darstellungsformen, Gruppenprozesse, Weinheim und München.

Niesyto, H. (2000) *Medienpädagogik und Soziokulturelle Unterschiede*, Baden-Baden: Ludwigsburg.

Niesyto, H. (2001) 'Youth research on video self-productions: reflections on a social–aesthetic approach', *Visual Sociology* 15: 135–153.

Niesyto, H. (ed.) (2003) *VideoCulture: Video und Interculturelle Kommunikation*, München: KoPäd.

Niesyto, H., Buckingham, D. and Fisherkeller, J. (2003) 'VideoCulture: crossing borders with young people's video productions', *Television and New Media* 4 (4): 461–482.

Notley, T. and Tacchi, J. (2005) 'Online youth networks: researching the experiences of "peripheral" young people using new media tools for creative participation and representation', *3C Media* 1, http://www.cbonline.org.au.

OECD (May 2006) *Where Immigrant Students Succeed: A Comparative Review of Performance and Engagement in PISA 2003*, OECD, Directorate for Education.

Ogan, C. (2001) *Communication and Identity in the Diaspora: Turkish Migrants in Amsterdam and Their Use of Media*, Lanham: Lexington Books.

Ohmae, K. (1995) *The End of the Nation State*, New York: Harper Collins.

Orellana, M.F., Thorne, B., Chee, A. and Lam, W.S.E. (2001) 'Transnational childhoods: the participation of children in processes of family migration', *Social Problems* 48 (4): 572–591.

Organisation for Economic Co-operation and Development (OECD) (2003) *Report on Main Trends in International Migration*.

Panagakos, A.N. (1998) 'Citizens of the trans-nation: political mobilization, multiculturalism and nationalism in the Greek diaspora', *Diaspora: Journal of Transnational Studies* 7 (4): 53–74.

Panagakos, A.N. (2003) 'Downloading new ethnicities: ethnicity, technology, and media in the global Greek village', *Identities: Global Studies in Culture and Power* 10: 201–219.

Phillips, M. (2001) 'The global Disney audiences project: Disney across cultures', pp. 31–61 in Wasko, J., Phillips, M. and Meehan, E. (eds) *Dazzled by Disney?*, London: Leicester University Press.

Piedra, J. (1994) 'Pato Donald's gender ducking', pp. 148–168 in Smoodin, E. (ed.) *Disney Discourse: Producing the Magic Kingdom*, New York: Routledge.

Pieterse, J. (2000) 'Globalization north–south: representations of uneven development in interaction modernities', *Theory, Culture and Society*, 17 (1): 129–138.

Pilkington, H. and Bliudina, U. (2002a) *Looking West: Cultural Globalization and Russian Youth Cultures*, Pennsylvania: Pennsylvania State University Press.

Pilkington, H. and Bliudina, U.(2002b) 'Cultural globalization: a peripheral perspective' in Pilkington, H., Flynn, M., Omel'chenko, E., Starkova, E. and Bliudina, U. (eds) *Looking West: Cultural Globalization and Russian Youth*, Penn State Press.

Pink, S. (2001a) *Doing Visual Ethnography: Images, Media and Representation in Research*, London: Sage.

Pink, S. (2001b) 'More visualising, more methodologies: on video, reflexivity and qualitative research', *Sociological Review* 49 (4): 586.

Pollock, D and van Reken, R. (2001) *Third Culture Kids: the Experience of Growing Up Among Worlds*, Chicago, IL: Intercultural Press.

Poole, E. (2001) 'Interpreting Islam: British Muslims and the British press', pp. 67–86 in Ross, K. and Playdon, P. (eds) *Black Marks: Minority Ethnic Audiences and Media*, Aldershot: Ashgate.

Portes, A. (2001) 'Introduction: the debates and significance of immigrant transnationalism', *Global Networks* 1 (3): 181–193.

Potts, D. (2001) 'Channeling girl power: positive female images in "The Power Puff Girls",' *Studies in Media and Information Literacy Education* 1:4, http://www.utpjournals.com/simile

Prout, A. and James, A. eds (1997) 'A new paradigm for the sociology of childhood: provenance, promise and problems', pp. 1–33 *Constructing and Reconstructing Childhood*, London: Falmer Press.

Punch, S. (2003) 'Childhoods in the majority world: miniature adults or tribal children?', *Sociology* 37 (2): 277–295.

Punch, S. (2007) 'Negotiating migrant identities: young people in Bolivia and Argentina', *Children's Geographies* 5(1): 99–112.

Putnam, R. (2000) *Bowling Alone: The Collapse and Revival of American Community*, New York: Simon and Schuster.

Rantanen, T. (2005) *The Media and Globalization*, London: Sage.

Refugee Council (2006) Refugee Council Briefing Nov 2006 Unaccompanied Children and the Dublin II Regulation, November 2006.

Richman, N. (1998) *In the Midst of the Whirlwind: A Manual for Helping Refugee Children*, United Kingdom: Trentham Books.

Riggins, S.H. (ed.) (1992) *Ethnic Minority Media: An International Perspective*, London: Sage.

Ritzer, G. (2004) *The McDonaldization of Society*, Thousand Oaks, CA: Pine Forge Press.

Rizzini, I. and Bush, M. (2002) *Editorial Childhood* 9 (4): 371–374.

Robertson, R. (1992) *Globalisation*, London: Sage.

Robertson, R. (1994) 'Globalisation or glocalisation?', *Journal of International Communication* 1 (1): 33–52.

Robertson, R. (1995) 'Glocalization: time – space and homogeneity – heterogeneity', pp. 250–244 in Featherstone, M., Lash, S. and Robertson, R. (eds) *Global Modernities*, London: Sage.

Robins, K. (1991) 'Tradition and translation: national culture, in global context', in Corner, J. and Harvey, S. (eds) *Enterprise and Heritage: Crosscurrents of National Culture*, London: Routledge.

Robins, K. (2000) 'Encountering globalization', pp. 191–195 in Corner, J. and Harvey, S. (eds) *The Global Transformations Reader: An Introduction to the Globalization Debate*, Malden: Polity.

Robins, K. and Aksoy, A. (2005) 'Whoever looks always finds: transnational viewing and knowledge–experience', pp. 14–42 in Chalaby, J. (ed.) *Transnational Television Worldwide*, London: I.B. Tauris.

Rogoff, B. (2003) *The Cultural Nature of Human Development*, Oxford: Oxford University Press.

Ross, K. (1996) *Black and White Media: Black Images in Popular Film and Television*, Cambridge: Polity.

Ross, K. (2000) 'In whose image? TV criticism and black minority viewers', pp. 133–148 in Cottle, S. (ed.) *Ethnic Minorities and the Media*, Buckingham: Open University Press.

Roth, M. (1996) 'A short history of Disney fascism', *Jump Cut* 40.

Rutter, J. (2006) *Refugee Children in the UK*, Maidenhead: Open University Press.

Said, E. (1993) *Culture and Imperialism*, London: Chatto and Windus.

Sakr, N. (2005) 'Maverick or model? Al-Jazeera's impact on Arab satellite television', pp. 66–95 in Chalaby, J. (ed.) *Transnational Television Worldwide: Towards a New Media Order*, London: I.B. Tauris.

Santianni, M. (2003) 'The movement for a free Tibet: cyberspace and the ambivalence of cultural translation', pp. 189–202 in Karim, K. (ed.) *Media of Diasporas*, London: Routledge.

Scannell, P. (1989) 'Public service broadcasting and modern public life', *Media Culture and Society* 10 (1): 135–166.

Scheidt, L.A. (2006) 'Adolescent diary blogs and the unseen audience', pp. 193–210 in Buckingham, D. and Willett, R. (eds) *Digital Generations: Children, Young People and New Media*, Mahwah, NJ: Erlbaum.

Schlesinger, P. (1987) 'On national identity: some conceptions and misconceptions criticised', *Social Science Information*, 26 (2): 219–264.

Schlesinger, P. (1991) 'Media, the political order and national identity', *Media, Culture and Society* 3 (3): 297–308.

Schneider, C. (1992) *Children's Television*, New York: Contemporary Books.

Sefton-Green, J. (ed.) (1999) *Young People, Creativity and New Technologies*, London: Routledge.

Seiter, E. (2005) *The Internet Playground: Children's Access, Entertainment, and Mis-Education*, New York: Peter Lang.

Selwood, S. (1997) 'Cultural policy and young people's participation in the visual arts', *Journal of Art and Design Education* 16 (3): 333–340.

Sernhede, O. (2002) *Alienation is my Nation. Hiphop och unga mäns utanförskap I det nya Sverige*, Stockholm: Ordfronts.

Shi, Y. (2005) 'Identity construction of the Chinese diaspora, ethnic media use, community formation, and the possibility of social activism', *Continuum: Journal of Media and Cultural Studies* 19 (1): 55–72.

Shim, D. (2006) 'Hybridity and the rise of Korean popular culture', *Media, Culture and Society* 28 (1): 25–44.

Shohat, E. and Stam, R. (1994) *Unthinking Eurocentrism: Multiculturalism and the Media*, London: Routledge.

Siew-Peng, L. (2001) 'Satellite TV and Chinese migrants in Britain', pp. 143–157 in Wood, N. and King, R. (eds) *Media and Migration: Constructions of Mobility and Difference*, London: Routledge.

Silj, A. (1988) *East of Dallas: The European Challenge to American Television*, London: British Film Institute.

Silverstone, R. (2001) 'Finding a voice: minorities, media and the global commons', *Emergences* 11 (1): 13–29.

Simpson, T.A. (1996) 'Constructions of self and other in the experience of rap music', in Grodin, D. and Lindlof, T.R. (eds), *Constructing the Self in a Mediated World*, London: Sage.

Smoodin, E. (ed.) (1994) *Disney Discourse: Producing the Magic Kingdom*, New York: Routledge.

Soep, E. (2005) 'Making hard-core masculinity: teenage boys playing house', in Maira, S. and Soep, E. (eds) *Youthscapes: Popular Cultures, National Identities, Global Markets*, Philadelphia, PA: University of Pennsylvania Press.

Solomon, T. (2005) ' "Living Underground is tough": authenticity and locality in the hip hop community in Istanbul, Turkey', *Popular Music* 24 (1): 1–20.

South Asian Popular Culture (2005) Special Issue on Bollywood Audiences, 3 (2).

Spence, J. and Holland, P. (eds) (1991) *Family Snaps: The Meanings of Domestic Photography*, London: Virago.

Spivak, G. (1987) *In Other Worlds: Essays in Cultural Politics*, London: Methuen.

Sreberny, A. (1999) *Include Me In: Rethinking Ethnicity on Television: Audience and Production Perspectives*, London: Broadcasting Standards Commission/Independent Television Commission.

Sreberny, A. (2000) 'Media and diasporic consciousness: an exploration among Iranians in London', pp. 179–196 in Cottle, S. (ed.) *Ethnic Minorities and the Media*, Buckingham: Open University Press.

Staubhaar, J. and Duarte, L. (2005) 'Adapting US transnational television channels to a complex world: from cultural imperialism to localization to hybridization', pp. 216–253 in Chalaby, J. (ed.) *Transnational Television Worldwide*, London: I.B. Tauris.

Stephens, S. (ed.) (1995) *Children and the Politics of Culture*, Princeton, NJ: Princeton University Press.

Stern, S. (2004) 'Expression of identity online: prominent features and gender differences in adolescents' WWW home pages', *Journal of Broadcasting and Electronic Media* 48 (2): 218–243.

Strelitz, L. (2004) 'Against cultural essentialism: media reception among South African youth', *Media, Culture & Society* September 1, 26 (5): 625–641.

Swedish Migration Board (Feb 2001). Report: Children in Aliens Processing System.

Tapscott, D. (1998) *Growing Up Digital: The Rise of the Net Generation*, New York: McGraw Hill.

Thompson, K. (2002) 'Border crossings and diasporic identities: media use and leisure practices of an ethnic minority', *Qualitative Sociology* 25 (3): 409–418.

Thornton, S. (1995) *Club Cultures: Music, Media and Subcultural Capital*, Cambridge: Polity Press.

Tobin, J. (ed.) (1992) *Remade in Japan: Everyday Life and Consumer Taste in a Changing Society*, New Haven: Yale University Press.

Tobin, J. (ed.) (2004a) *Pikachu's Global Adventure: The Rise and Fall of Pokémon*, Durham, NC: Duke University Press.

Tobin, J. (2004b) 'Conclusion: the rise and fall of the Pokémon empire', pp. 257–292 in Tobin, J. (ed.) *Pikachu's Global Adventure: The Rise and Fall of Pokémon*, Durham, NC: Duke University Press.

Tomkowiak, I. (2003) 'Vom Weltburger zum Global Player: *Harry Potter* als kulturubergreifendes Phanomen', *Fabula* 44 (1/2): 79–97.

Tomlinson, A. (1991) *Cultural Imperialism*, Baltimore, MD: Johns Hopkins University Press.

Tomlinson, J. (1999) *Globalisation and Culture*, Cambridge: Polity.

Toop, D. (1998) *Rap Attack*, London: Serpent's Tail.

Tsagarousianou, R. (1999) 'Gone to the market? The development of Asian and Greek – Cypriot community media in Britain', *Javnost* 6 (1): 55–70.

Tsagarousianou, R. (2001a) 'A space where one feels at home: media consumption practices among London's South Asian and Greek Cypriot communities', pp. 158–172 in Wood, N. and King, R. (eds) *Media and Migration: Constructions of Mobility and Difference*, London: Routledge.

Tsagarousianou, R. (2001b) 'Ethnic minority media audiences, community and identity: the case of London's South Asian and Greek–Cypriot communities', pp. 17–32 in Ross, K. and Playdon, P. (eds) *Black Marks: Minority Ethnic Audiences and Media*, Aldershot: Ashgate.

Tsagarousianou, R. (2004) 'Rethinking the concept of diaspora: mobility, connectivity and communication in a globalised world', *Westminster Papers in Communication* 1 (1): 52–66.

Tsaliki, L. (2003) ' "Globalisation and hybridity": the construction of Greekness on the Internet', pp. 162–176 in Karim, K. (ed.) *The Media of Diaspora*, London: Routledge.

Tufte, T. (2001) 'Minority youth, media uses and identity struggle: the role of the media in the production of locality', pp. 33–48 in Ross, K. and Playdon, P. (eds) *Black Marks: Minority Ethnic Audiences and Media*, Aldershot: Ashgate.

Tunstall, J. (1977) *The Media are American*, London: Constable.

Turner-Vorbeck, T. (2003) 'Pottermania: good, clean fun or cultural hegemony?', pp. 13–24 in Heilman, E. (ed.) *Harry Potter's World: Multidisciplinary Critical Perspectives*, London: RoutledgeFalmer.

Tyner, K. (ed.) (2003) *A Closer Look: Media Arts 2003*, San Francisco, CA: National Alliance for Media, Arts and Culture.

UNHCR (1994) Refugee Children: Guidelines on Protection and Care.

UNHCR (2000a) *The State of the World's Refugees: Fifty Years of Humanitarian Action*, Oxford: Oxford University Press.

UNHCR (2000b) Separated Children in Europe Programme Report.

UNHCR (2006a) Refugees by numbers, http://www.unhcr.org.

UNHCR (2006b) *2005 Global Refugee Trends: Statistical Overview of Populations of Refugees, Asylum Seekers, Internally Displaced Person, Stateless Persons and Other Persons of Concern to the UNHCR*, Geneva: UNHCR.

United Nations Convention on the Rights of the Child, Geneva, 1989.

Van Donselaar, J. and Rodrigues, P. (2001) *Monitor racisme en extreem-rechts*, Amsterdam: Anne Frank Stichting.

Van Hear, N. (2004) ' "I Went As Far As My Money Would Take Me": Conflict, Forced Migration and Class' (Working Paper 6), Oxford: University of Oxford (Centre on Migration, Policy and Society).

Veldkamp Marktonderzoek (1998) *Tijdbesteding en Mediagebruik Allochtone Jeugd 1997*, Amsterdam: Veldkamp Marktonderzoek.

Vera, M. (2002) 'Interpreters in the school setting', in *Serving English Language Learners with Disabilities: A Resource Manual for Illinois Educators*, Springfield, IL: Illinois State Board of Education.

Vertovec, S. (2003) 'Migrant transnationalism and modes of transformation', *International Migration Review* 37: 641–665.

Vertovec, S. (2004) 'Cheap calls: the social glue of migrant transnationalism', *Global Networks* 4 (2): 219–224.

Virta, E. and Westin, C. (1999) *Psychosocial adjustment of Adolescents with Immigrant Background in Sweden* (Occasional Papers, no. 2), Stockholm: CEIFO.

Von Feilitzen, C. and Carlsson, U. (1999) *Children and the Media: Image, Education, Participation*, Göteborg: UNESCO International Clearinghouse on Children, Youth and Media.

Von Feilitzen, C. and Carlsson, U. (eds) (2002) *Children, Young People and Media Globalisation*, Göteborg: UNESCO International Clearinghouse on Children, Youth and Media.

Wagnleitner, R. (1994) *Coca-colonisation and the Cold War: The Cultural Mission of the US in Austria After the Second World War*, Chapel Hill, NC: Duke University Press.

Warschauer, M. (2003) *Technology and Social Inclusion: Rethinking the Digital Divide*, Cambridge, MA: MIT Press.

Wasko, J., Phillips, M. and Meehan, E. (eds) (2001) *Dazzled by Disney?*, London: Leicester University Press.

Watson, J.L. (ed.) (1977) *Between Two Cultures: Migrants and Minorities in Britain*, Oxford: Blackwell.

Weibull, L. and Wadbring, I. (1999) *De Nya Svenskarna Möter Svenska Massmedier: Arbetsrapport nr. 91*, Göteborg: Göteborgs Universitet (Institutionen för Journalistik och Masskommunikation (JMG)).

Westcott, T. (2002) 'Globalisation of children's TV and the strategies of the "big three" ', pp. 69–76 in von Feilitzen, C. and Carlsson, U. (eds) *Children, Young People and Media Globalisation*, Göteborg: UNESCO International Clearinghouse on Children, Youth and Media.

White, A. (1997) *Rebel for the Hell of It: The Life of Tupac Shakur*, London: Quartet Books.

Whited, L. (2004) *The Ivory Tower and Harry Potter: Perspectives on a Literary Phenomenon*, St Louis, MO: University of Missouri.

Whiteley, S., Bennett, A. and Hawkins, S. (2004), *Music Space and Place: Popular Music and Cultural Identity*, Aldershot: Ashgate Publishing Co.

Willett, R. (2004) 'The multiple identities of Pokémon fans', pp. 226–240 in Tobin, J. (ed.) *Pikachu's Global Adventure: The Rise and Fall of Pokémon*, Durham, NC: Duke University Press.

Wood, N. and King, R. (2001) 'Media and migration: an overview', pp. 1–22 in Wood, N. and King, R. (eds) *Media and Migration: Constructions of Mobility and Difference*, London: Routledge.

Woodhead, M. (1997) (second edition) 'Psychology and the cultural construction of children's needs', in James, A. and Prout, A. (eds) *Constructing and Reconstructing Childhood: Contemporary Issues in the Sociological Study of Childhood*, London: Falmer Press.

World Tourism Organisation (2006) www.world-tourism.org site, accessed 26 January 2006.

Yano, C. (2004) 'Kitty litter: Japanese cute at home and abroad', in Goldstein, J., Buckingham, D. and Brougere, G. (eds) *Toys, Games and Media*, Mahwah, NJ: Erlbaum.

Yeoh, B. Huang, S. and Lam, T. (2005) 'Transnationalizing the "Asian" family: imaginaries, intimacies and strategic intents', *Global Networks* 5 (4): 307–315.

Zentrum für Türkeistudien (ed.) (1996) *Telefonbefragung zum Medienkonsumverhalten der Türkischen Wohnbevölkerung in der Bundesrepublik Deutschland. Medienanalyse zum Deutschlandbild Türkischer Fernsehsender. Endbericht*, Essen: ZfT.

Zipes, J. (1995) 'Fairy tales and the art of subversion', pp. 109–126 in Bazalgette, C. and Buckingham, D. (eds) *In Front of the Children: Screen Entertainment for Young Audiences*, London: British Film Institute.

Zipes, J. (2001) *Sticks and Stones: The Troublesome Success of Children's Literature form Slovenly Peter to Harry Potter*, New York: Routledge.

# Index